UNDERSTANDING INDIVIDUAL DIFFERENCES IN LANGUAGE DEVELOPMENT ACROSS THE SCHOOL YEARS

This volume presents the findings of a large-scale study of individual differences in spoken (and heard) language development during the school years. The goal of the study was to investigate the degree to which language abilities at school entry were stable over time and influential in the child's overall success in important aspects of development.

The methodology was a longitudinal study of over 600 children in the U.S. Midwest during a 10-year period. The language skills of these children – along with reading, academic, and psychosocial outcomes – were measured. There was intentional oversampling of children with poor language ability without being associated with other developmental or sensory disorders. Furthermore, these children could be sub-grouped based on their nonverbal abilities, such that one group represents children with specific language impairment (SLI), and the other group with nonspecific language impairment (NLI) represents poor language along with depressed nonverbal abilities.

Throughout the book, the authors consider whether these distinctions are supported by evidence obtained in this study and which aspects of development are impacted by poor language ability. Data are provided that allow conclusions to be made regarding the level of risk associated with different degrees of poor language and whether this risk should be viewed as lying on a continuum.

The volume will appeal to researchers and professionals with an interest in children's language development, particularly those working with children who have a range of language impairments. This includes Speech and Language Pathologists; Child Neuropsychologists; Clinical Psychologists working in Education, as well as Psycholinguists and Developmental Psychologists.

J. Bruce Tomblin, Ph.D., CCC-SLP is the D.C. Spriestersbach Distinguished Professor of Liberal Arts and Sciences at the University of Iowa. He is a Fellow and Honors recipient of the American Speech-Language-Hearing Association. He also received the Callier Prize in Communication Disorders. His research has been concerned with the causes, course, and consequences of developmental language impairments. This research has focused on children with specific language impairment and children with hearing loss.

Marilyn A. Nippold, Ph.D., CCC-SLP is Professor of Communication Disorders and Sciences at the University of Oregon where she has taught and conducted research since 1982. She is a Fellow of the American Speech-Language-Hearing Association (ASHA) and served as Editor (2010–2012) of the ASHA journal *Language, Speech, and Hearing Services in Schools* (LSHSS), which publishes articles that address communication disorders in school-age children and adolescents, including evidence-based intervention studies.

LANGUAGE AND SPEECH DISORDERS
BOOK SERIES
Series Editors:
Martin J. Ball, University of Louisiana at Lafayette
Jack S. Damico, University of Louisiana at Lafayette

This new series brings together course material and new research for students, practitioners, and researchers in the various areas of language and speech disorders. Textbooks covering the basics of the discipline will be designed for courses within communication disorders programs in the English-speaking world, and monographs and edited collections will present cutting-edge research from leading scholars in the field.

PUBLISHED

Recovery from Stuttering, Howell

Handbook of Vowels and Vowel Disorders, Ball & Gibbon (Eds.)

Handbook of Qualitative Research in Communication Disorders, Ball, Müller & Nelson (Eds.)

Dialogue and Dementia, Schrauf & Müller (Eds.)

Understanding Individual Differences in Language Development Across the School Yearsm, Tomblin & Nippold (Eds.)

FORTHCOMING

Applying English Grammatical Analysis: Clinical Language Assessment and Intervention, Jin & Cortazzi

Electropalatography for Speech Assessment and Intervention, McLeod, Wood, & Hardcastle

For continually updated information about published and forthcoming titles in the *Language and Speech Disorders* book series, please visit **www.psypress.com/language-and-speech-disorders**

UNDERSTANDING INDIVIDUAL DIFFERENCES IN LANGUAGE DEVELOPMENT ACROSS THE SCHOOL YEARS

Edited by
J. Bruce Tomblin and
Marilyn A. Nippold

Psychology Press
Taylor & Francis Group

NEW YORK AND LONDON

First published 2014
by Psychology Press
711 Third Avenue, New York, NY 10017

and by Psychology Press
27 Church Road, Hove, East Sussex BN3 2FA

Psychology Press is an imprint of the Taylor & Francis Group, an informa business

© 2014 Taylor & Francis

The right of J. Bruce Tomblin and Marilyn A. Nippold to be identified as editors of this work has been asserted by them in accordance with sections 77 and 78 of the Copyright, Designs and Patents Act 1988.

Library of Congress Cataloging-in-Publication Data
Understanding Individual Differences in Language Development Across the School Years / edited by J. Bruce Tomblin and Marilyn A. Nippold.
    p. cm.
    BF199.P54 2013
    150.19'434–dc23   2012033081

ISBN: 978-1-84872-532-4 (hbk)
ISBN: 978-1-84872-533-1 (pbk)
ISBN: 978-1-315-79698-7 (ebk)

Typeset in Minion
by Wearset Ltd, Boldon, Tyne and Wear

Printed and bound in the United States of America by Sheridan Books, Inc. (a Sheridan Group Company).

CONTENTS

FIGURES

TABLES

CONTRIBUTORS

Mindy Sittner Bridges, Assistant Research Scientist, Life Span Institute, University of Kansas.

Hugh W. Catts, Professor and Director, School of Communication Science and Disorders, Florida State University.

Marc E. Fey, Professor, Department of Hearing and Speech, University of Kansas Medical Center.

Laurence B. Leonard, Rachel E. Stark Distinguished Professor, Department of Speech, Language, and Hearing Sciences, Purdue University.

Carol A. Miller, Associate Professor, Department of Communication Sciences and Disorders, Pennsylvania State University.

Marilyn A. Nippold, Professor of Communication Disorders and Sciences, College of Education, University of Oregon.

J. Bruce Tomblin, DC Spriestersbach Distinguished Professor and Director of Child Language Research Center, Department of Communication Sciences and Disorders, University of Iowa.

Christine Weber-Fox, Professor, Department of Speech, Language, and Hearing Sciences, Purdue University.

Susan Ellis Weismer, Professor, Department of Communication Sciences and Disorders, Principal Investigator, Waisman Center, University of Wisconsin–Madison.

Xuyang Zhang, Associate Research Scientist, Department of Communication Sciences and Disorders, University of Iowa.

1

BACKGROUND OF THE STUDY

J. Bruce Tomblin

Systematic empirical research on individual differences in child language development and disorders emerged during the 1960s. Since that time, our understanding of the scope and nature of language across children and through development has expanded immensely. We now have rich theories and a wide range of methods for describing many features of individual differences of language in ways that are developmentally appropriate and theoretically well motivated. These theories and methods have yielded a much better understanding of the nature of language growth, the possible factors that contribute to individual differences and disorders in this growth, and the impact these differences have on the lives of children. The progress that has been made has largely come from the efforts of many individuals and small groups of academicians conducting research on relatively small samples of children sampled from clinical services units along with typically developing controls sampled as volunteers and thus often from advantaged homes. Furthermore, most of this research has employed cross-sectional designs with a focused set of research questions. Many of these characteristics arise naturally out of the limited resources available to most researchers in child language development and disorders.

In the pages that follow, we authors will describe a longitudinal project that spanned 10 years beginning in 1996 and terminating in 2006. This research project was concerned with advancing our understanding of individual differences in language development during the school years and represented a break from many of the earlier research practices described above. This research project represented a large-scale longitudinal collaborative study of children who were recruited using epidemiological sampling methods. Because of the size of the sample and the longitudinal design, the project could address questions that were often out of reach of the typical research study on language development and disorders. As such, this project may be viewed as an industrial-sized research effort, and in this regard, we acknowledge that size is not always a positive attribute. Because our research questions were wide ranging, we were not always able to examine all questions in depth or with the flexibility that one might have with a smaller, more focused project. Thus, we do not present this work with the claim that it is better than other research efforts, but rather that it provides complementary strengths to the existing literature.

In addition to this research project having an industrial-sized quality, it was admittedly opportunistic. As I will describe soon, this study arose from our having conducted a large-scale epidemiological study for the purposes of estimating the prevalence of specific language impairment (SLI). The availability of this sample presented a rare opportunity for large-scale research, and this required that a group of research collaborators be formed. Most research collaborations are formed around a common viewpoint and interests in a particular problem. Although we shared a common interest in language disorders, this collaboration was not formed around common perspectives or necessarily common theoretical viewpoints. We saw this diversity as an asset in that we would study a common cohort of children from a range of different perspectives. The pages that follow will provide the insights drawn from this common cohort of children, but will often be expressed with varied voices and perspectives.

A PERSPECTIVE ON THE IOWA LONGITUDINAL STUDY: DEFINING AND EXPLAINING LANGUAGE DISORDER

As I noted, the collaborators in this project were not required to "buy in" to a single common rationale for this research program. As the person who convened this collaboration, I had my own perspectives, which did shape the broad structure of the study. To some degree, the viewpoints that I held at the initiation of the project evolved further during the study, but the general thinking remained. In the late 1970s a major portion of my teaching was either in the clinic with students preparing to become clinicians or in the classroom with them. Much of my teaching had to do with the clinical management of developmental language disorders and yet I realized at that time that I did not explicitly address when or why we determine that a child presented with a language disorder. Furthermore, there was very little guidance in the literature on this topic. So I set about learning how other disciplines such as medicine or clinical psychology came to establish the basis for illnesses or disorders. My reading of this literature led me to develop a model for defining and explaining language disorders. A schematic of this model is shown in Figure 1.1. Over the years, I've presented various versions of this model (Tomblin, 1991, 2006; Tomblin & Christiansen, 2010), but the core ideas have remained. This core is that explaining and defining language disorder requires two types of explanation. One is concerned with how individual differences arise; the second is how and why individual differences are carved up into categories concerned with health and illness or normal and disordered conditions.

As shown in Figure 1.1, the central feature of this model concerns individual differences. It is an empirical fact that although language development is often described as a universal and uniform feature of humans, not all individuals within any language community are equally facile with language development or use. In some aspects of language, such as grammar, individual differences may be less apparent in adults, but even among adults, variability can be found in certain language usage tasks. Not only is it obvious that individual differences in language exist, it is also the case that without these differences it would not be possible to have a notion of disorder. If we perform a mind experiment in which all individuals are equal with respect to language performance, or any other trait for that matter, it would be impossible for us to consider the notion of a language disorder. Thus,

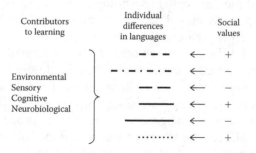

Figure 1.1 A characterization of causal sources for language impairment arising from the convergence of social values and learning systems onto individual differences.

the existence of individual differences is a necessary condition for any kind of construct of disorder.

If individual differences provide the basis for disorder, we can then ask the question "how do these arise?" This is one of the two explanatory questions I posed earlier. In many people's minds this question will also lead to answering it. If we ask the question about the cause of individual differences, it suggests that we believe that there are mechanisms or processes that give rise to these individual differences. However, many of those within important research disciplines concerned with language such as cognitive psychology and linguistics act as though these individual differences occur at random and thus represent noise in the causal mechanisms that give rise to language and cognitive development. This type of thinking is often found in cognitive psychology and linguistics and reflects a focus in these disciplines on universal (nomothetic) features of language and cognition. Thus, there are invariant mechanisms that operate in the same way and to the same degree in all individuals; however, noise enters into these operations, but it is unsystematic and uninteresting. In fact, it is much more likely that these individual differences across the range of development and function are principled and governed by systematic variations in the operations of natural biological and cognitive systems. These alternative views of individual differences are long-standing. Cronbach (1957) referred to them as representing two disciplines within psychology. The former view was common in experimental psychology and now in cognitive psychology. The alternative view, that individual differences are principled, is often found among those who work within the framework of differential psychology (psychology of individual differences). Cronbach noted that the differential psychologist "regards individual and group variations as important effects of biological and social causes" (Cronbach, 1957, p. 674). If we adopt the perspective of the differential psychologist, we could hypothesize that some forms of individual differences represent a "normal" state that arises from the proper operations of the mechanisms that contribute to language, and then there are other forms of individual differences that arise from defective mechanisms. That is, children with language disorder represent a subgroup of individual differences arising from a unique set of causes. Thus, if we study the causes of individual differences in language development using the appropriate scientific methods, we will be able to also discover and explain when and why some of these individual differences are disordered.

An alternative viewpoint, and one that I have preferred, acknowledges that there are principled causal mechanisms that give rise to individual differences; however, the variations in the operations of these mechanisms, as well as the functional variations in language that arise from them, are not inherently good or bad or represent states of health and illness. Instead, within this view, claims of health, illness, disorder, etc., are examples of cultural artifacts such as chairs, airplanes, or cooking pots. These are things invented by humans and reflect the social values of the inventor. In this regard, notions of illness and disorder are grounded in cultural values or norms that reflect what a society prizes or despises in its members. A very good example of this can be found in our field with regard to the health status of hearing loss. The Hearing culture views a hearing loss as a type of illness whereas the Deaf culture does not. Thus, within this perspective, forms of individual differences do not have an inherent quality of "normal" and "disordered" but rather these are culturally assigned. In some literature, this view is referred to as normativism, wherein the notion of norm refers to a social value. Figure 1.1 thus shows that these social values represent a separate causal path for explaining when and why some forms of individual differences come to be disordered. This path is distinct from the mechanisms that give rise to the individual differences.

In taking this view, my perspective in this research project was that we wanted to identify those situations in which children's lives are negatively affected by their language status. In this regard, studying outcomes is not just looking at by-products of language disorder, but rather become the means by which we determine when individual differences represent language impairment. In order to do this, we need to have longitudinal data about domains in children's lives that are culturally salient. I should also note that this viewpoint leads us to consider that the construct of language disorder as applied to any given child is at best probabilistic. Because I no longer view language disorder as a condition within the child, but rather a condition that exists between the child and the world the child will live in, we cannot say with certainty that the child will or will not face negative consequences during his/her life. Thus, our view of language disorder becomes a probabilistic statement rather than an absolute statement. In this regard, language disorder is not something children have in the same way that they have brown eyes or curly hair. These children may "have" certain language abilities and these may be enduring, but the particular ability the child possesses only confers some degree of risk for socially defined troubling outcomes. The risk and hence what we might consider disorder is probabilistic. In order for us to construct these probabilities, it is necessary to examine a large sample of children who span the range of language abilities and within these children we must measure both individual differences in language as well as individual differences in key outcomes. Then we need to examine the association between these. Indeed, this was one of the principal objectives of the longitudinal study.

DEVELOPMENTAL OUTCOMES AS COMPETENCE

Within this framework, some outcomes are more important than others. We are particularly interested in outcomes that are socially and personally valued. This introduces a new challenge to our research. How do we determine what developmental outcomes are socially valued? To some extent we are aided in this by the fact that we are members of the society into which these children are entering and therefore our intuitions can provide a reasonable guide. Another helpful source for framing this comes from researchers who have been examining threats to child development in the form of risks and factors that moderate these risks and as such lead to resilience. At the core of this research on risk and resilience has been the concept of developmental competence. Masten defined competence as "adaptation success in the developmental tasks expected of individuals of a given age in a particular cultural and historical context" (Masten et al., 1999). Societal expectations of individuals change as they age. This variation in expectation is incorporated in Zigler and Glick's notion of salient developmental tasks (Zigler & Glick, 1986). Roisman and colleagues have stated that "salient developmental tasks represent the benchmarks of adaptation that are specific to a developmental period and are contextualized by prevailing sociocultural and historically embedded expectation" (Roisman, Masten, Coatsworth, & Tellegen, 2004, p. 123). Because expectations vary with development, there are transitional points in life where old competences are diminishing in saliency and new ones are emerging to become salient (Roisman et al., 2004). As these new competences emerge, they build on the prior competences and also upon new cultural supports that motivate growth. For instance, within many cultures, it is likely that language development itself represents a salient developmental task of early childhood. Subsequently, during later childhood, academic and peer relations become salient tasks but these will be influenced in part by the earlier accomplishment of language development. Thus, as shown in Figure 1.2, competences can have a cascading relationship. Masten has proposed that failures in the development of competence at a later stage of development can often be traced to failures of development at earlier stages of development.

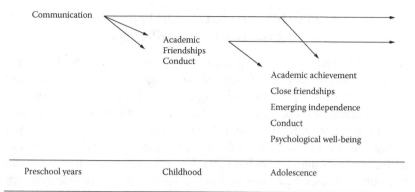

Figure 1.2 Developmentally salient competences across childhood demonstrating the cascade of communication competence over development.

Our current interest in this research program is the developmental period of childhood and adolescence. Therefore we can ask, within the culture of the United States, what are the developmentally salient tasks of childhood and adolescence around which we can define good or poor competence? During the elementary school years of childhood competence has been found to consist of three domains: "(a) getting along with peers (peer acceptance and having friends), (b) academic achievement, and (c) rule-abiding conduct (compliance with authority at home and school)" (Masten et al., 1995, p. 1335). These three domains of competence persist into adolescence but become refined. Academic competence in adolescence is reflected by level of education and school performance reflected in grades and teacher and parent report of school performance. Conduct during adolescence is reflected in rule following versus disruptive behaviors and rule violations at home, school, and in the community. Social competence is reflected in the adolescent's ability to develop close and lasting relationships. Additionally, in later adolescence, additional emerging competences are found in romantic relationships and the development of job-related skills.

During the course of this longitudinal study, data were gathered across these domains and this framework of competence provides a structure within which we can examine the developmental outcomes of the children in the study. An overriding question is whether individual differences in language have greater impact on one domain than the others. In addition to examining the strength of these relationships, we are also interested in identifying when limitations in language place children at worrisome risk for later poor competences. Finally, we can ask whether there are moderators of this risk.

CAUSES OF INDIVIDUAL DIFFERENCES IN
LANGUAGE DEVELOPMENT

Just as we needed a framework for structuring our study of the out-comes of individual differences in language development, we also needed a framework for considering the possible causes of these individual differences. Figure 1.2 provided a schematic of such causes, and we can see that there are several levels of study that could be brought to bear on this problem. In fact, there are so many causal domains and within each so many possible variables and constructs, that we could not consider a comprehensive look. As such, much of our research focused on the prominent cognitive accounts of individual differences in language development that were under consideration during the late 1990s and early 2000s.

Several closely related cognitive mechanisms were prominent in the literature at that time. The theory and the measures of these mechanisms came out of research on memory and information processing that emphasized those individual differences in the ability to store and process information that influenced the rate at which language was learned and the facility in the child's use of language. The individual differences then were the by-product of the integrity of one of these mechanisms. One cognitive account emphasized the rate of processing. Kail (1994) had shown that as tasks became more demanding, children with SLI appeared to experience a greater processing load than children who were typical language users. This load was reflected in response speed and thus the response rates of children with SLI slowed more rapidly as the task became demanding than did the typic-ally developing peers. Additionally, this slowing appeared to extend across modalities and kinds of stimulus-response material without regard to the speech or language content.

Two other closely related memory mechanisms were also under consideration as important contributors to individual differences in language development. One of these concerned the capacity of chil-dren to hold phonological information in immediate memory long enough and accurately enough to learn words and perhaps other aspects of language. This memory system had been proposed by Bad-deley (Baddeley, Gathercole, & Papagno, 1998) as an important mech-anism for language learning and was used by Gathercole and Baddeley as an explanation of language disorder (Gathercole & Baddeley, 1990). Baddeley's phonological memory comprised one part of a more general working memory system. Other models of working memory, particularly one by Carpenter and Just (Carpenter & Just, 1989; Just,

Carpenter, & Keller, 1996), have been developed around the task of comprehension and the cognitive demands that are placed on storage and computation needed to accomplish understanding. Both the phonological memory notions of Baddeley and Gathercole and the processing capacity accounts of Carpenter and Just were particularly useful schemes because they had been framed in individual differences accounts.

These cognitive processing accounts served as alternative, although not necessarily fully competing, hypotheses about the possible cognitive bases of individual differences in language development and disorders. As I noted earlier, we concentrated on cognitive explanations in this research. I should note that we also have been conducting a research program on the genetic contributions to individual differences. This research exploited the fact that we were gathering extensive phenotypic information on the children and that non-invasive methods for the collection of DNA were emerging at the time we conducted this study. Results of this research program are being reported in venues outside of this book.

SUMMARY

The ideas just discussed provided the broad "stage setting" for this rather large research project. The project itself required a group of colleagues who helped frame these ideas and the specific questions and methods used to obtain a vast array of data. In addition to assembling these investigators, I was fortunate to be able to bring together a team of research associates who – for over 10 years – managed the day-to-day aspects of the project and collected, stored, and analyzed the data.

REFERENCES

Baddeley, A., Gathercole, S., & Papagno, C. (1998). The phonological loop as a language learning device. *Psychological Review, 105*, 158–173.

Carpenter, P. A., & Just, M. A. (1989). The role of working memory in language comprehension. In D. Klahr & K. Kotovsky (Eds.), *Complex information processing: The impact of Herbert A. Simon* (pp. 31–68). Hillsdale, NJ: Lawrence Erlbaum Associates.

Cronbach, L. J. (1957). The two disciplines of scientific psychology. *American Psychologist, 12*, 671–684.

Gathercole, S. E., & Baddeley, A. D. (1990). Phonological memory deficits in language disordered children: Is there a causal connection? *Journal of Memory and Language, 29*, 336–360.

Just, M. A., Carpenter, P. A., & Keller, T. A. (1996). The capacity theory of comprehension: New frontiers of evidence and arguments. *Psychological Review, 103,* 773–780.

Kail, R. (1994). A method for studying the generalized slowing hypothesis in children with specific language impairment. *Journal of Speech and Hearing Research, 37,* 418–421.

Masten, A. S., Coatsworth, J. D., Neemann, J., Gest, S. D., Tellegen, A., & Garmezy, N. (1995). The structure and coherence of competence from childhood through adolescence. *Child Development, 66,* 1635–1659.

Masten, A. S., Hubbard, J. J., Gest, S. D., Tellegen, A., Garmezy, N., & Ramirez, M. (1999). Competence in the context of adversity: Pathways to resilience and maladaptation from childhood to late adolescence. *Development and Psychopathology, 11,* 143–169.

Roisman, G. I., Masten, A. S., Coatsworth, J. D., & Tellegen, A. (2004). Salient and emerging developmental tasks in the transition to adulthood. *Child Development, 75,* 123–133.

Tomblin, J. B. (1991). Examining the cause of specific language impairment. *Language, Speech, and Hearing Services in Schools, 22,* 69–74.

Tomblin, J. B. (2006). A normativist account of language-based learning disability. *Learning Disabilities: Research and Practice, 21,* 8–18.

Tomblin, J. B., & Christiansen, M. H. (2010). Explaining developmental communication disorders. In R. Paul & P. Flipsen (Eds.), *Speech sound disorders in children* (pp. 35–50). San Diego, CA: Plural.

Zigler, E., & Glick, M. (1986). *A developmental approach to adult psychopathology.* New York: John Wiley & Sons.

2

GENERAL DESIGN AND METHODS

J. Bruce Tomblin

As I noted in the first chapter, the research conducted during this project was multifaceted and in fact emerged over the duration of the project. Although there was a general framework within which the research was conducted, there were also many different and sometimes theoretically varied aspects to this project. Despite this flexible structure, one common and largely invariant property of the study was the sample of children who participated. In many respects much of our research was driven by our interest in taking advantage of a rare opportunity to have a large sample of children who were systematically sampled from the general population. We are taught in graduate school that the centerpiece of research is the research question. This should precede issues of method and certainly consideration of which and how many participants should be recruited for research. In this respect, we are guilty of doing things somewhat backward, but at times good science capitalizes on rare events, and we hope this is an example of such an opportunity.

The overall research project comprised two successive sub-projects. The first sub-project consisted of a cross-sectional study. For the purposes of this book, this sub-project serves as a backdrop for the second sub-project, which was a longitudinal study. The cross-sectional study was conducted as a research contract to the National Institute for Deafness and Other Communication Disorders (NIDCD) and its aims were largely to determine the prevalence and risk factors for specific language impairment (SLI). As such, this was an epidemiological study of SLI and therefore required that a population sampling method be used. Thus, this study can be viewed as a very large recruitment process that provided a large sample of children to be studied in the longitudinal project central to this book. Although the cross-sectional study is not the focus of this book, I will summarize the methods because they explain the source of the participants and the initial baseline data obtained for the longitudinal project.

CROSS-SECTIONAL STUDY DESIGN

The cross-sectional study was performed in order to address the question concerning the prevalence of SLI. Within the discipline of epidemiology, prevalence refers to the rate of affected individuals in a population at a particular point in time. In order to estimate this rate, it is necessary to obtain a cross-sectional representative sample of individuals within the defined population. We established that the population of interest would be children who are entering school – that is, children age-eligible for kindergarten. We selected this age group for several reasons. First, there is considerable evidence that during the preschool years, individual differences in language status are not stable. Children who are late talkers as 2-year-olds often show improvement by age 3 or 4 (Paul, 1993; Rescorla, Dahlsgaard, & Roberts, 2000; Thal, Tobias, & Morrison, 1991). In contrast, children identified with language impairment around 5 years of age or older appear to be much more likely to have persistent language impairments (Bishop & Edmundson, 1987; Aram, Ekelman, & Nation, 1984). Thus, children in kindergarten are more likely to have stable language abilities, and poor language status would be more likely to have long-term consequences to justify considering it as a language disorder. Second, kindergarten eligibility was selected as it represents a major developmental transition where children begin to use language as a tool for educational purposes as well as for social interaction. Thus it represents a natural boundary with regard to developmental expectations and demands. Third, and finally, was simple practicality. If we wanted to sample from a population of children, it would be much easier to do this once these children were attending school. Prior to kindergarten, it is very difficult to locate and recruit children. At the point that children are age-eligible for kindergarten, however, most enroll.

In addition to specifying the age of the children, we also specified that they were to come from monolingual English-speaking homes. The reason for this was simply that we did not know how to incorporate variations in language backgrounds into this study. All of our language instruments were in English and thus English-language skills were the developmental trait of interest. Children from homes where multiple languages are spoken that may include English are likely to differ from those who are monolingual speakers. One might assume that the English skills of these children would be poorer than the monolingual children; however, there is also emerging evidence that bilingualism may have benefits as well (Bialystok & Viswanathan, 2009; Siegal, Iozzi, & Surian, 2009). By limiting our sample to monolingual homes, we did not completely eliminate variations in the form of English used in the homes of the children. Socio-cultural dialects of English were allowed to remain. As we entered into this study, Vernacular Black English (VBE) was the most common variant we expected to find. As I will mention later, we attempted to accommodate VBE forms by using alternate scoring rules on our language measures. Even after this, we know that we were not fully successful at eliminating bias in our measures (Hammer, Pennock-Roman, Rzasa, & Tomblin, 2002).

Our final sampling constraint consisted of the place of residence of our participants. The NIDCD specified that our prevalence estimates be based on the type of living setting of the children: specifically, urban, suburban, and rural strata. To determine strata for this study, we used two variables: population density and distance from the urban center. Urban areas were within two miles of the central business district of an urbanized area. "Urban" also included areas that were between 2 and 3 miles from the central business district if the population density was 3,000 or more people per square mile. We used the business centers of four urbanized areas in Iowa: Cedar Rapids, IA; Des Moines, IA; Cedar Falls/Waterloo, IA; and the "Quad Cities" (Davenport, IA; Bettendorf, IA; Moline, IL; Rock Island, IL). The "Suburban" strata designation was assigned to areas having a population density greater than 2,000 persons per square mile and that did not qualify as being urban. "Rural" was considered to be areas with a population density lower than 2,000 persons per square mile.[1] By creating these three strata centered on each of the population centers, our sampling populations took on the form of clusters around a city center as shown in Figure 2.1.

The description above introduces another geographical constraint on the study population. Our sample was drawn from Iowa and a western edge of Illinois. Our goal was to arrive at a sample that was similar to the U.S. population at least with regard to mono-English-speaking kindergarten-age children. Ideally, to do this we would have sampled randomly across the United States. The logistics of doing this

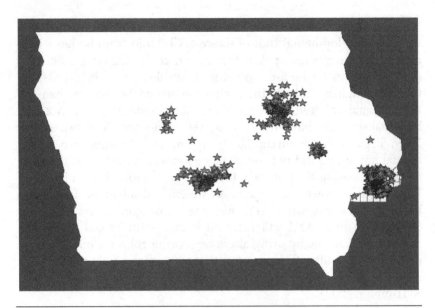

Figure 2.1 Geographic distribution of children in epidemiologic sample.

would have been considerable. It would have required a nationwide effort to organize information on kindergarten-age children, constructing a recruitment system across diverse governmental organizations, and then managing personnel over great distances. Instead, we opted to perform this study within a smaller catchment that was closer to home. Although Iowa is considered overall to be a rural state, by centering our sampling on major urban centers, this resulted in a population characteristic that was roughly approximate to national characteristics, as will be shown later. Essentially, we oversampled the Iowa urban sample and undersampled the rural populations.

Strata General Definition

The targeted 6,000 kindergarten children were equally distributed into the three residential strata – urban, suburban, and rural settings, as specified by the NIDCD contract – and we allowed the sampling of children across a spectrum of living and demographic conditions. To achieve this stratified sampling, the attendance zones of the school buildings from the four population centers were drawn and designated as being predominately urban, suburban, or rural. Subsequent to the study, each individual child was assigned to a stratum according to that child's home address, thus allowing for a more accurate assignment of residential strata.

Sampling Method

Our initial study design asked for 6,000 children, with 2,000 in each stratum. We employed a sampling method used in epidemiology called cluster sampling. Our goal was to sample children in each stratum for each of the population centers in order that every eligible child had an equal probability of participating in the study. The cluster sampling method accomplishes this by randomly sampling large units, such as city blocks, that will contain the participants of interest. In our case, the logical sampling unit was a kindergarten classroom. Therefore, initially all kindergarten classrooms in one of our targeted regions were eligible for sampling. Each school was assigned to one of the strata based on its catchment and thus this design is referred to as a stratified cluster sampling scheme. Once this was done, we had to gain access to the schools. We first contacted in writing the superintendent of each school district in the selected population centers. Along with a written explanation of the study was an invitation to participate during the course of this 2-year study. Receipt of a district superintendent's consent to participate allowed us to contact all of the principals of the school buildings in that district containing kindergarten classes to arrange to conduct the study. I should note that each kindergarten classroom was given a financial gift for its participation. A total of 41 districts were contacted; 21 (51.22%) superintendents consented to have their districts participate, 15 (36.59%) superintendents refused participation, and 5 (12.19%) superintendents did not respond. Only public school districts were sampled; there was no sampling of private schools or children being home-schooled. Private schools are largely affiliated with religious groups, and while we initially considered including these schools, the proportion of children in these schools was small, and the catchment areas of these schools were difficult to define.

As was described above, each participating school building was assigned a residential stratum (urban, suburban, rural) based on their attendance zones. Once we had our list of schools that had agreed to participate, each school was assigned a number for that stratum. Using a random number table, buildings were selected to obtain a minimum total sample of 1,000 students in each of the three strata across all population centers. Because the population of Iowa does not contain a substantial number of African Americans, this sampling strategy was modified to oversample the urban strata where there were more African Americans. Therefore, we sampled an additional 1,000 children in the urban areas across the study sites and thus our total sample size was 7,218 children who were actually recruited and screened. In order to study such a large sample, we spread the sampling across 2 years, creating two cohorts. Furthermore, we knew that some children who were age-eligible for kindergarten were being held out, a practice called "redshirting," and that these children could represent a sub-group who were developmentally less mature. As a result, for each of the two cohorts, we returned to the schools the following year and enrolled children who should have been in the prior year's class. These "redshirts" were then included with their age-mates of the prior year. Thus, at any point in time, the age of the children in this study covered a 2-year age span.

Assessment Procedures

In order to identify children with SLI within this large population, we employed a two stage design (see Figure 2.2). In this design, we screened the listening and speaking abilities of all consented children in each sampled kindergarten class. Using these screening results, we then recruited all children who had failed the screen and a random sample of those who passed for a more in-depth evaluation of their language, intellectual, hearing, and pre-reading abilities.

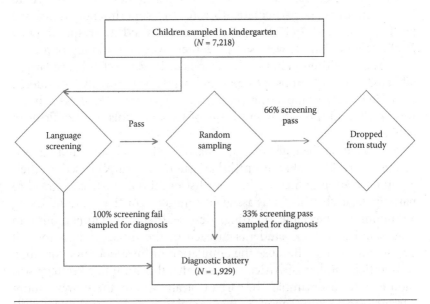

Figure 2.2 A flow diagram of the two-stage assessment consisting of screening followed by diagnostic assessment.

Screening Phase

Participants. All kindergarten children in a sampled school were participants in this phase. Parents were informed that this screening was being performed and were given the opportunity to withdraw their children from participation. The use of this negative consent procedure for this aspect of the study as well as all other aspects of this study was approved by the University of Iowa Institutional Review Board. A team of examiners was hired and trained to administer and score the screening measures. The examiners initially met with all children in the kindergarten classrooms, and they were shown the kinds of activities that they were to do in the screening. In this way, the children had some familiarity with both the examiners and the material. The children were then tested individually.

Screening Instrument. The screening procedure only involved language performance. Children were not screened for hearing, nonverbal intelligence, pervasive developmental disorder, or any other exclusionary condition for SLI. A language screening test was developed that had a very high predictive relationship with the diagnostic outcome. The screening tool consisted of 40 items from the Test of Language Development-2:P (TOLD-2:P; Newcomer & Hammill, 1988). This screening instrument was administered to each child individually and took approximately 10 minutes to complete.

Diagnostic Phase

Participants. All children who failed the screening and an equal-sized random sample of those who passed were invited to participate in the diagnostic phase of this study. The children in the control group were sampled from the same school as those who failed the screening in order to match the residential backgrounds of the children in the SLI and control groups. In this case, the children were re-consented using standard active consent. The screening failure rate was 27% (1,933) and therefore all of these children were recruited. We also recruited 1,944 children who passed the screening. Of this total of 3,877 children recruited, 2,084 were given permission by their parents to participate in the study. Of these children, 75 were reported by their parents to speak a second language, which was an exclusionary condition for this study. The rest of the 2,009 children constituted the final monolingual English-speaker sample. Of these 2,009 children, complete data were obtained for 1,929.

SLI Diagnostic Battery. The diagnostic assessment administered to these children was designed to identify those who represented SLI cases. We were challenged by the fact that there was not, nor in fact is there now, a "gold standard" for the diagnosis of SLI. Typically, when we define SLI, we employ two joint schemes. First, there is an inclusionary scheme that is concerned with the presence of language impairment. Second, the scheme consists of what are sometimes called exclusionary conditions that distinguish other forms of language impairment from SLI. The diagnostic battery was designed to provide for measures that could be used for both inclusion and exclusion.

The inclusionary information came from a set of listening and speaking measures. These measures were selected by a group of consultants, some of whom became investigators on the longitudinal study. These consultants decided that we wanted to measure both receptive and expressive aspects of language across the domains of words (vocabulary), sentences, and connected discourse that at this age level was in the form of narrative. This framework is shown in Figure 2.3. Because we needed to assess these children consistently, each of these aspects of language needed to be assessed within a standardized testing condition. We realized the value of a conversational language sample in most clinical settings; however, the amount of time needed to obtain the sample and to transcribe it for 2,000 children was deemed too great. We did, however, obtain spontaneous speech and language samples from a subset of 303 of these children and this was used in particular for analysis of speech sound production (Shriberg, Tomblin, & McSweeny, 1999).

MODALITY

	Reception	Expression	
	TOLD: Picture indentification	TOLD: Oral vocabulary	Vocabulary
LANGUAGE DOMAIN	TOLD: Grammatic understanding	TOLD: Grammatic completion TOLD: Sentence imitation	Sentence
	Culatta: Narrative comprehension	Culatta: Narrative recall	Discourse

Figure 2.3 Scheme characterizing the potential dimensions of language by modality and domain.

After looking at a variety of existing language tests, we found that the TOLD-2:P (Newcomer & Hammill, 1988) fit the framework well, although it did not contain a connected discourse task. Thus, we added a narrative story task involving both comprehension and production (Culatta, Page, & Ellis, 1983). The TOLD-2:P comprised six subtests: Picture Vocabulary, Oral Vocabulary, Grammatic Understanding, Sentence Imitation, Grammatic Completion, and Word Articulation. The team of consultants decided that speech sound production would not be incorporated within the construct of SLI and thus, although we administered the Word Articulation subtest, it was not used to make the language diagnosis. A complete description of these measures and their scoring can be found in Tomblin *et al.* (1997). As shown in Figure 2.3, these tests could be cast into a two-dimensional matrix formed by language modality (receptive, expressive) and the domain of the language unit (word, sentence, discourse) being tested.

As noted earlier, some of the children in the study were users of Vernacular Black English (VBE); therefore, there was a concern that these children might be falsely identified as having language deficits. Scoring guidelines were developed that contained examples of acceptable VBE responses to the test stimulus items based upon judgments provided by local members of the African American communities within which the study was conducted. These forms were not counted as errors on these subtests for VBE speakers. A child was considered a VBE speaker if the examiner noted examples of these VBE forms in informal conversation with the child or if two or more responses on Grammatic Completion and Sentence Imitation subtests were consistent with VBE.

This protocol operationalized our notion of language for this study, but we still needed to establish criteria to determine language impairment. A range of criteria existed in the literature but again no established guidelines were available. Therefore, we conducted a study (Tomblin, Records, & Zhang, 1996) in which we asked clinicians from around the country to evaluate hypothetical scores from our test protocol. We then evaluated different schemes for interpreting these judgments. We arrived at a fairly straightforward scheme that was based on computing a set of composite scores that summarized performance in each modality (receptive, expressive) and each language domain (vocabulary, sentence, discourse). Using a cut-off of the 10th percentile and requiring failure of at least two of the five scores captured the clinical judgments of the clinicians well. Thus, this became our standard for diagnosing language impairment.

Because the construct of SLI often involves the exclusion of children with low nonverbal IQ or hearing loss, we also tested the children's hearing and nonverbal IQ. We also added a small set of additional measures of speech, language, and motor performance. These measures are described below.

Nonverbal IQ. Nonverbal IQ was estimated using the Block Design and Picture Completion subtests of the Wechsler Preschool and Primary Scale of Intelligence–Revised (WPPSI; Wechsler, 1989b). For this study, children with nonverbal IQs within or above 1 standard deviation of the mean (IQ = 85) were considered as falling in the normal IQ range.

Audiometric Testing. All children in the diagnostic phase were screened for hearing using both pure tone audiometric screenings and acoustic immittance/impedance audiometry. The latter measures were used to differentiate between persistent hearing loss and one caused by an ear infection. Pure tone screening was conducted for 500, 1, 2, and 4 kHz at 20 dB.

Pre-reading Tasks. Early literacy skills were examined as important ancillary measures. The Letter Identification subtest of the Woodcock Reading Mastery Tests–Revised (Woodcock, 1987), the Word–Sound Deletion Task and the Random Animals–Colors Task (Catts, 1993) were used to measure pre-reading skills.

Motor Skills. Two gross measures of motor skills were obtained: gait and handedness. The examiner observed the child walking to the examining room, and noted if there were any obvious gross motor problems when walking. The child was also asked to write her/his name, and the examiner made a note of which hand the child used.

Diagnostic outcomes were determined based on language performance as well as hearing and nonverbal intellectual performance. Based on the diagnostic results, the children were assigned to one of five diagnostic categories: (1) specific language impaired (SLI; failed language testing using two out of five criteria, but passed hearing and nonverbal cognitive testing where passing was a score of 85 or greater); (2) normal control (C; passed all language, hearing, and nonverbal cognitive testing); (3) nonspecific language impaired (NLI; failed the language testing and nonverbal cognitive testing, but passed hearing testing); (4) low cognitive (LC; passed language and hearing testing, but failed nonverbal cognitive testing); and (5) hearing failure (HF; failed both hearing screenings and did not continue for further testing). Although most of the measures we employed had norm tables for children of the age we were studying, we decided that it was wiser for us to develop our own norms that were specific to this population and perhaps unique methods of test administration and scoring.

LONGITUDINAL COHORT STUDY

The cross-sectional study generated a large pool of children (1,929) who had been systematically sampled and tested in kindergarten. The data from this study allowed us to estimate the prevalence of SLI (Tomblin et al., 1997), the prevalence of speech sound disorder (Shriberg et al., 1999), and a variety of other features of SLI including risk factors (Hammer et al., 2002; Hammer, Tomblin, Zhang, & Weiss, 2001; Hewitt, Hammer, Yont, & Tomblin, 2005; Tomblin, Smith, & Zhang, 1997; Tomblin, Hammer, & Zhang, 1998; Zhang & Tomblin, 2000). As we were concluding the epidemiological study, we considered the large sum of public money and effort that had been expended on obtaining this sample that was quite unique due to the fact that it represented a population sample containing a large number of children identified as having poor language skills. Therefore, a group of collaborators who had been studying child language disorders was convened, and plans were made to follow many of these children into the school years.

As I discussed earlier, the research program was aimed at examining questions concerned with causes and consequences of individual differences in language development, with a particular interest in children with poor language abilities. Therefore, we wanted to follow children with a wide range of language abilities, but also to have a substantial number of children who had poor language skills in kindergarten. The first step in developing this longitudinal study involved the creation of a registry from which we could select our longitudinal cohort members. To do this, we approached all parents of the participants in the diagnostic phase of the cross-sectional study and asked them if we could enter their children into a research registry that would allow us to contact them in the future. Of the 1,929 children who participated in the diagnostic phases of the cross-sectional study, 1,328 children were enrolled in this registry by their parents. A comparison of the participants and non-participants in the registry showed no differences with respect to language and IQ status.

This registry was then used for sampling and recruitment of children for this longitudinal study. The longitudinal study was initiated when the Cohort 1 children were beginning second grade and the Cohort 2 children were in first grade. The study was designed to follow 600 children. To accomplish this, 686 children were sampled from the registry and asked to participate. Positive responses came from 608 (89%). All children ($N = 348$) in the registry who had been diagnosed in the cross-sectional study as being language impaired (SLI or NLI) at kindergarten were invited to participate in the longitudinal cohort and 70% (244) agreed to join. Among the NLI children, 15 had performance IQ scores below 70 based on the Wechsler Intelligence Scale for Children–III (WISC-III; Wechsler, 1989a) performance scale and hence might be considered to be mentally retarded; however, we retained these children but excluded them from some analyses. Also, 442 children in the registry who had normal language status (NL or LC) were randomly sampled and asked to participate, and 315 (71%) agreed to join the cohort. None of these children had diagnoses at kindergarten entry of developmental disorders including mental retardation, autism, or neuromotor or sensory impairments such as blindness or hearing impairment. Table 2.1 summarizes the sample size, nominal grades and ages of the children at each wave of assessment.

The key characteristics of this cohort can be seen in Table 2.2. The diagnostic categories reflect their status when these children were in kindergarten, and therefore the language and performance IQ scores of the groups reflect the degree to which scores changed from kindergarten (Wave 1) to Wave 4 due to regression to mean effects and possible true change. Because slightly more than 40% of these children had spoken language skills below –1.25 SD in at least two areas of language when they were kindergarteners, the overall longitudinal cohort contained an overrepresentation of children entering school with poor language skills. This oversampling of children with poor language skills was planned in order to increase the information available concerning these children. The children with normal language skills were included in the study for several reasons:

1. This study was intended to evaluate alternative diagnostic schemes for LI and SLI; thus, it was important to include children that were not LI in the EpiSLI system, but could be in an alternative system.
2. A part of this study was concerned with reading disorder (RD) in children with and without spoken language impairment; thus, a moderately large sample of NL children were needed.

Table 2.1 Cohort characteristics and sample size across the waves of the study

	Wave 1	Wave 2	Wave 3	Wave 4	Wave 5
Nominal Grade	Kindergarten	2nd	4th	8th	10th
Mean Age	5.9	8.0	9.9	13.9	15.9
Range	5.3–6.7	7.1–9.0	9.1–10.9	13.1–15.4	14.9–16.4
Number	604	604	570	527	504

Table 2.2 Characteristics of the children with language impairment and normal language status at Wave 4 (eighth grade) with respect to gender, language ability, performance IQ, mother's education, and race

Group	#	% Males	Composite Language Score (z-score)	Perf. IQ	Mother's Education (years)	Race		
						White	Black	Other
Normal Language (NL)	338	57.10	-0.02	99.62	13.8	299	30	9
Language Impairment (LI)	189	54.50	-1.80	83.75	13.2	150	34	5

Notes:
Normal Language status (NL): No more than 1 language composite score out of 5 possible below –1.25 SD for age.
Language Impairment (LI): 2 or more language composite scores below –1.25 SD for age, normal hearing, absence of other developmental disorders such as autism, cerebral palsy, or mental retardation.

3. Normal language controls were needed for several studies and in particular were needed in order to allow the development of local norms for norm referenced interpretation.

Design of Data Collection Across Time

Figure 2.4 provides an overview of the course of the longitudinal study. As shown, the children enrolled in the longitudinal study were initially studied as kindergarteners when they were part of the cross-sectional study. Recall that the initial cross-sectional sample comprised two cohorts, one enrolled in 1993–1994 (Cohort 1) and the other in 1994–1995 (Cohort 2). Subsequent to this initial wave of data collection, these children were followed across 10 years. Data for all members of each cohort were obtained 2, 4, 8, and 10 years after this initial participation. In general, these correspond to their grade placement in 2nd, 4th, 8th, and 10th grades, although some children were held back along the way and thus were not always attending the grade expected for their age. Figure 2.4 also shows the number of children who participated at each of these data-collection waves. Because we recruited from the cross-sectional study prior to the Year 2 wave of observation, we had full participation at both kindergarten and Year 2. After that, we did lose a very modest number of children, with an overall attrition of 16.6%. The data-collection scheme shown in Figure 2.4 represents time points where language, reading, selected cognitive, and psychosocial and educational status information were obtained on all children. We also gathered data concerning selected subsets of these children at other time intervals. In particular, a large array of data concerning speed of processing and processing capacity was obtained on a subsample of children between Waves 2 and 3.

As noted earlier, the children sampled for this longitudinal study did not constitute a random sample of the original 7,218 children due to our effort to ensure a large sample of children with poor spoken language. Often in our research, however, we have needed to evaluate the data with this bias corrected. Fortunately, because we knew how each child came to be included in the longitudinal cohort from the original sample, we were able to correct for this bias by the use of differential weights that reflected differences in sampling probabilities. Specifically, each child in the cohort was a member of a subgroup of the original sample based upon whether s/he had passed or failed the initial screening and whether or not the child was found to be language impaired or normal in the diagnostic phase. The degree to which the final cohort contained an over- or underrepresentation of these subgroups was determined and children's scores were weighted according to this

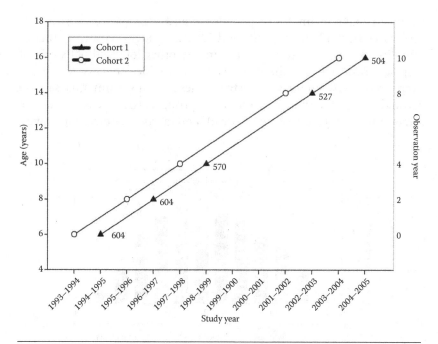

Figure 2.4 An overview of the scheduling of assessments for each cohort and the sample sizes at each assessment interval.

sampling bias. Figure 2.5 shows the distribution of weighted and unweighted language screening scores for the members of the longitudinal cohort and the distribution of scores for the total group of 7,218 children. The skewed shape of the original sample was the result of our use of a screening measure that was intentionally less sensitive to children with high language scores. As shown in the bottom panel of Figure 2.5, the weighting scheme for the children in the longitudinal sample resulted in a distribution that was similar to the original population sample. Additional evidence that this weighting system generated a normal and representative distribution can be seen by examining the distribution of weighted and unweighted performance IQ scores using the WISC-III norms. In the second grade, the mean unweighted performance IQ was 94.48 (SD 15.14), but the weighted IQ score for our cohort was 100.04 (SD 15.05). Thus the weighted scores on the WISC-III correspond to the values expected from a well-sampled normal population such as that used for the norms of this test. These results show that it was possible with this sample to obtain parameter estimates for a typical population of children who are monolingual English speakers. This capacity provided us with the ability to make estimates of prevalence and estimates of norms that generalize beyond this cohort, and identify general contributions of sampling biases that are not found in any other longitudinal study of language impairment. The capacity to create local norms cannot be overstated. Our ability to construct these norms from this sample allowed us to use the same reference group across measures at the same time point (assessment wave) and across assessment waves.

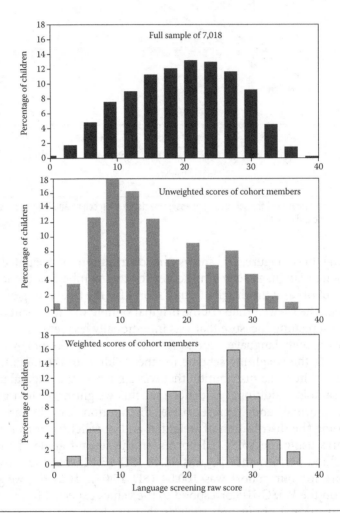

Figure 2.5 The top panel shows the distribution of language screening scores in original sample of 7,218 children. The middle panel shows the distribution of unweighted screening scores for the 604 children in the longitudinal sample and study cohort. The bottom panel provides the distribution of scores after weighting the scores to correct for oversampling of children with low language.

Typically, norms developed for standardized tests are based upon cross-sectional data. Changes across tests and across ages in such norm referenced scores can reflect differences in the referent groups. However, by using the same group over time, this source of variance is eliminated. Thus, the use of common local norms was particularly helpful when the research question asked for an ipsative (within child profile) perspective and thus asked for a profile analysis. In most research, this is very difficult to do because the sample size is small.

Constructs Measured Across the Longitudinal Study

During the course of this longitudinal study, the members of this cohort have been systematically observed in order to address the causes and outcomes of individual differences in language. Table 2.3 summarizes the broad domains that were evaluated across the study within the general categories of causes and outcomes. The measures of outcome focused on various communication skills involving listening, speaking, reading, and writing. Additionally, we obtained information from parents, teachers, and the youth themselves regarding the academic performance and psychological/behavioral status of these children. As we approached this study, there were also prominent theories regarding cognitive factors that might cause poor spoken language ability as well as poor reading ability. These theories centered upon the status of phonological processing (metaphonological skills) for reading, speed of information processing, the capacity of information processing, and/or the robustness of phonological memory. Additionally, some of these processing constructs were examined within online

Table 2.3 Constructs reflecting individual differences in language and their causes and consequences and the time points during the study when measures were obtained

	Construct	K	2	3	4	8	10
Individual Differences in Language	Spoken Language	X	X		X	X	X
Causes	Speed of Processing			X			X
	Processing Capacity			X	X		
	Phonological Memory		X		X		
	Phonological Processing	X	X		X	X	X
Consequences	Written Language			X	X	X	X
	Psychological/Behavioral		X		X	X	X

Notes:
General Data Collection Procedures.
Setting for Collection of Data.

language processing tasks, including measures of event-related potentials. An additional causal domain that has been explored in this project concerned genetic contributions to these individual differences in language. In this regard, DNA was obtained from most of the children and, in many cases, from their parents as well. The results of this research will not be covered in this book in part because these data are still being analyzed as this book is being written and also because of the considerable space needed to introduce and interpret these data.

Because the children in this study had originally been sampled in three different regions within the state of Iowa, it was necessary to develop data-collection methods that were efficient and that would lead to high levels of participation. This led us to develop an approach to data collection where the personnel who gathered the data went to the homes and/or schools of the children rather than asking them to travel to a central site. This general approach led us to employ three examiners who lived in the regions where the children resided and who were trained as either speech-language clinicians or special education specialists. Thus, all personnel had experience with children and were generally trained in administration of standardized tests. Because these examiners were traveling to the children's homes, we determined that the most efficient way to collect data was to provide each examiner with a vehicle for travel and as a testing suite. We were aware of companies that converted minivans into traveling offices and found that these were quite suitable for most of our testing needs. These vehicles provided a relatively quiet setting (see Figure 2.6). Initially, we planned to perform all the testing at the children's homes; however, this limited the amount of time available for testing since these children were in school much of the day. Therefore, we approached the school authorities and generally found that they were willing to have the child tested at school in the minivan, so long as the parents provided permission. In these cases we worked with the teachers to select times that would have minimal impact on instruction. The availability of the minivan in this case meant that we did not have to arrange for physical space in the school.

Training and Reliability of Examiners

The use of multiple examiners and a wide range of tasks required us to develop methods for data collection that would minimize systematic examiner effects and would yield reliable and valid data. To accomplish this, a system was developed to first train the examiners on the specified protocols and establish consistency between themselves. Additionally, after training, our procedures employed a systematic

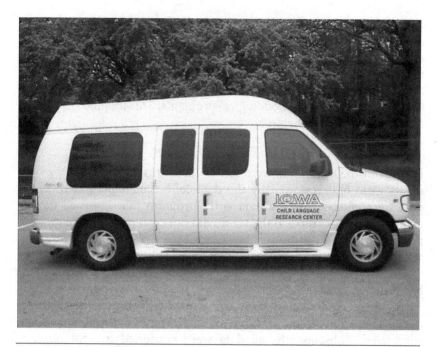

Figure 2.6 Minivan used for collection of data.

monitoring of the examiners' conduct of the protocols including scoring. In order to implement this training and monitoring, the project employed an experienced SLP who also had served as a research assistant for several years. This person was responsible for documenting the protocols, training examiners, and monitoring ongoing data collection.

Training began with the investigators developing detailed descriptions of the research methods. This description was then reviewed by the data-collection manager. She then ran a small number of pilot children of the appropriate range of development; where necessary, the testing sessions were videotaped and sent back to each investigator to be reviewed for accuracy. Once each protocol was piloted and the methods had been clarified and standardized, the field examiners were brought in for a period of training. Training was distributed over a span of several weeks and included opportunities to practice administering the protocols. After the completion of training, an initial set of two participants was scheduled by each examiner. Each of these sessions was observed by the data-collection manager to ensure compliance with the protocol and consistency across examiners. During these sessions, those procedures that produce responses requiring examiner interpretation were scored blindly by the data-collection manager and the examiner. Subsequently, a minimum of 5% of the examination sessions were monitored in this way to prevent drift in protocol administration and to check interrater reliability. Furthermore, mid-year sessions were conducted to allow the field examiners to assess and clarify methodological problems. This method resulted in data that were very reliable.

Data Entry and Storage

Data from the examiners were sent to the central lab. All of the data sheets were first reviewed by the data-collection manager. Then the data were entered using a data entry program that involved double entry of all information. If the values did not correspond, the data were not accepted, and the discrepancy needed to be resolved. This program also contained range checking so that illegal values were blocked.

Once the data were entered, they were merged into a research database. Many of the variables involved test scores. In these cases only raw scores were entered and then computer algorithms computed the norm referenced scores. Thus, errors in examiner table look-ups were eliminated. Subsequently, all data were examined to spot outliers. These outliers were checked to verify that they were not the product of coding or errors in data entry. The methods described above pertain to most of the data obtained during the project. An exception to this procedure occurred with those data collected using computer-managed experiments including the ERP as well as measures that required transcription of audio files.

Measuring Individual Differences in Language

The examination of individual differences in language ability and patterns of stability and change in ability was a central theme of the research in this study. The consequences and causes all converged on these differences. Therefore, as we designed this study, we set out to systematically measure these individual differences throughout the study period via a common scheme that was consistent with our model of language established in kindergarten. We also believed that this framework incorporated most of the principal aspects of the construct of language spanning listening and speaking across units of words, sentences, and discourse.

One aspect of language clearly missing from this core set of measures was pragmatics. If we define pragmatics as the use of language form and content for the accomplishment of social communicative function, then the standardized measures employed sampled very little of this. The connected discourse tasks from second grade on, as will be described, were tasks that required the child to provide information in different age-appropriate genres (narration, explanation, and conversation), but the aspects of language measured in these tasks did not emphasize features of social communication adequacy or appropriateness. Much of our rationale for this paucity of pragmatic information concerns the challenges of measuring pragmatics within this age range and within standardized protocols that could be done in a reasonable amount of time. The only standardized measures of pragmatics available for children of this age were measures that tapped meta-pragmatic performance. That is, the child would be asked how s/he would perform in a particular setting, but it is not clear that such performance is predictive of how the child would actually perform. At the same time that this project was being initiated, Bishop was developing the *Children's Communication Checklist* (Bishop, 2003) that was aimed at assessing pragmatic disorder. This is a parent report instrument, and we did employ it during Years 6 and 7 because we were not seeing these children in person. Additionally, some of the parent and teacher report instruments concerned with behavior and psychosocial status indirectly provided information about communication. However, it will be clear that our core measures of language operationalize language as the use of words, sentences, and discourse for the purposes of understanding and making messages of various forms and content.

We wanted to measure language, as just defined, across a broad period of development. Although by the age of 6, most children have acquired a considerable command of language, there is still a substantial amount of additional growth that occurs during the school years (Nippold, 2007). This means that measures that are appropriate for kindergarten age children are often inappropriate for older children. This is particularly the case with respect to measures of sentence use and discourse. Thus, as we constructed the language assessment protocol across time, we needed to select measures that were parallel with each other, that is, were measuring the same construct. At the same time, these measures needed to be sensitive to individual differences at each age group and thus needed to be appropriately difficult. These are basic psychometric issues that can be solved and have been solved in some areas of psychological measurement such as intelligence testing. Unfortunately, the field of language has not had the benefit of this kind of effort. Therefore, we had to rely on our judgment and intuition rather than data in order to select the measures to be used. It should also be emphasized that there was a practical constraint on the development of this protocol. Each investigator wanted to gather as much information as possible from these children, but we needed to manage the burden of assessment in order that the child was not excessively tested and thus likely to withdraw, and we had limited personnel to do the data collection. Our aim was to keep the assessment time of any child to approximately 4 hours spread over two assessment sessions. With all of these factors shaping the language assessment instruments used, we arrived at a core set of instruments as summarized in Table 2.4.

Most of these measures were standardized language tests, and our administration followed the instructions provided by the test manuals. In several places, we had to develop extensions to these manuals when situations arose that were not addressed in the manuals. This was particularly necessary with regard to scoring of language production tasks such as expressive vocabulary. In these cases, our scoring rules were always guided by the existing examples and rules. The raw scores obtained from these standardized measures were transformed into norm referenced scores using the local norming methods described for the kindergarten measures. Furthermore, these individual tests were combined to form composite scores for each of the modalities and the three domains and an overall composite score in the same manner as was done for the kindergarten measures.

The measures of discourse were not always obtained via widely available tests and furthermore these measures provided several different summary measures. Therefore, these measures require more description at this point. Our use of the term discourse here refers to the use of language where multiple propositions are arranged within some type of organizational framework that governs the sequential organization of the propositions in the discourse. A common classification of these frameworks or genres consists of two forms of monologic discourse – narration and explanation – and then the general multiple talker (dialogic) discourse found in conversation. Each of these genres is characterized by a macrostructure (Van Dijk & Kintch, 1983) that governs the global semantic content of the discourse. The monologic genre that has received the most study is narrative. Children in the early years of school demonstrate considerable growth in their skills at narrative comprehension and production, and narratives are very common in the classroom during the primary grades. It was for these reasons that we assessed narrative comprehension and production in Years 2 and 4. Narratives are structured around episodes that have a strong temporal organization. In contrast, expository discourse typically is organized around different logical frameworks and functions to inform or explain some subject matter. The

Table 2.4 Core measures of spoken language obtained across the longitudinal study

Year	Modality	Word	Sentence	Discourse
2	Rec	PPVT-R	CELF-III Sentence Structure Concepts & Direct.	CELF-III List. To Paragraphs
	Exp	CREVT-Expressive	CELF-III Recalling Sentences Word Structure	Fey/Catts: Story Generation
4	Rec	PPVT-R	CELF-III Concepts & Direct.	CELF-III List. To Paragraphs
	Exp	CREVT-Expressive	CELF-III Recalling Sentences Formulated Sentences	Fey/Catts: Story Generation
8	Rec	PPVT-R	CELF-III Concepts & Direct.	QRI: Expository Listening Comprehension Recall
	Exp	CREVT-Expressive	CELF-III Recalling Sentences	QRI: Expository Recall
10	Rec	PPVT-R	CELF-III Concepts & Direct.	QRI: Expository Listening Comprehension Recall
	Exp	CREVT-Expressive	CELF-III Recalling Sentences	QRI: Expository Recall

Notes:
CELF-III: Clinical Evaluation of Language Fundamentals (3rd ed.)
CREVT: Comprehensive Receptive & Expressive Vocabulary Test
PPVT-R: Peabody Picture Vocabulary Test-Revised, Form L
QRI: Qualitative Reading Inventory

macrostructure of expository discourse can be more demanding, and because logical relations are important in exposition, the microstructure becomes crucial and more complex. Not surprisingly, expository discourse is a later developing form of language and becomes more common in school curricula during the higher grades and throughout high school (Nippold & Scott, 2010). Thus we elected to assess expository discourse at Years 8 and 10.

The narrative protocol used in Years 2 and 4 employed the Clinical Evaluation of Language Fundamentals, Third Edition (CELF-III; Semel, Wiig, & Secord, 1995) Paragraph Comprehension subtest to measure discourse comprehension. Thus, this aspect of discourse took advantage of an existing published test. We were unable to do the same for narrative production. Therefore, a narrative production task was developed by Marc Fey and Hugh Catts at the University of Kansas (Fey, Catts, Proctor-Williams, Tomblin, & Zhang, 2004). This task was designed to examine narrative production in either the spoken or written mode. The task provided the child with three pictures of key elements of an episode: the setting, the problem, and the resolution. Also the child was given an example of a story that could be generated from a different set of pictures. The child was then shown a different picture set and then was asked to name the key elements in the story. After this, the child generated a story based upon the picture set. Two spoken and two written story samples were obtained across the two testing sessions. Several measures were obtained from transcriptions of these stories (for details, see Fey et al., 2004). For the purposes of computing the narrative composite scores, we elected to use the measure of total clauses produced in the narrative as an index of the quality of the narrative.

The expository assessment protocol used in Years 8 and 10 was drawn from the Qualitative Reading Inventory–II (QRI; Leslie & Caldwell, 1995). This test provides passages of varying difficulty that are graded according to the child's age. The passages can be read either to the child or by the child. After hearing/reading the passage, the child is asked to retell the passage. Following this, some questions are asked to assess comprehension. We selected two passages for the listening and speaking task in Year 8 (Lewis & Clark and City of Constantine) that were appropriate for children in the seventh and eighth grade. In Year 10, we used a different set of passages (Biddy Mason, Malcolm X) that were appropriate for this grade level. The answers to the comprehension questions provided scores for discourse comprehension. The passage recall for each child was transcribed, and the total number of clauses was used as an index of discourse production.

This core language protocol provided data that could be used to describe the language abilities of the children as a continuous quantitative trait, and also we could assign the children to categories of impaired versus normal language using the same EpiSLI scheme employed in kindergarten. Although all the children in the study began with normal hearing, we did continue to check hearing status throughout the study. None of the children acquired a persistent hearing loss during the course of the study. We also asked for information concerning new diagnoses of other exclusionary conditions based on parental report. Some children were reported as having intellectual disability, autism, or brain injury. The children with brain injury were dropped from the study. The children with intellectual disability or autism were retained, but excluded from the SLI diagnosis. Also, in order to differentiate SLI from NLI, we administered nonverbal IQ tests in Years 2 and 8. In Year 2, we tested the children using the full performance scale of the WISC-III. In Year 8, nonverbal IQ was reassessed using the Block Design and Picture Completion subtests of the WISC-III.

Other Measures of Listening and Speaking. The measures described above were used to systematically describe language ability in our children using generally well-known tasks that in many cases have been used for the clinical assessment of language. We also, however, obtained a number of other measures of language that were often designed to examine particular features of language in all or some subset of these children. These measures are described below.

Extended Optional Infinitive Use (EOI). As we initiated this study, Mabel Rice and her colleagues had proposed that children with SLI have particular difficulty acquiring a full command of the obligatory marking of tense on finite verbs. Rice and Wexler (Rice & Wexler, 1996a, 1996b; Rice, Wexler, & Cleave, 1995) proposed that this difficulty was based on impairments in the maturation of this aspect of a universal grammar and that this deficit may be a sensitive marker of SLI. Additionally, it was unclear whether children with SLI would ultimately develop full maturity. Thus, measures of tense marking were obtained during the study period.

Measures of tense usage were obtained using a set of structured probes of tense use. These consisted of two elicitation probes for tense marking. One probe task measured third person singular present tense -*s* and the other measured past tense regular and irregular. The third person singular task (3Ps) provided the child with 12 pictures that showed a person engaged in a prototypical activity associated with an occupation. The examiner would show the child a picture and say,

"This is a bus driver. If I'm a teacher and I teach, he's a bus driver so he [drives]," and the child completed the utterance. The past tense probe task presented the child with pairs of pictures that contrasted with respect to whether the action was ongoing or completed. The examiner would say "Here the boy is washing [referring to the first picture]. Now he is done [referring to the second picture]. Tell me what he did to the dishes." The tasks were the same as those used by Rice and her colleagues (Rice & Wexler, 1996a, 1996b; Rice et al., 1995) and were also very similar to the tasks contained in the Rice/Wexler Test of Grammatical Impairment (Rice & Wexler, 2001). In addition to scores on each probe task, a composite tense score was computed by taking the mean of the 3Ps and the two tense probes (regular and irregular). As shown in Table 2.5, these measures were obtained on a subset of children with SLI.

Use of Discourse Genre in Adolescence. The core language measures used to characterize individual differences as well as the EOI probes were all employed in elicited language contexts. Within the core measures, we did incorporate a discourse measure, but particularly at Years 8 and 10, this was conducted with an elicited recall task. In order to expand the scope of language and in particular to allow us to contrast conversational versus expository discourse, we added a set of spoken discourse tasks at Years 8 and 10.

These discourse tasks were conducted in 20-minute sessions that were audiotaped. During these sessions, the examiner presented the student with tasks that required the use of expository discourse. Additionally, the examiner employed a standard script to engage the student in a conversation. Details of the elicitation procedures for these tasks are provided in Chapter 4.

Cognitive Causes of Individual Differences in Language

As noted in Chapter 1, we based our research concerning cognitive associates of SLI on a set of theories regarding the influence of storage and processing of information systems on language development. One account emphasized the speed or rate of processing (see for instance:

Table 2.5 Children assessed on EOI probe measures

Grade at Testing	TLD	SLI	NLI
Kindergarten	90	78	70
Grade 1	97	87	80
Grade 2	98	91	83
Grade 3	99	95	85

Kail, 1994; Kail & Salthouse, 1994). Within this account, the constraint on speed was not limited to linguistic or even auditory information and thus was domain and modality independent. Several measures of response speed to a range of linguistic and nonlinguistic stimuli were therefore included in our research. As shown in Table 2.6, these measures of speed were obtained on a subsample of 77 children with and without LI in Years 3 and 8.

An alternative account of the constraint on processing capacity examined in this study was that language learning was influenced by the availability of working memory resources that in turn limit computational capacity during language learning. One type of resource that was of great interest was that of phonological memory (PM). The Nonword Repetition Task (Dollaghan & Campbell, 1998) was used to measure PM in both Years 2 and 8. Processing capacity can also be reflected in tasks that entail simultaneous processing of two tasks. The Dual Processing Comprehension Task asked students to enact the meaning of two sentences spoken by a male and female that had been heard at the same time. The Competing Language Processing Task (CLPT; Gaulin & Campbell, 1994) was also used. This task requires the child to listen to sentences and make true/false judgments and then later recall the last word of each sentence heard. These two dual

Table 2.6 Tasks used for measurement of response speed

Nonlinguistic		
Motor	Tapping	Tap one or two keys as quickly as possible for 5 s.
	Simple RT	Strike a key in response to "***."
Nonverbal Cognitive	Visual Search	Strike one key if target is present, another if absent.
	Mental Rotation	Strike one key if second matches target, another if mirror image.
Linguistic		
Lexical	Picture Matching	Strike one key if two pictures match on criterion, another if not.
	Picture Naming	Speak name of picture shown
Grammatical	Truth Value	Strike one key if picture matches sentence heard, another if not.
	Grammaticality	Strike one key if sentence is correct, another if incorrect.
Phonological	Judge Rhymes	Strike one key if stimuli rhyme, another if not.
	Judge Initial Consonants	Strike one key if stimuli star with same sound, another if not.

processing tasks were administered in Years 3 and 8 to the same children who participated in the speed of processing tasks.

Measures of Consequences of Individual Differences in Language

I noted earlier that a key issue in this study concerned the relationship between individual differences in language ability and important domains of developmentally relevant life function. As described in Chapter 1, Masten and colleagues have referred to these life functions as competences (Masten et al., 1999; Masten & Coatsworth, 1998; Pellegrini, Masten, Garmezy, & Ferrarese, 1987). During the school years, these authors have identified three competence domains: academic achievement, behavioral conduct (rule following), and peer social competence (friendships). When we began this study, we knew that most of these domains of competence were associated with individual differences in language. There was already an existing literature documenting the academic and in particular the reading problems associated with poor language. We sought to understand this relationship within emerging models of reading that emphasized the importance of constructs of phonological awareness, decoding, and reading comprehension. We also wanted to incorporate spelling and writing within the broader view of written language. With respect to existing research concerning behavior and social development at the time we began this study, it was clear that much of the work examined these traits in the form of psychopathology. We continued to be interested in psychopathologies as co-morbid conditions with SLI and NLI, but we also wanted to look at the broader range of competence. With these general perspectives in mind, protocols for the assessment of competence in the academic, behavioral, and social domains were constructed.

Written Language and Academic Performance

Our examination of academic performance was heavily oriented toward written language; however, data from teacher and parent reports of school achievement and school-administered achievement testing were also obtained. Table 2.7 summarizes the written measures obtained across the study period. Further description of these measures will be provided in Chapter 6.

As was the case with the spoken language measures that made up the core assessment, most of these measures were standardized tests. In these cases, the tests were administered according to the test

Table 2.7 Measures of written language

Construct	2nd Grade	4th Grade	8th Grade	10th Grade
Phonological Awareness	Sound deletion	Sound deletion	Pig Latin Phoneme Delet.	Pig Latin Phoneme Delet.
Decoding	WRMT-R Word Attack Word ID GORT-III (rate & accuracy)	WRMT-R Word Attack Word ID GORT-III (rate & accuracy)	WRMT-R Word Attack Word ID Reading Rate GORT-III (rate & accuracy)	WRMT-R Word Attack Word ID GORT-III (rate & accuracy)
Comprehension	Woodcock Reading Mastery Test Pass. Comp. GORT-III (passage score) DAB-2	WRMT-R Pass. Comp. GORT-III (passage score) DAB-2	WRMT-R Pass. Comp. GORT-III (passage score)	Woodcock Pass. Comp. GORT-III (passage score)
Spelling	TWS-3	TWS-3		
Writing	Fey/Catts: Written story generation	Fey/Catts: Written story generation		

Notes:
WRMT-R: Woodcock Reading Mastery Test- Revised
GORT-III: Gray Oral Reading Tests (3rd edl)
DAB-2: Diagnostic Achievement Battery (2nd edition)
TWS-3: Test of Written Spelling (3rd edition)

manual. For some purposes, the scores were referenced to the national norms provided with the tests, and in other cases we used local norms computed in the same manner as was done for the spoken language measures. As can be seen from the table, some of these measures were not standardized, and therefore we will describe the basic methods for these measures.

Phonological Awareness and Rapid Naming. Phonological awareness reflects the ability of the child to consciously represent and manipulate sublexical phonological information. During kindergarten, Year 2, and Year 4, phonological awareness was assessed by a syllable/phoneme deletion task, an adaptation of Rosner's Auditory Analysis Test (Rosner & Simon, 1971). In this task, participants were required to delete a syllable or, in some cases, a phoneme of a word and to say the remaining sound sequence. By Year 4, many of the children were reaching ceiling, and therefore in Years 8 and 10, phonological awareness was assessed by an alternate phoneme deletion task and a pig Latin task. The phoneme deletion task required participants to repeat 46 nonwords individually and then delete a phoneme to derive a real word. Nonwords were presented via headphones and a high-quality audio recorder and the participants' responses were recorded. The pig Latin task required participants to strip the initial phoneme from a spoken word, move it to the end of the word and add "ay." There were 27 items, 15 one-syllable and 12 two-syllable words. Within each syllable condition, half (or approximately half) of the items began with a single consonant and the remainder with a consonant cluster. Words were presented live voice, and the participants' responses were recorded. Both of these phonological awareness measures were adapted from Gayan and Olson (2003).

Rapid naming is also a skill that has been consistently associated with reading achievement. Throughout the study, this skill was measured via the Rapid Naming of Animals task (Catts, 1993), which requires participants to name as rapidly as possible the color and name of a series of pictured animals (e.g., blue horse, red cow, black pig). Both the number of correct responses and the total time taken to name all the pictures were obtained. The latter served as the primary index of performance on the measure.

Written language passages were obtained in parallel with the discourse samples during the spoken language protocol. During Years 2 and 4, we obtained writing samples using the same Fey and Catts narrative elicitation described earlier for the spoken narrative sampling; however, in this case the child was shown an example written passage for a set of story pictures and then asked to produce a written story for two more sets of pictures. These passages were analyzed in the same manner as the spoken language sample.

Behavioral and Social Competence

Our original plan with respect to the measurement of the behavioral and social domains was quite extensive. We had hoped to obtain interviews from the children and their parents and to obtain a survey of social status and friendships via a sociometric method. Unfortunately, we were not able to obtain funding for this dimension of our project. As a result, we mainly relied on questionnaires to obtain this information.

Two batteries of questionnaires were used. The first was the Social Skills Rating System (SSRS; Gresham & Elliott, 1990). The SSRS was completed by the parents and teachers in Years 2 and 4 and by the parents in Years 8 and 10. This scale is designed to measure a wide range of social competences and thus does not emphasize psychopathology. It contains subscales concerning cooperation, assertion, responsibility, empathy, and self-control. The second battery consisted of questionnaires from the Achenbach System of Empirically Based Assessment (ASEBA; Achenbach & McConaughy, 1995). This system comprises several questionnaires. One of these, the Child Behavior Checklist (CBCL), is completed by the parents. One section of the CBCL asks about academic performance, friendships, etc. The second and principal part of the CBCL asks the parents about the presence of a wide range of behaviors indicative of various psychopathologies. These questions are then used to compute a variety of scores reflective of different forms of psychological problems. One scale (Total Problems) is simply an overall score. Subscores for Internalizing and Externalizing, as well as a range of syndrome scales such as one for attention deficit hyperactivity disorder, are also provided. The CBCL was also completed by the parents in Years 2, 4, 8, and 10. A second scale in the ASEBA system is the Teacher's Report Form (TRF). This scale is similar to the CBCL, except that it is completed by the child's teacher. It provides largely the same summary scales as the CBCL. The TRF was administered in Years 4 and 10. In Year 10, we faced the challenge of each child having several different teachers, and some of these teachers may have had limited contact with the target youth. Therefore, in this case, we allowed the young persons to select the teachers they believed knew them best. Finally, the ASEBA also contains a Youth Self-Report (YSR) questionnaire that is administered to the child. Again, it has many of the same questions and provides for the same summary scales. Because this is a written questionnaire, we did not administer it until

Wave 5; thus, the children were more likely to be able to read and provide this information. Thus, in Year 10, we administered the whole ASEBA battery that provides information from the child and the teacher and the youth's perspective.

Perception of Self-Worth. The TRF administered in 10th grade provided us with an opportunity to learn about the way the youth in our study perceived themselves. The TRF, however, as noted earlier, was particularly concerned with troubling behavior. Therefore, we constructed a computer-based interview that addressed the perceptions that these youth had of themselves that reflected their self-worth and provided some general indicators of quality of life.

Most of the items pertaining to self-worth were based upon Harter's measures of self-esteem and self-worth in adolescents (Harter, 1988). Harter employs a 4-point scale formatted as shown in Figure 2.7. In this case, the student is given two polar examples of self-perception and asked to determine which kind of student he or she is more like. Then the student indicates how closely he or she feels similar to this student. Because some of our children were poor readers, we adapted this scale by presenting this in both auditory and text form via ePrime software running on a computer. The student then entered the responses on a button box.

We also used the Satisfaction with Life Scale (SWLS; Pavot, Diener, Colvin, & Sandvik, 1991; Pavot & Diener, 1993), which is a simple five-item scale that asks for ratings on statements such as "I am satisfied with life" or "If I could live my life over, I would change almost nothing."

Thus, the early measures of social/behavioral outcomes were largely derived from parent and teacher report provided by the CBCL, TRF, and the SSRS scales. Social/behavioral perspectives of the student were obtained at the last observation interval. Collectively, these measures provided a broad perspective on several facets of social/behavioral development. Indeed, the number of different variables provided by

Some students like writing papers for school.		Other students don't like writing papers for school.	
Really true for me	Sort of true for me	Sort of true for me	Really true for me

Figure 2.7 Format of the Self Report questionnaire.

these instruments can be extensive and thus has required the use of multivariate analysis methods to reduce the size of the data set. This work will be described in later chapters.

SUMMARY

This chapter provides the methodological backdrop to the longitudinal study. As such, the focus was on the general structure of the study and in particular the manner in which the participants were sampled. In the subsequent chapters we will provide more details on the particular methods as well as the key findings that have come from this effort.

NOTE

1. The Quad Cities are bisected by the Mississippi River and thus we only used population density in this site. Urban was considered to be greater than 3,000 people per square mile, suburban was between 2,000 and 3,000 people per square mile, and rural was designated as areas having fewer than 2,000 people per square mile. The Cedar Rapids site was only used to sample "urban" children and was generally treated as part of the Cedar Falls/Waterloo site.

REFERENCES

Achenbach, T. M., & McConaughy, S. H. (1995). *Empirically based assessment of child and adolescent psychopathology: Practical applications.* London: Sage.

Aram, D. M., Ekelman, B. L., & Nation, J. E. (1984). Preschoolers with language disorders: Ten years later. *Journal of Speech and Hearing Research, 27,* 232–244.

Bialystok, E., & Viswanathan, M. (2009). Components of executive control with advantages for bilingual children in two cultures. *Cognition, 112,* 494–500.

Bishop, D. (2003). *Children's Communication Checklist, Version 2 [CCC-2].* London: Psychological Corporation.

Bishop, D. V. M., & Edmundson, A. (1987). Language-impaired 4-year-olds: Distinguishing transient from persistent impairment. *Journal of Speech and Hearing Disorders, 52,* 156–173.

Catts, H. W. (1993). The relationship between speech-language impairments and reading disabilities. *Journal of Speech and Hearing Research, 36,* 948–958.

Culatta, B., Page, J., & Ellis, J. (1983). Story retelling as a communicative performance screening tool. *Language Speech and Hearing Services in Schools, 14,* 66–74.

Dollaghan, C., & Campbell, T. (1998). Nonword repetition and child language impairment. *Journal of Speech, Language, and Hearing Research, 41,* 1136–1146.

Fey, M. E., Catts, H. W., Proctor-Williams, K., Tomblin, J., & Zhang, X. Y. (2004). Oral and written story composition skills of children with language impairment. *Journal of Speech, Language, and Hearing Research, 47,* 1301–1318.

Gaulin, C. A., & Campbell, T. F. (1994). Procedure for assessing verbal working memory in normal school-age children: Some preliminary data. *Perceptual and Motor Skills, 79,* 55–64.

Gayán, J., & Olson, R. K. (2003). Genetic and environmental influences on individual differences in printed word recognition. *Journal of Experimental Child Psychology, 84*(2), 97–123.

Gresham, F., & Elliott, S. (1990). *Social Skills Rating System.* Circle Pines, MN: American Guidance Service.

Hammer, C. S., Pennock-Roman, M., Rzasa, S., & Tomblin, J. B. (2002). An analysis of the Test of Language Development: Primary for item bias. *American Journal of Speech-Language Pathology, 11,* 274–284.

Hammer, C. S., Tomblin, J. B., Zhang, X. Y., & Weiss, A. L. (2001). Relationship between parenting behaviours and specific language impairment in children. *International Journal of Language & Communication Disorders, 36,* 185–205.

Harter, S. (1988). *Manual for the self-perception profile for adolescents.* Denver, CO: University of Denver.

Hewitt, L. E., Hammer, C. S., Yont, K. M., & Tomblin, J. B. (2005). Language sampling for kindergarten children with and without SLI: Mean length of utterance, IPSYN, and NDW. *Journal of Communication Disorders, 38,* 197–213.

Kail, R. (1994). A method for studying the generalized slowing hypothesis in children with specific language impairment. *Journal of Speech and Hearing Research, 37,* 418–421.

Kail, R., & Salthouse, T. A. (1994). Processing speed as a mental capacity. *Acta Psychologica, 86,* 199–225.

Leslie, L., & Caldwell, J. (1995). *The Qualitative Reading Inventory–II.* New York, Longman.

Masten, A. S., & Coatsworth, J. D. (1998). The development of competence in favorable and unfavorable environments: Lessons from research on successful children. *American Psychologist, 53,* 205–220.

Masten, A. S., Hubbard, J. J., Gest, S. D., Tellegen, A., Garmezy, N., & Ramirez, M. (1999). Competence in the context of adversity: Pathways to resilience and maladaptation from childhood to late adolescence. *Development and Psychopathology, 11,* 143–169.

Newcomer, P., & Hammill, D. (1988). *Test of Language Development-2: Primary.* Austin, TX: Pro-Ed.

Nippold, M. A. (2007). *Later language development: School-age children, adolescents, and young adults* (3rd ed.) Austin, TX: Pro-Ed.

Nippold, M. A., & Scott, C. M. (2010). Overview of expository discourse: Development and disorders. In M. A. Nippold & C. M. Scott (Eds.), *Expository discourse in children, adolescents, and adults: Development and disorders* (pp. 1–11). Austin, TX: Pro-Ed.

Paul, R. (1993). Patterns Of development in late talkers: Preschool years. *Communication Disorders Quarterly, 15,* 7–14.

Pavot, W., & Diener, E. (1993). Review of the Satisfaction with Life Scale. *Psychological Assessment, 5,* 164–172.

Pavot, W., Diener, E., Colvin, C. R., & Sandvik, E. (1991). Further validation of the Satisfaction with Life Scale: Evidence for the cross-method convergence of well-being measures. *Journal of Personality Assessment, 57,* 149–161.

Pellegrini, D. S., Masten, A. S., Garmezy, N., & Ferrarese, M. J. (1987). Correlates of social and academic competence in middle childhood. *Journal of Child Psychology and Psychiatry and Allied Disciplines, 28,* 699–714.

Pennington, B. F., Vanorden, G. C., Smith, S. D., Green, P. A., & Haith, M. M. (1990). Phonological processing skills and deficits in adult dyslexics. *Child Development, 61,* 1753–1778.

Rescorla, L., Dahlsgaard, K., & Roberts, J. (2000). Late-talking toddlers: MLU and IPSyn outcomes at 3; 0 and 4; 0. *Journal of Child Language, 27,* 643–664.

Rice, M. L., & Wexler, K. (1996a). A phenotype of specific language impairment: Extended optional infinitives. In M. L. Rice (Ed.), *Toward a genetics of language* (pp. 215–237). Mahwah, NJ: Lawrence Erlbaum Associates.

Rice, M. L., & Wexler, K. (1996b). Toward tense as a clinical marker of specific language impairment in English-speaking children. *Journal of Speech and Hearing Research, 39,* 1239–1257.

Rice, M. L., & Wexler, K. (2001). *Rice/Wexler Test of Grammatical Impairment.* San Antonio, TX: Pearson.

Rice, M. L., Wexler, K., & Cleave, P. L. (1995). Specific language impairment as a period of extended optional infinitive. *Journal of Speech & Hearing Research, 38,* 850–863.

Rosner, J., & Simon, D. P. (1971). The Auditory Analysis Test: An initial report. *Journal of Learning Disabilities, 4,* 384–392.

Shriberg, L. D., Tomblin, J. B., & McSweeny, J. L. (1999). Prevalence of speech delay in 6-year-old children and comorbidity with language impairment. *Journal of Speech, Language, and Hearing Research, 42,* 1461–1481.

Siegal, M., Iozzi, L., & Surian, L. (2009). Bilingualism and conversational understanding in young children. *Cognition, 110,* 115–122.

Thal, D., Tobias, S., & Morrison, D. (1991). Language and gesture in late talkers: A 1-year follow-up. *Journal of Speech and Hearing Research, 34,* 604–612.

Tomblin, J. B., Hammer, C. S., & Zhang, X. Y. (1998). The association of parental tobacco use and SLI. *International Journal of Language & Communication Disorders, 33,* 357–368.

Tomblin, J. B., Records, N. L., Buckwalter, P., Zhang, X., Smith, E., & O'Brien, M. (1997). Prevalence of specific language impairment in kindergarten children. *Journal of Speech, Language, and Hearing Research, 40,* 1245–1260.

Tomblin, J. B., Records, N. L., & Zhang, X. (1996). A system for the diagnosis of specific language impairment in kindergarten children. *Journal of Speech and Hearing Research, 39,* 1284–1294.

Tomblin, J. B., Smith, E., & Zhang, X. (1997). Epidemiology of specific language impairment: Prenatal and perinatal risk factors. *Journal of Communication Disorders, 30,* 325–344.

Van Dijk, T. A., & Kintch, W. (1983). *Strategies of discourse comprehension.* New York: Academic Press.

Wechsler, D. (1989a). *Wechsler Intelligence Scale for Children* (3rd ed.). San Antonio, TX: The Psychological Corporation.

Wechsler, D. (1989b). *Wechsler Preschool and Primary Scale of Intelligence, revised.* San Antonio, TX: Psychological Corporation.

Woodcock, R. (1987). *Woodcock Reading Mastery Tests–Revised.* Circle Pines, MN: American Guidance Service.

Zhang, X., & Tomblin, J. B. (2000). Factors related to receipt of speech-language therapy. *American Journal of Speech-Language Pathology,* 345–357.

3

THE CHARACTER AND COURSE OF INDIVIDUAL DIFFERENCES IN SPOKEN LANGUAGE

J. Bruce Tomblin, Marilyn A. Nippold, Marc E. Fey, and Xuyang Zhang

In the previous chapters, we established that individual differences in spoken language constitute a necessary condition for language impairment. All would agree that children with language impairment, including those who are defined as having specific language impairment (SLI), occupy a region of low language ability. From this simple starting point, however, things become complex rather quickly. How do we characterize this space that contains SLI? How many different ways are children, including those we say have SLI, free to vary with respect to language development? How stable are these individual differences? And how are these individual differences organized in this space – is the variation spread out along a dimension in a continuous fashion or is it lumpy, suggesting distinct types? These are all big questions that could not be completely answered, but at least addressed within the scope of the longitudinal Iowa Project. Ideally, we would have measured these children in a wide variety of ways so that our picture of language could encompass various theoretical perspectives on the nature of language in children. As described in Chapter 2, we did collect measures of a wide range of language behaviors and did so over a substantial period of child development. In this case, however, we were constrained to a study of language development in mid- and later childhood. By the time children enter school, a substantial amount of language development has occurred. In fact, most of the literature on child language development has been concentrated on the early childhood years during which time very rapid growth occurs and somewhat variable rates of language growth have been shown. There has been much less focus on these later years of childhood. We know that language abilities during the school years continue to expand and become much more refined. New forms of language genre emerge often in the service of academic and literary activities.

Longitudinal studies covering the school years that have focused on spoken language have been rare. Most of the studies that existed when this study was initiated consisted of longitudinal studies of clinically identified groups of children rather than children sampled from the general population (Stothard, Snowling, Bishop, Chipchase, & Kaplan, 1998; Aram, Ekelman, & Nation, 1984; Stark et al., 1984). In all cases, these studies had a very limited number of follow-up periods, either terminating in the early school years or following up only once in adolescence. One longitudinal study led by Joseph Beitchman (Beitchman et al., 1994) was based upon an epidemiological sample; however, this study also did not examine the early and middle school years, and the focus of this study was on the psychiatric sequelae of language impairment. Thus, the longitudinal study provided a rare opportunity to look at the issues of continued language growth throughout the school years within a broad sample of children, many of whom began school with poor language. Using this sample of children and the array of language measures described in Chapter 2, we are able to address a range of questions concerning the way that individual differences in language are manifested across development during the school years.

DIMENSIONALITY OF INDIVIDUAL DIFFERENCES IN LANGUAGE

We will begin our exploration of school-age spoken language by asking how these individual differences organize across the potential domains or dimensions of language. For the past 50 years, most of the conceptual models of language that have driven our assessment and description of child language have come from linguistic theory. Linguistic theories provide a rich and sometimes competing array of subsystems of language. These theories have evolved from efforts to understand systematic properties of spoken languages. To be a satisfying theory, the account needs to provide economy and generality within and across languages; however, most contemporary linguistic theories do not address individual differences in language. In fact, individual differences are usually treated as extralinguistic phenomena. Also, for our purposes of broad characterization of language, we need to acknowledge that there is no encompassing theory of language, but rather we have linguistic theories that are concerned with subsystems of language such as semantics, grammar, phonology, and pragmatics; in fact, dominant theories within the generative framework explicitly claim that these subsystems are distinct, albeit interactive. Even within these subsystems there are many potential components that can represent relatively independent systems in their own right. Therefore, the theories provide a very rich set of possible ways that language users could differ, but provide very little guidance about how independent these subsystems actually are with respect to individual differences. If we are to attempt to characterize individual differences in language and to study their developmental course, we need to grapple with the problem of how to measure language or perhaps at least what our measures of language can tell us. Linguistic theories may predict that language will be carved into subsystems, but our measures may either fail to reveal these subsystems or provide evidence that the theoretical subsystems are not valid. This problem is made even more complex when we consider that children's language changes over time. Thus, the very kind of language representations very likely change qualitatively and/or quantitatively over time, making the description of language growth even more difficult.

These are issues that lie at the very roots of research on child language, and certainly this study will not be able to resolve them. However, we can inspect our data in order to determine the extent to which our measures of language provide a rich or sparse array of language dimensions and how children with poor language are placed in this array. This issue concerning the dimensionality of the individual differences reflected by our measures bears directly on our ability to generate categories and in particular subcategories of language status using these measures. As described in Chapter 2, a general framework for the diagnosis of SLI was established for the determination of the prevalence of SLI in kindergarten. This framework was developed to reflect the possible ways that children with poor language were thought to possibly vary. Thus, we established a dimension of receptive versus expressive language (modality) and another dimension that reflects the principal domains of language structure – words, sentences, and discourse. Specific language tests were then nested within this framework to measure the intersection of domains and modality. This diagnostic framework then was used throughout the longitudinal study to examine the language status of our children over time. Given the centrality of this framework and the measures adopted to implement it, we believe it is essential to examine these core measures across the time period using basic psychometric methods to aid our interpretation of the data provided by them. Thus, we will examine the core measures used within the diagnostic framework. Also, we will incorporate the additional measures of language that we obtained in order to aid in determining what the core measures of language do and do not tell us about individual differences in language.

PRINCIPAL COMPONENTS STRUCTURE OF LANGUAGE

Over the past century, researchers interested in individual differences have come to rely on a set of well-developed tools that all in one way or another draw on correlational methods. Two measures that are correlated are assumed to measure much the same thing in these participants because the relative standing of the participants is retained across the two measures. By extension, if we have several measures performed on the same participants, we may hypothesize that these measures are likely to be interrelated and thus share variance. Principal components analysis (PCA) provides a means of organizing the measures with respect to this shared variance into a set of composite variables formed by combinations of these variables. Each new composite variable can be made to be independent of the other composite variables and thus PCA can reveal the amount of independent information provided by the individual measures. We will use this method to examine the core language measures within the diagnostic framework as well as the additional language measures collected at each age interval.

KINDERGARTEN

Recall that the first phase of the Iowa Project provided a much larger sample of 1,929 children who were used in the EpiSLI study. These children were assessed with language measures described in Chapter 2 and also listed in Table 3.1. One feature of oral communication not included in this model was speech sound production; however, one of the purposes of this initial epidemiological study was to examine the rate of speech sound disorders in children with SLI, and thus we also obtained a measure of speech sound production using the TOLD-2:P Word Articulation test (Newcomer & Hammill, 1988). Because we did so, we are able to incorporate this measure into our consideration of the dimensionality of language in such a way as to consider how closely associated speech sound production is to other aspects of spoken language.

Table 3.1 Principal components analysis of language and speech measures in kindergarten

	Component 1	Component 2	Component 3
Picture Vocabulary	0.70*	0.15	0.02
Oral Vocabulary	0.75*	0.27	−0.01
Sentence Imitation	0.76*	0.21	0.23
Grammatic Understanding	0.75*	0.05	−0.03
Grammatic Closure	0.79*	0.24	0.14
Narrative-events recalled	0.10	0.90*	0.01
Narrative-Comprehension	0.40*	0.67*	0.09
Articulation	0.08	0.05	0.98*

Notes:
* Loading values greater than 0.34 are flagged to signify that the measure has sufficient loading to be considered in the interpretation of the Factor.

A PCA of these measures resulted in three principal components with Eigenvalues above or very near 1.0. These principal components were employed in a three-component PCA with orthogonal rotation; the results are shown in Table 3.1. We can see Component 1 clearly represents receptive and expressive vocabulary and sentence use. Component 2 comprises the two tasks involving narration, while Component 3 is quite clearly a speech sound production factor reflected in the Articulation test score. Usually, in PCA it is desirable for at least three measures to load on a component in order for us to have a good sense of what this component represents. Therefore, it is difficult to interpret the third component containing the single measure of speech sound production task other than to say that it does not load on the language components.

Component 1 is quite clearly one that represents tasks that tap into various aspects of what is commonly viewed as "language." Within this component, identifying words, defining words, and producing and understanding sentences cohere together, and this could be taken as evidence that when children are skilled in one aspect of word and sentence use, they are likely to be similarly skilled at other aspects. Even though these measures in some cases were purely receptive (Picture Vocabulary and Grammatic Understanding) and others were purely expressive (Oral Vocabulary), there was no support for a receptive-expressive dimension. Also, there was no differentiation between word and sentence use in this analysis; and in fact even narrative comprehension loaded on this first principal component as well as loading on the second. These data do seem to suggest that the narrative task involved additional sources of variance that were not common to the first component. This was particularly reflected in the number of clauses expressed during the narrative recall.

Within the kindergarten test battery, we also included two other tasks for the purposes of examining pre-reading abilities. These were the Deletion Task (DT) and the Rapid Automatized Naming (RAN) task. We might expect to see these either form a separate principal component or perhaps combine with the Articulation measure based on a common phonological trait. However, when these were added to the PCA, they did not load with the Articulation measure but rather loaded with the Component 1 (RAN loaded at –0.50 and DT loaded moderately at 0.76). Thus, although these tasks do involve phonological knowledge, this aspect of phonological knowledge does not overlap with speech sound production. These findings are consistent with the recent conclusions of Pennington and Bishop (2009) with respect to the weak relationship between speech sound production and early word reading as well as spoken language.

SECOND GRADE

One principal objective of this research was aimed at evaluating variations in individual differences across ages, and therefore within this expanded set of measures we wanted to retain the same framework for diagnosis used at kindergarten. This need for measurement continuity was challenged by the fact that the particular tests used in kindergarten measures were approaching ceiling at second grade. Thus, we needed to alter the specific set of measures to avoid these ceiling effects. This problem with ceiling effects also led us to no longer assess speech sound production due to the fact that the study was focusing on language and that speech sound production in most children has reached ceiling levels by 8 years of age. Because the sample size of the longitudinal study was reduced, we were also able to examine the language status of these children using a wider range of language measures. Thus, we had the opportunity to evaluate the dimensionality of a different set of core measures of language. Furthermore, we could use the additional measures to aid our understanding of what is and is not measured by the core diagnostic battery. Using the same approach as in kindergarten, we initially examined the dimensionality of the core language measures along with the additional measures using PCA.

As can be seen in Table 3.2, when the core measures of language used for diagnosis of language impairment (LI) were submitted to a PCA, two factors were suggested. The first component with an eigenvalue of 4.36 was formed by all the measures except for the total clauses measure. As in the kindergarten data, the narrative comprehension measure loaded with the other word and sentence tasks. Also

Table 3.2 Principal components of the core measures used at second grade for diagnosis of language impairment

Language test	Component 1	Component 2
PPVT	0.81*	0.10
CREVT	0.74*	0.06
CELF-Sent. Struct.	0.66*	0.10
CELF-Concepts and Directions	0.83*	0.07
CELF-Word Structure	0.83*	0.08
CELF-Recall Sentences	0.84*	0.09
CELF-Listening to Paragraphs	0.74*	0.10
Number of Clauses in Narrative	0.11	0.99*

Notes:
* Loading values greater than 0.34 are flagged to signify that the measure has sufficient loading to be considered in the interpretation of the Factor.

similar to the kindergarten data, a second factor was suggested by the total clauses measure; however, this principal component had an eigenvalue of 0.94 and accounted for only an additional 12% of the variance.

This analysis shows that the dimensionality of the second grade diagnostic protocol was very similar to the one used at kindergarten in that one dominant general language ability seemed to underlie most of the measures, but a second component representing the amount of information provided in the narrative formed a second component. The interpretation of the second component was made difficult by the fact that we had only one measure loading on this component.

Fortunately, unlike the kindergarten protocol, we had more measures of language at this wave of assessment. We added these measures to this analysis to aid us in the interpretation of what this diagnostic battery is and is not measuring with respect to tasks and measures ordinarily considered to reflect language. One measure that was added was the Berry-Talbot morphology test. This test is not in common use currently, and in fact is not in print. However, it provided a very classic way of assessing inflectional and derivational morphology. This test is simply an adaptation of the classic Berko Cloze test. The Berry-Talbot test presents the child with novel-named objects performing novel-named actions. Additionally, the Narrative Elicitation Task developed by Fey (Fey, Catts, Proctor-Williams, Tomblin, & Zhang, 2004) was used to provide the narrative production score in the form of total clauses; however, this task also provides several different measures of language facility drawn from the narrative. In this task, there are six key measures of language usage that are potentially independent:

number of total words, number of C-units produced, mean length of utterance (MLU), clausal density, percentage of C-units with mazes, and percentage of C-units that are grammatical.

The measures in the diagnostic battery and the additional ones from the Berry-Talbot and the narrative generation tests did not measure the social/conversational aspect of language and communication nor did they provide information about the perceptions that listeners have of these children. Social communication is often considered as separable from aspects of language measured by our tests. Bishop (2000) has referred to the latter as structural language and proposed that this represents a different dimension of language. Ratings of behaviors that are reflective of social communication were sampled from two rating systems that asked children's teachers to rate the children's communication along with a variety of other behaviors. Some of these behaviors (see Table 3.3) to be rated were embedded in the teacher form of the Social Skills Rating System (SSRS; Gresham & Elliott, 1990). In each case, the teachers were asked to rate these behaviors from 0 (never) to 2 (often). Because this system was designed to assess social skills, you can see that the content of these questions focuses on some specific behaviors involving social/interpersonal use of communication. An additional set of items were included on a form asking teachers about the child's performance in the classroom. These items are shown in Table 3.4. Again, these items were concerned with the child's communicative performance in and around the classroom. Separate scores based on the SSRS questions and the Classroom Communication questionnaires were computed in order to provide multiple measures of social communication. Finally, included in the classroom questionnaire was a request for the teacher to rate the child on a five-point scale with regard to the child's standing relative to classmates with respect to general speaking ability.

These additional language variables from the Berry-Talbot test, the narrative generation task, and the social communication ratings from the teachers were entered into a PCA, along with the core diagnostic

Table 3.3 Items from the Social Skills Rating System concerned with communication

Introduces herself or himself to new people without being told
Says nice things about himself or herself when appropriate
Invites others to join in activities
Initiates conversations with peers
Appropriately tells you when he or she thinks you have treated him or her unfairly
Gives compliments to peers

Table 3.4 Items concerned with communication from classroom performance ratings by teacher

Shares equally in conversations

Communicates in conversations in a manner that is similar to peers

Maintains topic of conversation

Answers conversational questions appropriately

Demonstrates different conversational behaviors with peers and adults

---

language measures in order to aid us in understanding what trait is being assessed in our diagnostic measures and what aspects of communication might be left out. The PCA yielded four principal components with eigenvalues of 1 or greater. The eigenvalues for these components were 5.54 (35% of the total variance), 2.01 (13%), 1.47 (9%), and 1.09 (7%). Thus, the four-factor solution was chosen and is shown in Table 3.5.

We can see that Component 1 appears to be reflective of semantic and grammatical language maturity in general, cutting across lexical size and grammatical/syntactic skills. The two supplementary measures that loaded on this component were both concerned with grammatical skill and morphology in particular. Component 2 is reflective of measures of amount of language generated when the task allows spontaneous expression as reflected by the number of clauses and different words. This component could be labeled loquaciousness. Component 3 appears to reflect utterance complexity (MLU and clausal density) and disfluency in the narrative generation. Importantly, maze rate and the measures of utterance complexity were all positive, and therefore this component reflects a construct of greater mazing and utterance complexity. Also, we see that along with these features, the rate of grammatical C-units was weakly negatively loaded on this component. That is, grammatical accuracy declined with increases in utterance complexity and maze rate. The association of disfluency and grammatical errors with utterance complexity seems counterintuitive, but perhaps reflects a vulnerability to processing that comes with greater complexity. Even though this component is concerned with sentence complexity, it seems to be distinct from grammatical skill and accuracy that is captured by the first component. Note that the rate of grammatical accuracy was significantly loaded in a positive direction on Component 1. At this point, interpreting what the language variance reflected in this third component is not straightforward. In contrast, Component 4 reflects the two ratings from teachers and could be viewed as a dimension concerned with social communication.

Table 3.5 Varimax rotated principal components for core measures and supplemental measures of language in second grade

Language measure	Component 1	Component 2	Component 3	Component 4
PPVT-R	0.80*	0.11	0.01	0.06
CREVT	0.72*	0.07	-0.02	0.22
CELF-Sent. Struct.	0.63*	0.11	0.03	0.07
CELF-Word Struct.	0.83*	0.07	0.01	0.11
CELF-Concept & Dir.	0.80*	0.08	0.3	0.17
CELF-Recalling Sent.	0.82*	0.10	0.0	0.11
CELF-List to Para.	0.71*	0.12	0.10	0.10
Berry-Talbot	0.72*	0.03	0.05	0.01
Number of Clauses in Narr.	0.06	0.97*	0.03	0.09
Number of Different Words	0.18	0.93*	0.12	0.10
MLU	0.21	0.05	0.87*	-0.08
Clausal Density	0.18	0.30	0.77*	0
Percent C-units with maze	-0.08	-0.08	0.46*	0.07
Percent grammatical C-units	0.38*	-0.02	-0.30	0.14
SSRS-Social Comm.	0.25	0.12	-0.04	0.86*
Classroom Comm.	0.43*	0.05	-0.03	0.77*

Notes:
* Loading values greater than 0.34 are flagged to signify that the measure has sufficient loading to be considered in the interpretation of the Factor.

What this additional analysis provides is a better understanding of the initial PCA performed with just the diagnostic battery. There we saw that there were two kinds of ability reflected in the measures on the core battery, and these continue to be shown in the first two components of this analysis – general language maturity and verbosity. The skills reflected in Component 3 having to do with utterance complexity and Component 4 concerned with social communication are not reflected in this battery. We can conclude that most of the individual differences in tasks involving activities that we call language use are organized on a small number of dimensions and that our core language diagnostic measures covered much of this dimensionality.

One last question we can raise has to do with how these four components are associated with the teachers' rating of overall speaking ability in the classroom. When this rating was correlated with factor scores generated for each of the four principal components, we find that the correlations of this rating were 0.48, 0.09, 0.07, and 0.46. Thus, the teachers' overall views of the children were equally influenced by their general language maturity and the teachers' rating on social communication. This latter correlation is no doubt inflated by the fact that the same rater contributed to both. What is striking is that the trait derived from the standardized language test was well correlated with this rating, thus adding further external validity to this first principal component.

FOURTH GRADE

The fourth grade language protocol was very similar to the second grade protocol with the exception of some of the Clinical Evaluation of Language Fundamentals, Third Edition (CELF-III; Semel, Wiig, & Secord, 1995) subtests. The Word Structure and Sentence Structure tests approach ceiling at this age and therefore these were deleted from the protocol and the Formulated Sentences test was added to provide information on expressive syntax. Given that the Word and Sentence Structure subtests were loaded on the first component in second grade along with several other of the standardized language tests, this change was not expected to alter the information provided by our assessment. Indeed a PCA similar to the one performed in second grade on both the core measures and the supplementary measures confirmed this, as shown in Table 3.6.

We see again that four components had eigenvalues greater than 1 and that the first component was largely formed from the standardized tests of the core diagnostic battery along with the rate of grammatical

Table 3.6 Principal components analysis of fourth grade core and supplementary measures of language

Language measure	Component 1 4.09	Component 2 1.74	Component 3 1.73	Component 4 1.56
PPVT-R	0.81*	0.08	0.05	0.21
CREVT	0.74*	0.06	0.10	0.09
CELF-Concept & Dir.	0.78*	0.08	0.12	0.06
CELF-Recalling Sent.	0.80*	−0.03	0.20	0.11
CELF-List to Para.	0.73*	0.03	0.02	0.14
CELF-Formulated Sent.	0.77*	0.05	0.22	0.13
Number of Clauses in Narr.	0.16	0.02	0.87*	0.12
Number of Different Words	0.15	0.07	0.86*	0.03
MLU	0.22	0.85*	0.10	0.01
Clausal Density	0.30	0.76*	0.29	−0.01
Percent C-units with maze	−0.16	0.52*	−0.12	0.07
Percent grammatical C-units	0.47*	−0.37*	0.04	0.07
SSRS-Social Comm.	0.13	0.04	0.06	0.89*
Classroom Comm.	0.31	0.02	0.09	0.87*

C-units produced in the narrative task. The second component at this time point was formed by the utterance complexity measures and mazing rate. This component was the same as Component 3 in second grade. The third component was formed by the same measures of verbosity (number of C-units, number of different words) that constituted Component 2 in second grade, and the social communication measures formed the fourth component. Thus, the dimensional structure of this set of measures appears to be quite robust in that it is very clearly replicated across a 2-year period.

EIGHTH GRADE

The language testing protocol employed in the eighth grade was both similar to and different from the previous waves of assessment. We continued to use the basic model of language that provided for comprehension and production of words, sentences, and connected discourse. The tests of word and sentence use continued to be the same except that we dropped the CELF-III Sentence Formulation test. We changed the discourse measures substantially by dropping the CELF-III Listening to Paragraphs and the earlier narrative generation task. In place of these, we added a more lengthy assessment of discourse comprehension and production based on the Qualitative Reading Inventory–II (QRI; Leslie & Caldwell, 1995) (as described in Chapter 2). The nature of the discourse in these cases was more strongly academic and expository. Also, the discourse production task was one involving retelling rather than generation. This discourse task provided the same measures of discourse-based language production obtained in the narrative generation task used in second and fourth grades. Thus, we used measures of utterance complexity (MLU, dependent clauses per C-unit) and verbosity (number of clauses) provided during the discourse recall. At this time, the grammaticality of utterances was not included. In addition to the QRI recall task, we were able to derive the same measures from the expository samples where the children talked about their favorite game or sport. Thus, at this point, we had three discourse tasks – recall and favorite game or sport (FGS) and conversation.

The children in eighth grade were now attending schools where they had multiple teachers, and therefore the classroom performance assessment was dropped. In place of this, we adopted the Children's Communication Checklist-2 (CCC-2; Bishop, 2003). This form was sent home to the parents of the 527 children who remained in the study at this grade level; 394 were returned. This parent questionnaire asks about a range of communication behaviors covering both structural language (articulation, syntax, and semantics) as well as pragmatic/social language use. Bishop has shown that the pragmatic score (Social Interaction Deviance Composite; SIDC) represents an independent dimension from the structural language score reflected by the General Communication Composite (GCC), and we might expect these two scales to load on separate principal components.

Again, the measures above were entered into a PCA. As in the second and fourth grades, a four-factor solution appeared to be the most appropriate (Table 3.7). Again the first component was formed by the core measures of receptive and expressive word and sentence use. Of particular interest is the loading of the CCC-2:GCC on this factor. This is reminiscent of the loading of the teachers' judgments of language ability obtained in the second and fourth grades and provides very important validation concerning the nature of language measured by this component. These findings show that this language trait represents semantics and grammatical performance that is available to parents in everyday communication. Unlike the prior solutions in the second and fourth grades, the MLU measure derived from the QRI narrative recall loaded modestly on this first component rather than a component concerned with utterance complexity that appears to constitute the second component analysis among these measures. The two measures of utterance complexity from the expository discourse task did form this second, now familiar, utterance complexity variable. It is likely that the QRI MLU did not load on this factor because variance in this measure was linked to the QRI comprehension task, and this covariance was absorbed on Component 1. The third component, also quite familiar by now, comprised measures of total number of utterances in either the expository or the QRI discourse, and thus again the variable of verbosity appears. Finally, the fourth component was formed solely by the SIDC. Thus, although we do not have multiple measures of pragmatics, this is consistent with the prior solutions in the earlier grades supporting a separate dimension for pragmatics.

The additional fourth component with an eigenvalue of 1.0 was formed by the SIDC alone. This variable loaded on the other factors at less than +/–0.20. The GCC measure loaded heavily (0.67) on Component 1 and with loading less than +/–0.10 on the remaining

Table 3.7 Principal components analysis of core and supplementary language measures at 8th grade

	Component 1 4.50	Component 2 1.50	Component 3 1.13	Component 4 1.00
PPVT-R	0.80*	0.08	0.28	0.11
CREVT	0.72*	0.14	0.21	0.03
CELF-CD	0.75*	0.11	–0.08	–0.04
CELF-RS	0.82*	0.02	0.07	–0.04
QRI-Compreh.	0.73*	0.25	0.41*	–0.02
QRI-Total Utt.	0.38*	0.13	0.70*	0.05
QRI-MLU	0.49*	0.25	0.22	0.25
EXP-MLU	0.19	0.85*	0.21	0.02
EXP – Clause Density	0.05	0.91*	–0.01	–0.06
EXP – Total Number of Independent Clauses	–0.02	0.06	0.84*	–0.08
CCC-2:GCC	0.67*	0.06	–0.04	0.07
CCC-2:SIDC	0.84	–0.08	–0.03	0.97

Notes:
* Loading values greater than 0.34 are flagged to signify that the measure has sufficient loading to be considered in the interpretation of the Factor.

components. We also see that the kinds of inappropriate use of language for communication reflected in the SIDC is generally not associated with this structural language trait.

What we can see from this is that the standardized language measures all converge on the quality of language knowledge displayed, but not how verbose the child will be. Interestingly, Component 2 also seems to reveal an aspect of language reflective of language sophistication with regard to sentence complexity indicators; however, these were specific to the more unconstrained discourse setting rather than being common to the standardized measures. It should be noted, however, that this should not be taken as evidence that these measures of grammatical/syntactic skill in expository discourse are independent of the measures on Component 1. Rather these data from the PCA suggest that there may be a particular ability concerning sentence generation in expository discourse that is separate from an ability that contributes to the standardized language test performance. The PCA showed that even MLU in expository discourse was loaded at 0.48 on the unrotated first principal component. Thus, when we think of these measures as reflecting common variance, all but expository clause density and number of independent clauses were substantially loaded on Component 1.

TENTH GRADE

The 10th grade language test protocol was the same as that used in the eighth grade. Additionally, the expository discourse sample employed the same measures. Again, we used the same summary measures from an expository generation task that in this case consisted of an explanation of a conflict resolution problem rather than a favorite game or sport. At this point, the children were approaching 16 years of age and therefore the CCC-2 was not used.

Again, we conducted the same kind of analysis as used in the prior grades for these 10th grade data. Table 3.8 summarizes the PCA of these various measures of language, cutting across the language tests and discourse tasks. The resulting solution yielded three principal components very much like in the eighth grade. Because we did not have a social communication measure, there was no fourth component. The first component had an eigenvalue of 4.18 and accounted for 42% of the variance. The next two had eigenvalues of 1.59 and 1.02 and added 16% and 10% of the variance respectively. When these factors were rotated using varimax, the loadings on these three factors revealed a very similar story to what was seen in eighth grade. The first factor comprised the standardized language measures including the comprehension measure as well as the total number of utterances from the QRI. The MLU of the QRI recall was only weakly loaded on this factor in this case, but this time was loaded on the second factor along with MLU and the clausal density from the expository discourse task. As in the eighth grade, the third factor was formed by the measures of total utterances produced in the two discourse tasks with the addition this time of a weak clausal density loading from the expository task.

Again, as in the prior analyses, we see evidence of one dominant language factor that represents the extent of lexical knowledge displayed on the standardized tasks as well as ability to use sentences for listening and expression. The second factor, as in the eighth grade, appears to be one largely concerned with utterance complexity in discourse. We might have expected to see the Recalling Sentences subtest on the CELF-III also load on this, but it appears that this measure, at least at this age, does not tap the same kind of language ability. Finally, as was seen across the different protocols, the third factor appears to represent verbosity.

ALTERNATIVE PERSPECTIVES ON DIMENSIONALITY OF LANGUAGE MEASURES

The analysis of dimensionality just provided reveals little evidence of any substructure within the language test battery that we used throughout the study. These findings are largely consistent with data

Table 3.8 Principal components analysis of tenth grade core and supplementary language measures

Language measure	Component 1	Component 2	Component 3
PPVT-R	0.86*	0.10	0.02
CREVT	0.78*	0.15	0.13
CELF-CD	0.76*	0.02	0.15
CELF-RS	0.78*	0.12	0.08
QRI-Compreh.	0.77*	0.21	0.22
QRI-Total Utt.	0.41*	0.09	0.73*
QRI-MLU	0.34	0.65*	−0.37
EXP-MLU	0.17	0.81*	0.31
EXP-Clause Density	0.01	0.77*	0.41*
EXP – Total Number of Independent Clauses	0.08	0.23	0.72*

Notes:
* Loading values greater than 0.34 are flagged to signify that the measure has sufficient loading to be considered in the interpretation of the Factor.

that we published on this topic (Tomblin & Zhang, 2006). In that article, however, we reported that across time a dimension formed around the distinction between vocabulary and sentence use and became apparent at the eighth grade. This distinction was not present in the kindergarten, second grade, or fourth grade data but did emerge at the eighth grade assessment period. We did not find this emergence of a sentence–vocabulary distinction in the current analysis. There are several reasons why this might be. First, the Tomblin and Zhang analysis was a factor analysis rather than a principal components analysis. In this regard, the focus was on the dimensionality of latent ability in the children rather than the dimensionality of individual differences of the measures themselves. Second, the data used in the Tomblin and Zhang study were scores based on an Item Response Theory (IRT) analysis that were designed to reflect language ability. Later, more details will be given about the nature of these scores. However, a key feature of these IRT scores when compared with standard scores such as z-scores is that the means and variances of these scores can change over development, whereas standard scores are designed to have a constant mean and a constant variance. We can see the effect of this in Figure 3.1. Ability in vocabulary and sentence use was equated at

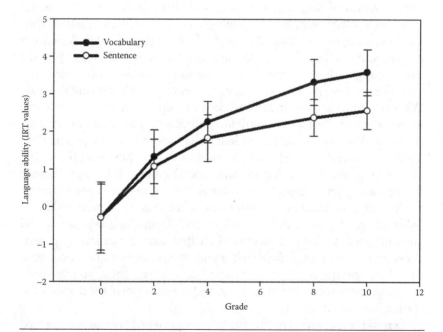

Figure 3.1 Patterns of growth in vocabulary and grammar ability scores across grade levels.

kindergarten, but then could change independently. We can see that vocabulary shows a greater rate of growth across time than sentence use. Given the nature of the two skills, this is not surprising. Vocabulary is largely an open system in which more words can be created and learned, while the grammar and syntax of sentences appears to be closed, at least on standardized tasks. Thus, we see that by adolescence, there is little room for more growth in sentence use, as measured by standardized tasks, and the variance at this point is somewhat smaller. Vocabulary growth slows but continues to progress. This evidence of a separation in absolute ability between the two systems was reflected in the factor analysis. What the current PCA shows, however, is that even though the ability levels of vocabulary and sentence use diverge, the relative standing of children in each of these domains as reflected in the standard scores is very similar; in other words, there is a strong correlation between these two systems.

SUMMARY OF DIMENSIONALITY

We began with the recognition that individual differences in language performance was a potentially highly dimensional phenomenon. As such, we might find that children would be free to vary in terms of different aspects of language subsystems such as speech sound production, vocabulary, syntax, morphology, etc., as well as whether they were listening or speaking. Although the majority of these skills were measured in our protocol at most age intervals, the data do not provide strong support for this high dimensionality. This does not mean that such dimensionality does not exist, as this requires accepting the null. We can say that our measures do not capture unique sources of information in the form of individual differences to show this dimensionality. We do see some evidence that speech sound production, ability to understand and produce words and sentences, and the ability to use language in accordance with social conventions seem largely free to vary. That is, children who are skilled in one area are not necessarily skilled in another. Additionally, what may be viewed as knowledge of word and sentence content and form (language form and content) measured on standardized elicited tasks is not strongly associated with the amount (verbosity) and complexity of utterances produced in spontaneous unconstrained discourse. Thus, standardized language assessment methods seem to provide information about the former but not the latter.

Across the age range of this study, Component 1 was largely formed from standardized tests. This raises the question as to whether what is being measured here reflects general language ability or perhaps test-taking ability. Evidence in support of the former rather than the latter comes from the fact that grammatical accuracy measured in the narrative and expository tasks were also loaded on this component. Additionally, teacher and parent reports of language facility were correlated with this component. This question of what this Component 1 is actually measuring is a question about its validity. Validity is a notion that requires converging evidence from many sources. Given the item content of the tests that load on Component 1 and these other pieces of evidence, it seems reasonable to believe that Component 1 is reflecting a construct of language content and form ability.

The dimensionality we did find is largely consistent with common clinical distinctions between speech sound disorders (phonological disorders), language disorders (form and content), and pragmatic disorders. However, the absence of separate dimensions concerning receptive and expressive language or between lexical and sentence skills calls into question subtypes of language impairment that would require these distinctions. It is possible that the two dimensions concerned with verbosity and utterance complexity reflect a dimension that could contain an expressive language disorder, but recall that even these dimensions did not contain the variable of grammaticality in expressed utterances.

Our data analysis also presented a rather striking picture of continuity of this dimensionality of language across the 10 years of the study despite the fact that many of the specific aspects of the assessment protocol changed over time. This stability does make for a much easier job of examining questions of change in individual differences over time, as it suggests that within these dimensions it will be possible to view variation as quantitative. As such, we can now turn to this topic of variation/stability in language status across time.

LANGUAGE CHANGE: STABILITY AND GROWTH ACROSS THE SCHOOL YEARS

In the prior section, we inspected our measures of language across the course of the longitudinal study with respect to what we were measuring at each time point and whether what we were measuring remained the same. This analysis showed that our battery of language tests used to diagnose language impairment largely converged onto one construct that can be described as content and form. We could see some evidence for two other dimensions concerned with form and content – verbosity and utterance fluency and complexity that could be reflected in the expressive discourse measure. The manner in which the discourse measure was incorporated into the diagnostic battery reflected the verbosity dimension via measures of total number of clauses. Thus, our diagnostic battery provided quite good coverage of content and form, and showed that a simple composite score of these measures can be justified. The battery also included additional dimensions concerned with language and communication. Speech sound production and social communication appear to be separate dimensions, and these dimensions are not ordinarily incorporated in the notion of LI, but rather are represented within the diagnostic categories of speech sound disorder and pragmatic disorder.

Of particular importance within a longitudinal study was the evidence that these dimensions of language and communication emerged at each time period despite some changes in how we measured them. Thus, as we begin to consider patterns of change across time, we are able to have some assurance that we are measuring the same construct across time and thus quantitative treatment of our measures is reasonable.

RELIABILITY AND DEVELOPMENTAL STABILITY

Research on individual differences focuses on understanding how individuals differ from one another with respect to notions such as performance, achievement, and ability. Not all aspects of the differences among individuals are equally interesting. It is common to differentiate between differences that are transient and those that are at least somewhat enduring. Sometimes the transient variation is viewed as reflecting state characteristics of the person whereas the enduring are viewed as trait characteristics. Kraemer, Gullion, Rush, Frank, and Kupfer (1994) define a trait as existing when "the dependent variable is relatively consistently expressed within each subject over the span of time under consideration and, in addition, differentiates individuals within the population from each other." They define state variation as occurring when "the dependent variable fluctuates within individuals during that time span" (Kraemer et al., 1994, p. 57). Trait properties are reflected in relative stability in within-person performance relative to other individuals, whereas trait variation reflects within-person variation over time and setting. Most of our interest in developmental psychology and communication sciences and disorders has been toward understanding traits, and this will be our focus here. This is not meant to imply that trait research is more valuable or more informative than studies of state variation. The latter is well exemplified by those who employ Vygotskian-influenced methods such as dynamic assessment. Indeed the trait versus state contrast is rather clearly revealed in the differences between traditional psychological measurement via standardized tests and dynamic assessment.

If we are interested in measuring the language trait status of children, then we need to determine how much of our measured variable is reflective of this stable trait and how much of it reflects state variance and unsystematic measurement error. Then we can begin to consider how stable this trait is across time.

RELIABILITY OF KINDERGARTEN LANGUAGE STATUS

Many of our research questions concerning the language status of the children in this study began with the child's language status at kindergarten. This was what influenced whether the child was sampled into the longitudinal study, and to a great extent this is the time point from which we wanted to project outcomes and examine the level of risk associated with poor language at kindergarten entry. Thus, early on we recognized a need to determine the reliability of our kindergarten language battery, and so we conducted a test–retest reliability study for the language measures (TOLD-2:P and narrative story task). All composite language scores of children tested at one point in time during the diagnostic phase were transformed into decile scores. The decile scores were listed in rank order, and 54 children were selected to receive a second language testing session, with four to five children randomly selected from each decile. The selected children were retested an average of 24 days after the first testing, with a range of 13 to 29 days. In this sample, 53.7% were female, and 46.3% were male. Pearson correlation coefficients for the subcomposite scores were used to make the LI diagnosis, and the overall composite scores are shown in Table 3.9. The reliability coefficients for the subcomposite scores ranged from 0.72 to 0.87, and the composite score was 0.89. These values are similar to those reported for the TOLD-2:P. This study also showed that there was 90.74% agreement in language diagnosis from test to retest, and 9.26% disagreement. No child diagnosed as having normal language skills at the first testing was diagnosed as having SLI at the second testing. However, five children diagnosed as having SLI at the first testing were diagnosed as having normal language skills at the second testing. Thus, our diagnosis is not error free even across a very short period. We will revisit this topic when we look at diagnostic stability across age intervals; however, this suggests that changes in

Table 3.9 Correlation values among language composite scores across assessment waves

	Wave 1	Wave 2	Wave 3	Wave 4
Wave 2 (2nd grade)	0.80			
Wave 3 (4th grade)	0.78	0.86		
Wave 4 (8th grade)	0.76	0.82	0.86	
Wave 5 (10th grade)	0.71	0.79	0.83	0.91

diagnostic status are not due to systematic variation in development since these changes occurred within a month.

These data provide us with a measurement baseline as we examine patterns of change, stability, and growth across time. Reliability levels for the subcomposite score shown in Table 3.9 are quite respectable, and the overall composite score would be considered very good for most psychometric instruments. Despite this, the overall composite score still contains about 20% non-trait-like (state and error) variance. Thus, some variation over time in the measure of language status in these children can be expected even though the underlying trait status may be unchanged. If we look at only two time points, it is difficult to determine how much variation between times is due to systematic change in the language trait and how much is due to random error, although we have already noted that there seems to be little time for much systematic change in these data.

STABILITY OF LANGUAGE COMPOSITE SCORES ACROSS TIME

Because we have good evidence that the various language measures used in our test battery are all measuring the same thing, we can use the overall composite score as our best estimate of each child's language status at each time point. We just observed that this composite measure in kindergarten had a test–retest correlation of 0.89. Thus, we would not expect correlations above this for any correlation involving the kindergarten composite score and later measures of language. Table 3.9 provides the correlations among the composite scores across the study period.

We can see from the correlations in Table 3.9 that overall there is considerable stability in the individual differences in language status across the 10-year period of this study. Thus, children who entered the study as kindergarteners generally remained in their relative position within the distribution of language abilities in this sample. We also can see that the correlations across adjacent waves of assessment were all at 0.80 or greater. Thus, the long-term reliability of our measurement of language status is quite good and is not much lower than the very short-term reliability obtained in kindergarten. When we look at the trend in correlations across the waves of assessment by going down each column in the table, we can see that the values decline in each case. The magnitude of this change is not great. For instance, the shared variance (r^2) between kindergarten and second grade was 0.64 whereas it was 0.49 between kindergarten and 10th grade, but it does leave some room for changes in children's standing over time. This was of particular interest in our research, as this change could reflect gains in language status for children with poor language in kindergarten. This will be examined further in Chapter 4.

ARE ABSOLUTE MEASURES OF LANGUAGE ABILITY STABLE?

The analyses concerning stability of scores of relative standing above suggest that by the time a child reaches school age, his/her language status is largely fixed. Scores of relative standing, however, require that gains by one child result in declines by another. There are ways, however, that change in one member of the group does not have to come at the cost of another. If we consider the status of a trait such as language in terms of absolute ability, such as in the total words known or grammatical morphological skill, changes in this ability do not have to come at the price of another. This would particularly be the case when the variability between individuals changed over time as when the ability reaches an asymptote and thus variance declines. This is quite evident in children's speech sound production where, by early school age, most children have near-perfect performance. Thus, it would be very useful to look at language skill using a metric that reflects ability in an absolute sense. In this case, we need a way to represent language ability so that it can reflect change in ability independent of the ability status of other children in the sample. We also need a way to estimate this ability from a variety of tests used across age, and that this ability be placed on a uniform scale. Fortunately, modern psychometrics provide just such a metric in the form of IRT ability scores.

IRT provides estimates of both the difficulty of test items and abilities of the examinees. Difficulty is a property of items based on performance of examinees and ability is a property of examinees based on items. Thus, each of these variables is based on the other. Item difficulty represents the proportion of individuals of a given ability who would pass an item. Thus, item difficulties can be computed by holding the examinees' ability constant and then varying items. Items passed by most of these examinees are easy and those passed by few would be difficult. Likewise, the ability of examinees can be determined by holding item difficulty constant and varying examinees. Examinees who fail more items have less ability than those who pass more items. The purpose of IRT modeling is to achieve estimates of item difficulty and examinee ability that are independent of each other. Because items can be scaled with regard to difficulty, IRT provides a means of calibrating items from different tests. In this way measures from a test given to 14-year-olds can be placed on the same scale as items given to kindergarteners. Once all items across the age range are calibrated with regard to difficulty, then it is possible to assign ability scores to examinees across the age range. These ability scores allow us to track changes in absolute language ability across time. This process of computing IRT scores is explained in more detail in the Appendix. It should be noted that underlying an IRT analysis is the assumption that the items being scaled are measuring the same underlying ability.

The computation of IRT ability scores provided the basis for the data in Figure 3.1. This shows the distribution of IRT scores for vocabulary and grammar measures at each wave of assessment. We can also compute a single language ability score across time and this is shown in Figure 3.2. The most important thing to note is that unlike the z-scores of relative standing that have been used up to this point, the variance of these scores does not have to remain the same. We can see that there is a considerable shift in variance between kindergarten and second grade. This is due in large part to the fact that we sampled the children after kindergarten and thus we see again the effects of regression to the mean. From 2nd, 4th, 8th, and 10th grades, the standard deviation shifts from 0.63, 0.50, 0.49, 0.50. Therefore, although these scores could fan out or narrow down, there is little of either.

The primary reason for our deriving the IRT ability scores was that these scores allow us to measure the changes in absolute language ability across time for each child in the form of growth trajectories or growth curves. Variability in growth curves among children would be indicative of a form of instability in language status across time. Therefore, we employed a mixed model to analyze the amount of individual differences found in our children with regard to initial language status (intercept) and rate of change (slope) after kindergarten. Because the data in Figure 3.2 show a clear nonlinear shape, it was necessary to transform the data. We elected to transform the IRT scores via a square transformation; however, because some of the initial values

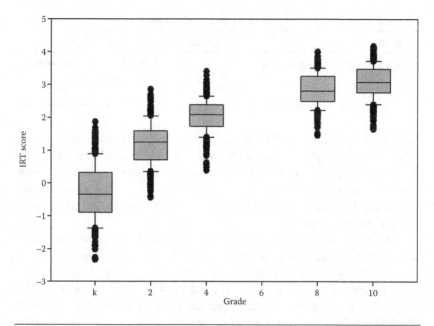

Figure 3.2 Box plots of Item Response Theory language ability scores.

were negative it was necessary to add a constant of three to all scores in order that the lowest score exceeds zero. Also, we set the intercept point at 6 years of age, which was the average age of the children at the first assessment.

The model that was tested was purely a random effects model (unconditional model) without any predictors of individual differences. Thus, this model provided an intercept testing whether scores in kindergarten were significantly different from 0, and a slope parameter that tested whether the growth in language was greater than 0. The effect estimates and the significance test results for this unconditional model are presented in Table 3.10. From this model, we learn that for all the children combined, the average starting ability level in kindergarten was significantly greater than 0. Since the IRT scores are on an interval scale where 0 is arbitrary, these results are not too interesting. The average rate of change per year of growth (2.85) was also significantly different from 0. Thus, not surprisingly, the children in general showed gains in language ability. When compared with a model that only contained the intercept (means model), this model containing the age variable accounted for 91% of the variance of the means model. This value represents the proportion of within-subject variance accounted for by age, and

Table 3.10 Parameter values for growth curve analysis of language

Fixed effect	Coefficient	se	t-value	Df	p
γ_{00}: Intercept at 6 years for $(IRT+3)^2$.	11.29	0.21	52.21	484	<0.0001
γ_{10}: Growth rate of IRT score $(IRT+3)^2$ per unit increase in age.	2.85	0.01	128.52	1454	<0.0001

Singer and Willett (2003) describe this measure as a Pseudo R^2. Therefore, the square root of this value (0.95) provides an estimate of the reliability of our language measure across the school years. This is a very good summary measure telling us that these ability scores are very stable once we account for the individual differences present at kindergarten.

This model also provides estimates of the amount of residual variance representing potential individual differences that remain to be accounted for by background characteristics of the children. The unaccounted-for variance in the intercept was 14.13 ($z = 7,85$, $p = 0.0001$) whereas the unaccounted-for variance of the slope was 0.04 ($t = 3.88$, $p < 0.0001$). The residual error variance was 13.32. Thus, of the total variance reflective of between-subjects variance, 51% was concentrated in the intercept – that is, the child's language ability at the beginning of the study. Quite surprisingly, only 0.1% of the total variance across individuals can be traced to variation in slope. This tells us that although our sample contained considerable variation in the language skills of these children, the majority of this variation is represented by the kindergarten status of these children, and a very small fraction of these individual differences can be found in differences in rates of growth after kindergarten.

CONCLUSIONS REGARDING STABILITY AND GROWTH IN LANGUAGE

The data we have just examined tell a rather coherent and somewhat surprising story. The data concerning reliability of the scores of relative standing showed that children's relative status in language remains steady across the school years. We worried that some of this stability could be due to the fact that at each time point, we transformed language skill into scores of relative standing. Our use of the IRT scores provided a way to avoid this by tracking language change using values that represented absolute ability. The variance over time was not constrained in this way. Even with this metric, we still find considerable stability in language ability across time.

These findings tell us that however children become different with regard to language ability, it happens during the years preceding school entry. There have been several studies of language development during the preschool years. Many of these have focused on children who were late talkers (Ellis Weismer, Murray-Branch, & Miller, 1994; Fischel, Whitehurst, Caulfield, & DeBaryshe, 1989; Rescorla, Dahlsgaard, & Roberts, 2000; Rescorla, Roberts, & Dahlsgaard, 1997; Thal & Reilly, 1997). These studies suggest that the language status of children is not at all stable during the preschool years and that there is considerable change in relative standing and variability in growth rates. The absence of this variation in the school years is remarkable and for those of us who are interested in altering the trajectories of growth during the school years, it should be troubling. The data suggest that with respect to individual differences in language, the cards have been dealt and now it is just a matter of the child playing the hand. It must be said that this study made no effort to change language growth; however, it is reasonable to assume that among these children there were many varied experiences. None of these appears to have had an impact on the growth rates. Had this happened, we would have found a much higher rate of variance among the children with regard to language growth. Less than 1% of the total variance in language skills of children between 6 and 16 is attributable to systematic, linear differences in rates of language growth. In contrast, more than 50% of this variance in language is associated with their language ability when they were in kindergarten. There does remain a substantial amount of variance that is not explained by linear within-subjects and between-subjects sources of variance. Some of this may simply be the kind of variation referred to earlier as state variation. This would show up in unsystematic variation across time. We know that even with very good reliability this could be of modest size. Thus, as with all claims of small or negligible effects, we need to recognize that there is still the potential for some systematic patterns of change; however, it seems unlikely to be very large – perhaps at best 20%. If so, this may provide the range of variance that interventions directed at changing fundamental language abilities could tap into. Fortunately, not all of the interventions provided to school-age children are intended to change general ability. Instead, often the focus is on either very specific skills that are unlikely to be tapped by standardized language measures such as those used in this study, or they are directed at developing compensatory skills and curricular adaptations. The data from this study would suggest that these approaches may be the most likely to provide improvements in language function.

APPENDIX

Computation of Item Response Theory (IRT) Ability Scores

Our goal in performing an IRT analysis was to come up with a way to measure language ability across the waves of assessment using a common scale. We selected 28 item scores (0 or 1) for each of the two language areas. When selecting items, raw item difficulty, i.e., pass rate, was considered. While a pass rate around 0.5 is ideal, we considered pass rates between 0.1 and 0.9 acceptable. This resulted in selected items that were different from one grade to the next, because the difficulty of different items was appropriate for one grade but too low for the next grade.

Effort was also made to have item overlap in each language area between adjacent grades (e.g., between second and fourth or fourth and eighth). Table 3.11 presents the item list for each grade and the overlap between adjacent grades. The overlap items were used as anchors to calibrate the average growth from one grade to the next based on the pass rate increase on the same items. From 2nd grade to 4th, to 8th, and to 10th grade, the average growth was based on the common items given at adjacent grade levels. Because of the calibrating, the change in performance on the common items from one grade to the next can be considered to be due to change in ability level, and individual differences in performance in the common items can be considered to be due to individual differences in ability levels. Due to extensive growth of receptive vocabulary from fourth to eighth grade, there was no overlap in the appropriate PPVT-R items between these two grades. Thus, the average vocabulary growth from fourth grade to eighth grade was estimated only on the basis of overlapping items in CREVT. From 8th grade to 10th grade, calibrating was not necessary, because adolescents in both grades completed the same set of items.

As shown in Table 3.11, there was no overlap between the test items given at kindergarten and at second grade. Hence, the average growth from kindergarten to second grade could not be estimated based on the pass rate increase on the overlapping set of items given at both grades. To calibrate the difficulty of all the items on the same scale, we administered the two sets of language tests, kindergarten and second grade sets, to 80 second graders and with the order of two sets counterbalanced. Based on the data from these 80 children, we calibrated the difficulty of the two sets of items on the same scale so that the average item difficulty difference and the average growth of the latent ability from kindergarten to second grade could be separated.

Table 3.11 Items used for Item Response Theory (IRT) analysis and construction of item equivalency

Test Items	Grade					# of items	Modality R = Receptive E = Expressive	Domain V = Vocabulary S = Sentence Use
	K	2nd	4th	8th	10th			
TOLD 2:P								
Picture vocabulary Item 9 to 22	X					14	R	V
Oral vocabulary Item 2 to 15	X					14	E	V
Grammatic Understanding Item 11 to 24	X					14	R	S
Sentence Imitation Item 4 to 10	X					7	E	S
Grammatic Completion Item 6 to 12	X					7	E	S
PPVT-R								
Item 70, 71, 74 to 79		X				8	R	V
Item 80 to 83		X	X			4	R	V
Item 84		X				1	R	V
Item 85		X	X			1	R	V
Item 86 to 94			X			9	R	V
Item 138 to 151				X	X	14	R	V
CREVT								
Item 2 and 3		X				2	E	V
Item 4 to10		X	X			7	E	V
Item 11 to 15		X	X			5	E	V
Item 16 and 17			X	X	X	2	E	V
Item 18 to 24				X	X	7	E	V

continued

Table 3.11 Continued

Test Items	K	2nd	4th	8th	10th	# of items	Modality R = Receptive E = Expressive	Domain V = Vocabulary S = Sentence Use
CELF								
Word Structure Item 26 to 32		X				7	E	S
Recalling Sentences Item 6 to 8		X				3	E	S
Recalling Sentences Items 9 and 10		X	X			2	E	S
Recalling Sentences Items 11 and 12		X	X	X		2	E	S
Recalling Sentences Item 13 to 15			X	X		3	E	S
Recalling Sentences Item 16 to 24				X		9	E	S
Formulated Sentences Item 6 to 12			X			7	E	S
Sentence Structure Item 14 to 20		X				7	R	S
Concept & Direction Item 17 to 23			X	X	X	7	R	S
Concept & Direction Item 24 to 30			X	X	X	7	R	S

We performed the above analysis using the computer program BILOG (Mislevy & Bock, 1998). The difficulty of the test items was controlled so that the group means and standard deviations of the difficulty estimates for the common test items were held constant across the grade levels. We achieved this by adjusting the location and scale parameters for the IRT model. Thus, the performance level increase on the same set of items from one grade level to the next could be totally attributed to the ability increase. After the average increase in the ability and the standard deviation change from one grade level to the next were determined (i.e., location and scale parameters were correctly specified), the IRT modeling procedure automatically estimated the difficulty and discrimination power for all items. As there were no common test items in the kindergarten and second grade testing, 80 of the 485 children in the second grade were given both the kindergarten and the second grade set of items. When the means and standard deviations of the ability for the 80 children were held constant across the two sets of items, the average pass rate difference between the two sets was attributed to the difficulty difference. After the average difficulty difference between the two sets was determined, IRT modeling procedure automatically estimated the item difficulty and discrimination power for each item.

REFERENCES

Aram, D. M., Ekelman, B. L., & Nation, J. E. (1984). Preschoolers with language disorders: Ten years later. *Journal of Speech and Hearing Research, 22*, 232.

Beitchman, J. H., Brownlie, E. B., Inglis, A. L., Wild, J., Mathews, R., Schachter, D., et al. (1994). Seven-year follow-up of speech/language-impaired and control children: Speech/language stability and outcome. *Journal of the American Academy of Child & Adolescent Psychiatry, 33*, 1322–1330.

Bishop, D. V. M. (2000). Pragmatic language impairment: A correlate of SLI, a distinct subgroup, or part of the autistic continuum? In D. V. M. Bishop & L. B. Leonard (Eds.), *Speech and language impairments in children: Causes characteristics, intervention and outcome* (pp. 99–113). Hove: Psychology Press.

Bishop, D. (2003). *Children's Communication Checklist, Version 2 [CCC-2]*. London: Psychological Corporation.

Ellis Weismer, S., Murray-Branch, J., & Miller, J. (1994). A prospective longitudinal study of language development in late talkers. *Journal of Speech and Hearing Research, 37*, 852–867.

Fey, M. E., Catts, H. W., Proctor-Williams, K., Tomblin, J. B., & Zhang, X. (2004). Oral and written story composition skills of children with language impairment. *Journal of Speech, Language, and Hearing Research, 47,* 1301–1318.

Fischel, J. E., Whitehurst, G. J., Caulfield, M. B., & DeBaryshe, B. (1989). Language growth in children with expressive language delay. *Pediatrics, 83,* 218–227.

Gresham, F., & Elliott, S. (1990). *Social Skills Rating System.* Circle Pines, MN: American Guidance Service.

Kraemer, H. C., Gullion, C. M., Rush, A. J., Frank, E., & Kupfer, D. J. (1994). Can state and trait variables be disentangled? A methodological framework for psychiatric disorders. *Psychiatry Research, 52,* 55–69.

Mislevy, R., & Bock, R. D. (1998). *Bilog 3.* Lincolnwood, IL: Scientific Software Inc.

Newcomer, P., & Hammill, D. (1988). *Test of Language Development-2: Primary.* Austin, TX: Pro-Ed.

Pennington, B. F., & Bishop, D. V. (2009). Relations among speech, language, and reading disorders. *Annual Review of Psychology, 60,* 283–306.

Rescorla, L., Dahlsgaard, K., & Roberts, J. (2000). Late-talking toddlers: MLU and IPSyn outcomes at 3; 0 and 4; 0. *Journal of Child Language, 27,* 643–664.

Rescorla, L., Roberts, J., & Dahlsgaard, K. (1997). Late talkers at 2: Outcome at age 3. *Journal of Speech Language, and Hearing Research, 40,* 556–566.

Singer, J. D., & Willett, J. B. (2003). *Applied longitudinal data analysis: Modeling change and event occurrence.* London: Oxford University Press.

Stark, R., Bernstein, L., Condino, R., Bender, M., Tallal, P., & Catts, H. (1984). Four-year follow-up study of language impaired children. *Annals of Dyslexia, 34,* 49–68.

Stothard, S. E., Snowling, M. J., Bishop, D. V. M., Chipchase, B. B., & Kaplan, C. A. (1998). Language-impaired preschoolers: A follow-up into adolescence. *Journal of Speech, Language, and Hearing Research, 41,* 407–418.

Thal, D. J., & Reilly, J. S. (1997). Origins of language disorders. *Developmental Neuropsychology, 13,* 233–237.

Tomblin, J. B., & Zhang, X. (2006). The dimensionality of language ability in school-age children. *Journal of Speech, Language, and Hearing Research, 49*(6), 1193–1208.

Tomblin, J. B., Zhang, X., Buckwalter, P., & O'Brien, M. (2003). The stability of primary language impairment: Four years after kindergarten diagnosis. *Journal of Speech, Language, and Hearing Research, 46,* 1283–1296.

4

FEATURES OF LANGUAGE IMPAIRMENT IN THE SCHOOL YEARS

J. Bruce Tomblin and Marilyn A. Nippold

In the previous chapter, we examined the measurement characteristics of our battery of language variables used in this study to provide a clear understanding of what these variables were measuring (validity) and the features of stability of these measures. This allowed us to understand what our measures could and could not tell us about individual differences in language across the age span that we studied for children across the ability spectrum. This analysis revealed some striking features of the language data gathered in this project. First, the number of different aspects of language measured by our various standardized and nonstandardized tasks was quite small. Much of the variance was concentrated on a general language component we might view as knowledge and maturity of lexical sentential aspects of language. Additional dimensions reflecting connected discourse behaviors, social communication, and speech sound production were also found. We also saw that the character of these dimensions remained similar across the time span, even though we used somewhat different tasks at different assessment waves. Finally, we examined the stability and growth characteristics of the major language dimension for all children. The data showed quite striking stability of individual differences for the total sample and very little evidence of individual differences in rates of language growth across time. The child's relative standing in the sample remained very stable across time, and furthermore, when we employed an index of absolute language ability based on Item Response Theory, we found little change in variance across the age range and thus little evidence for some children to fall further back or to catch up. We see in the current chapter that these findings have implications for what we can learn about the nature of language impairment (LI) in general and specific language impairment (SLI) in particular.

The conclusions above were concerned with individual differences in language across ability levels and development. These analyses did not focus on the individual differences that we deemed to represent LI. In this chapter, we will turn to a set of questions concerned with some of the fundamental characteristics of LI in school-age children. The first had to do with the degree to which children with LI show recovery. We also expected to evaluate predictors that would differentiate and thus identify those who showed recovery and those who did not. We now know that the general level of stability across the 10-year period for the sample as a whole is considerable and thus recovery in children with LI would be an exception. A second question we asked was whether common subtypes of LI used in clinical and research settings could be found in this larger sample of children who were sampled from a general population rather than a clinical sample, and whether we could find evidence for a qualitative distinction of children with LI from typically developing children. Finally, given the paucity of research published on spoken language impairment during adolescence, we established a goal of characterizing the features of language impairment in adolescents with LI.

STABILITY AND PROGNOSIS OF LANGUAGE IMPAIRMENT

As just noted, we have found strong evidence of stable patterns of individual differences from kindergarten through the 10th grade for children in general. This pattern of high stability is less clear in the literature on children with LI. If this is true, and in particular if children with early LI systematically improve rather than just fluctuate, then we must consider that some important developmental processes are in play for children with LI that are not operating in typically developing children. In addition, the issue of diagnostic and trait stability is clinically significant. Clinical intervention is predicated on the assumption that the clinical status of a child, as based upon the clinical examination, will persist unless intervention is provided. If there is spontaneous resolution, then appropriate clinical action would be to withhold intervention. However, if spontaneous resolution is not expected, the withholding of treatment – assuming an efficacious intervention is available – would not be defensible. If a reasonable number of children with LI do show recovery without intervention, then we will need to find ways of predicting who these children might be. Our understanding of the stability of LI is made more complex by the report of potential "illusory" periods of recovery (Scarborough & Dobrich, 1990) in which children with prior histories of LI appear to recover. Later, these same children present language impairment again, albeit sometimes in other language domains. Prior to this study, several longitudinal studies have enrolled children with language impairments at or around the time of school entry and followed them into the school years (Aram & Nation, 1980; Baker & Cantwell, 1987; Bishop & Edmundson, 1987a; Silva, McGee, & Williams, 1983; Stark et al., 1984). Additionally, two other studies were conducted at the same time as this one (Conti-Ramsden & Botting, 1999; Rice, Wexler, & Hershberger, 1998). These studies show varying levels of stability of LI during the early school years. Some authors suggest that 81–89% of children continue to present a language problem throughout their school years (Silva, 1987; Stark & Tallal, 1988). Other authors have reported lower levels of persistence in the range of 54–56% (Bishop & Edmundson, 1987b; Cole, Schwartz, Notari, Dale, & Mills, 1995).

This stable pattern of language status relative to age mates over extended periods was reported by Stothard and colleagues (1998). In their study, 71 young British adolescents (15–16 years) who had been clinically identified as language impaired at age 4 were recruited and examined. These children had participated in a short-term longitudinal study across ages 4 to 8 (Bishop & Edmundson, 1987b). A new comparison group of 52 children who had not participated in the earlier study was also recruited. Children who had language impairment persisting to 5-and-a-half years were very likely (76%) to continue to be language impaired in adolescence. These authors noted that children with apparently normal phonological and grammatical skills, but limited narrative abilities at kindergarten, were more likely to decline in language over the 10-year period. These data and others led the authors to note that language status at 5 years appeared to be crucial in setting a course of academic and linguistic development. Specifically, they stated:

> Children whose verbal skills were within the satisfactory range by age 5;6 were able to benefit from language learning situations to maintain or accelerate their vocabulary development. In contrast, children who started out with poorer vocabulary knowledge at 5;6 became increasingly more handicapped over time.
> (Stothard, Snowling, Bishop, Chipchase, & Kaplan, 1998)

These conclusions are of particular importance to the Iowa Project because they refer to patterns of differential growth through the school years where children with LI show slower growth than typically developing children. These patterns have often been the object of speculation. However, none of the previous studies obtained systematic longitudinal data through the elementary school years where these differential growth patterns would be expected to arise. Stothard and her colleagues, including Bishop, hypothesize that growth rates, thus slopes, will differ between subgroups of children with language limitations.

One of the most common ways that language impairment has been diagnosed has been via measures of relative standing. Thus, if children's relative standing with regard to language is quite steady as suggested by our correlational analysis, it is likely that we should see stability in the diagnosis of language impairment. That is, most children diagnosed with LI would remain LI at subsequent intervals. This kind of prospective stability is reflected in the notion of predictive value positive. In this longitudinal study, we established a child's status with respect to LI by placing cut-points at the 10th percentile on the five measures represented in the EpiSLI diagnostic system. Thus, the diagnosis is based on dichotomizing a continuous metric. When we look at the rate of LI (SLI and NLI combined) at 2nd, 4th, 8th, and 10th grades in children diagnosed with LI in kindergarten, we find that the predictive power positive is between 54 and 58% (see Table 4.1). That is only slightly more than half of the children in kindergarten who were LI remained so later on. We first reported results like this in an article that examined the stability of language diagnosis from kindergarten through fourth grade (Tomblin, Zhang, Buckwalter, & O'Brien, 2003). This rate of persisting LI at subsequent intervals seems lower than we might expect given the rather high reliability of the measures. These findings would seem to suggest that many of these children recovered from LI after kindergarten. However, in the Tomblin et al. article, we contended that this was not the appropriate interpretation. To begin with, if the predictive value positive numbers in Table 4.1 reflect true improvement, it would also mean that there should be a large number of new cases of LI appearing later. Remember that our diagnosis is based on scores of relative standing. Thus, for one child to improve another one has to do less well and therefore there would have to be quite a bit of variation among children with and without LI. Our reliability data do not suggest that there is this much reshuffling going on. Instead of viewing the moderate levels of diagnostic change as recovery, we argued in Tomblin et al. (2003) that this pattern of apparent recovery was in fact due to a phenomenon called regression to the mean. Regression to the mean will occur when a sample at one tail of a normal distribution is selected and then remeasured subsequently. On the second measure, the sample will have scores that average closer to the mean than they did on the first testing. This can be explained by the fact that the measure has error and when you sample on one side or the other of the normal distribution, this error is not symmetrical. Thus, you end up with a sample with more people who have erroneously low scores than high scores. When you look at the sample the next time, the children with erroneous low scores are likely to move back toward their correct score and thus appear to have improved. We provided several lines of support for this conclusion in the article; however, the data in Table 4.1 provide even more. Note that the rate of subsequent LI in the sample does not systematically diminish across time as would be expected if this were recovery. Indeed, we would have to assume that nearly all the recovery occurred between kindergarten and second grade. This would mean that after second grade, LI should be stable. If we rediagnose children in second grade, however, 61% of the children with LI persist to 10th grade. This is about the same recovery rate as we saw between kindergarten and second grade. So now we would say that the point of recovery happens after second grade. Recall also that in Chapter 3, where we talked about the reliability of our language measures, we showed that there was a similar high rate of recovery even after less than a month between two diagnoses. What becomes clear is that recovery seems to happen each time we categorize the children into diagnostic categories and indeed this is what the regression to the mean phenomenon predicts.

Since this article was published, often we have been asked how we can overcome this. The only solution would be to have measures of language that have no measurement error. But given that our measures have rather low error rates and still this problem surfaces, the solution is for us to acknowledge that our assignment of children to categories such as LI is an educated guess and there will be error. We can take comfort, however, in the knowledge that most of the children who contribute to

Table 4.1 Probability of a diagnosis of LI at subsequent grades

Grade	Predictive power positive from LI in kindergarten (%)
2nd	58.7
4th	56.7
8th	56.9
10th	54.8

this error have language skills that are close to the cut-point used. In Figure 4.1 we show the distribution of composite language scores across the subsequent assessment waves. The box and whisker plots display the upper and lower quartiles via the box and the range is shown via the whiskers. We can see from the graph that at any time interval, around 75% of the children who were LI in kindergarten were around the –1 standard deviation level or below. We can also see in Table 4.2 that only 24% of these children were consistently diagnosed as "normal" throughout the study and 57% were LI on at least two subsequent occasions. Thus, we may be making diagnostic errors, but the errors are not likely to be of great consequence since these error cases are likely to be on the margins and these children with marginal scores would benefit from any type of efficacious intervention for LI.

In Chapter 3, we introduced a growth curve analysis in which we examined the rate of change across the children in the study using the IRT ability scores for language. In that analysis we found that there was a very high rate of homogeneity in growth trajectories among the children in this study. We can return to this analysis and ask whether there is evidence of differential growth rates in children with LI when compared with the typically developing children. Recall that the analysis in Chapter 3 was an unconditional (level 1) analysis.

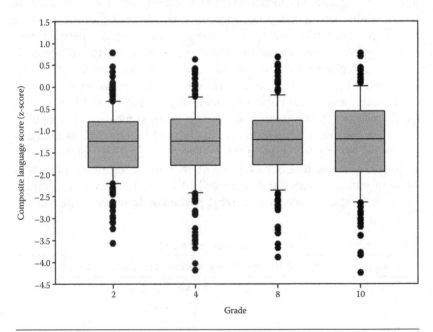

Figure 4.1 Distribution of language scores for children with LI at 2nd, 4th, 8th, and 10th grade.

Table 4.2 Proportion of children in normal and LI groups receiving 0, 1, 2, 3 or 4 diagnoses of language impairment after kindergarten

	Number of diagnoses of LI subsequent to kindergarten				
Group	0	1	2	3	4
Normal	73.61	15.3	5.8	2.9	2.4
LI	24.0	18.67	14.67	16.44	26.22

Notes:
Searching Further for Signs of Recovery – Differential Growth in Children with LI.

A growth curve analysis using a mixed model where we now introduce a fixed effect (level 2) representing the kindergarten language diagnosis resulted in a model that did not account for any additional variance over and above the unconditional model described in Chapter 3 earlier. The residual variance in the conditional model was slightly greater (13.33) than the unconditional model (13.32). Although the children with LI had different intercepts from the typical group ($t(483) = \_11.84,\_ p < 0.0001$), the groups did not differ with respect to slopes.

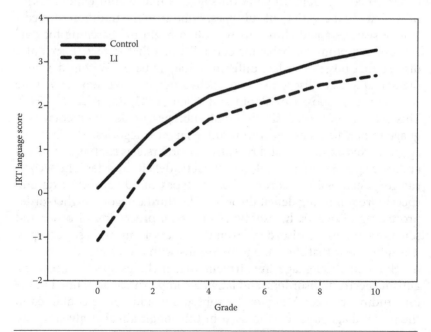

Figure 4.2 Language ability scores (IRT) across waves for children with language impairment (LI) and controls.

What is particularly surprising in these data is the observation that the children with LI show rates of growth that are very similar to that found in the typical language learners. This is very different from the prediction made by Stothard et al. (1998) where it was expected that the children with LI would continue to fall further behind. The predictions by Stothard et al. seem quite reasonable. Children at 5 to 6 years of age with poor language ability had to have poorer language growth during the preschool years than the typically developing children. Why wouldn't we expect this to continue during the school years? Something seems to change between the preschool years and the school years with regard to language growth. If children who enter school with poor language ability can achieve very typical growth rates during the school years, why is this not happening during the preschool years? There are no clear answers to these questions, but the answers should provide important insights into ways to improve language outcomes in children.

SUBTYPES OF LANGUAGE IMPAIRMENT

A common statement regarding children with LI is that they are a heterogeneous group. This notion suggests that within children with LI we may find a variety of subtypes. Following the tradition of medicine, researchers and clinicians will often begin by searching for patterns of symptoms or behavior constellations that suggest forms of a disease that possibly reflect different etiologic bases. Within developmental language disorders, two such schemes have emerged. One scheme was proposed by Rapin and Allen (1983; Rapin et al., 1996). This scheme proposed six different subtypes of developmental language impairments nested within three larger categories. The first category, mixed expressive and receptive disorders, has subtypes of verbal auditory agnosia and phonologic/syntactic deficit disorder. The second category, expressive disorders, has subtypes of verbal dyspraxia and speech programming deficit disorder. The third category, higher-order processing disorders, has subtypes of lexical processing disorder and semantic pragmatic disorder. From the descriptions of these subtypes, it is quite clear that this taxonomy begins with a very broad notion of developmental language impairment that includes speech disorders, autism spectrum disorders, and language impairment as defined in the longitudinal project. Many of the subtypes would not be contained in the initial diagnostic scheme used in this longitudinal study since we did not include measures of speech sound disorders or pragmatic disorders in the EpiSLI scheme. In the previous chapter, we did see supportive evidence that in the full sample of children, speech sound production and social communication appeared to be separate dimensions that lay outside the core diagnostic framework. Given the low prevalence of several of the subtypes in the Rapin and Allen system and the fact that we screened for poor lexical and sentence use but not speech or pragmatic problems, this project is not well suited to test the Rapin and Allen scheme. Recently, others (Conti-Ramsden, Crutchley, & Botting, 1997; Conti-Ramsden & Botting, 1999) have provided evidence that these categories and subcategories do emerge from children who are receiving clinical services in the United Kingdom.

Subtypes of LI Based on Modality

Prominent within the Rapin and Allen scheme is the distinction between receptive and expressive disorders. This use of modality as a major basis for forming taxonomic categories of LI has a long history (Eisenson, 1972; Myklebust, 1954) that continues today within the DSM-IV (American Psychiatric Association, 2000). Within this system, children are characterized as being expressive-only or receptive-expressive. The notion of a receptive-only subtype is not proposed, as it seems to be uncommon in the studies that have reported these groups. Bishop and Edmundson (1987a) employed a form of this taxonomy along with speech sound disorder and concluded that these subtypes could be viewed as belonging on a single dimension of severity where expressive-only disorders reflected milder cases than expressive-receptive disorders. Thus, expressive-only disorders were also more common than expressive-receptive disorders. The fact that these subtypes form a continuum suggests that, rather than distinct types based on modality, there is just a single dimension of language ability that varies in magnitude. The results that are summarized in Chapter 3 revealing limited dimensions of the standardized tests are consistent with this. Furthermore, in a large validation study of the Rapin and Allen system, little evidence was found to support subtypes of LI based on modality (Rapin et al., 1996).

Modality Subtypes in Kindergarten. The data obtained in the kindergarten sample provide an opportunity to test further whether there are subtypes of children with LI organized around the modality of language use. Recall that at this time point, we diagnosed 1,929 children. Of these children, 420 were diagnosed as LI (SLI or NLI). When expressive-only was defined as an expressive subscore < -1.25 with receptive equal to or greater than -1.25, 24% (102) of our LI sample fell into this category. Using the same criteria for receptive disorder, we obtained 18% (74) and by far the most common subtype (53%; 224) was a mixed form of expressive and receptive disorder. A small number (20) did not fall into the impaired level on either modality. These were children who had earned two scores below –1.25 in the vocabulary, sentence, or discourse domains of our scheme. The approach to subtyping in this example assumes that any difference between expressive and receptive scores that spans the cut-off value of –1.25 is a reliable difference, which we know is not the case. The solution to this is to require that children who are considered to have deficits in only one modality have a discrepancy between expressive and receptive language that is significant based on the known measurement error of each test. Fortunately, for these language measures obtained in kindergarten, we had obtained test-retest reliability and therefore we could compute the 95% confidence interval for a difference in these two tests. When we compute subtypes in this way, we find that 7% of the children with language impairment were expressive only, 6% were receptive only, and 85% were mixed expressive-receptive. Again, a small number of children (eight) did not fall into the region of impairment on either expressive or receptive skills. We can see that when we build measurement error into the analysis, there is very little evidence of specific deficits in a modality of language. Unlike the findings of Bishop and Edmundson, the mixed subtype is the most common, and expressive-only disorders are rare. These data are consistent with the earlier evidence of no modality dimension in our measures and generally support the notion that as far as these measures are concerned, there are no subtypes of LI defined in terms of modality differences in language.

Subtypes of LI Based on Performance IQ

Another popular way that subtypes of children with poor language have been formed has been on the basis of their language ability relative to their intellectual abilities. Since intelligence has often been measured via language performance, nonverbal or performance IQ has usually been used as the indicator of intelligence in order to avoid a confound. Thus, children may have poor language and poor IQ, or they may have poor language but normal IQ. The former group often are viewed as not having impaired language because their language was in accord with their intellectual or cognitive abilities. That is, these children are acquiring language in accord with their intellectual status and thus are not defective learners. This thinking reflects a view described in the first chapter wherein impairment or disease derives from a defect in the causal system. Following this philosophical stand, the children with poor language but intact intelligence (and hearing, etc.) must have something wrong with their language learning machinery because they have the capability to learn nonverbally. Note that this account seems to assume that the language development system is modular, that is, independent of general cognitive systems. The defect that causes the language impairment lies within this modular system. However, it also assumes that in the normal case, language is based on the function of nonverbal cognitive systems, that language is normally dependent upon cognition. Indeed, this thinking reflected a notion called the Cognitive Hypothesis, which held that cognitive development set the limits on language development (Cole, Dale, & Mills, 1990). The Cognitive Hypothesis emerged during the 1970s when Piagetian theory was in ascendance in the field of child development. At the same time, the use of discrepancies between achievement and ability were being advocated by many in the fields of learning disabilities and reading disorders. Again, the notion was that a learning disability or reading disorder could be defined by some form of discrepancy between intelligence and academic achievement (see, for instance, Fletcher, Francis, Rourke, Shaywitz, & Shaywitz, 1992; Shepard, 1980). This notion of a discrepancy for defining language impairment became a prominent practice for defining language impairment after Stark and Tallal (1981) proposed a diagnostic standard for LI that incorporated a nonverbal mental age–language age discrepancy. In recent years, several authors (Cole et al., 1990; Lahey, 1990; Plante, 1998) have argued that the use of cognitive referencing is neither conceptually well founded nor supported by empirical data. These arguments parallel those that have been expressed about the use of IQ–reading achievement discrepancy standards for dyslexia (Jorm, Share, MacLean, & Matthews, 1986; Shaywitz, Fletcher, Holahan, & Shaywitz, 1992). Recently, a panel of experts, convened by the National Institute for Deafness and Other Communication Disorders (NIDCD), has proposed that the use of a performance IQ be examined to determine if this standard should be retained (Tager-Flusberg & Cooper, 1999).

One of the goals of our research program was to examine whether there were any grounds for distinguishing between children with poor language who had language IQ discrepancies (children with SLI) and children with poor language without such discrepancies (children with NLI). This issue was raised in the subproject concerned with cognitive processing (Chapter 6) and with reading disorder (Chapter 5). In this section, we will look for evidence within the language data gathered. We have already published some data on this question using the kindergarten data. In this case (Tomblin & Zhang, 1999), we found that children with SLI and children with NLI have the same profiles of language deficits and differed only in terms of overall severity of impairment. In this case, we were using the subscale scores of the kindergarten standardized test battery, and we now know that these measures are all examining a common source of variance. Thus, these findings are quite expected. Within this section we will search further for any evidence that these two groups comprise different types of language learners.

To begin, it may be helpful to see how the children with SLI and NLI compare with respect to language and performance IQ. Figure 4.3 provides a scatter plot of the composite language and performance IQ scores for a random sample of 500 children tested in kindergarten. We can see that the children with SLI and NLI occupy the regions on the left side of the scatter plot. We see that although the performance IQ nominally does not involve language, language abilities remain correlated ($r = 0.48$, $p < 0.001$) with performance IQ. This correlation means that when we select children with low language but average performance IQ as we do with SLI we will constrain the range of the language scores to be higher than when this constraint is not in place. Thus we will find that the children with SLI have significantly higher language abilities (Mean = 77, SD 6.3) than children with NLI (Mean = 73, SD 8.0), as shown in the inset of Figure 4.3. Thus, we see that the language skills of these two groups differ with respect to severity.

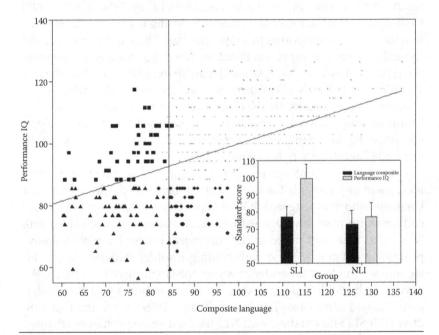

Figure 4.3 Scatter plot of relationship between language and performance IQ for children in second grade. Square symbols show children with SLI; triangles are children with NLI.

Figure 4.3 also shows us that the SLI and NLI children are continuously distributed across the range of IQ scores and language scores. Thus, as we know, these categories are arbitrarily formed by dichotomizing the continuous variables. We know from our analysis of the reliability of LI that categories formed from dichotomizing a continuous distribution, particularly at the tails, can result in poor reliability. In this case, we have the added issue of dichotomizing on two correlated variables (language and performance IQ). If we look at Figure 4.3, the children with SLI all fall away from the regression line, and thus these are children with high residual scores. These residual scores are more likely to contain high levels of measurement error than the scores of the NLI children who have low residual scores. Since the regression line functions like a bivariate mean, we can expect that on a second testing, these extreme scores will have a greater likelihood of regression back toward the regression line. As such, we can expect that the children with SLI will be less stable across time than the children with NLI. Indeed, when we compared the stability of SLI and NLI from kindergarten to second grade (see Tomblin et al., 2003), we found that only 42% of children initially diagnosed as SLI in kindergarten were also SLI in second grade. In contrast, 75% of the NLI children in kindergarten remained NLI in second grade. Furthermore, the majority of the children with SLI who changed categories changed to the normal language group; that is, their language scores moved in the predicted direction toward the regression line. We see a similar pattern between second and eighth grades where 33% of SLI remain stable and 50% of the NLI group does so.

These data show that a feature of children who are selected because of a discrepancy between language and nonverbal IQ is that their language status is more likely to be underestimated than among children with no such discrepancy. This has consequences both for research and clinical work. Within research, it is often thought that it is advisable to match the LI children on IQ with normal language controls. Even if we are not assuming that children with discrepancies are qualitatively different from those without discrepancies, this design may be viewed as providing the opportunity to remove the effects of IQ in the study and thus facilitate interpretation of the results. The evidence that children with SLI as a group have a larger degree of measurement error for language shows that this practice of matching on nonverbal IQ comes at a cost. Specifically, the higher level of measurement error in children with language–nonverbal IQ discrepancies will reduce the overall power of the language effect in a research design since the effect size reflects the ratio of a systematic effect (differences between group means or between two variables) and the overall variance. The increased error variance will fall into the denominator of this ratio and thus reduce the effect size. A researcher must think carefully about why nonverbal IQ needs to be controlled in a study. Francis and colleagues (Francis, Fletcher, Shaywitz, Shaywitz, & Rourke, 1996) cautioned that, in fact, there are few ways that nonverbal IQ would actually function as a confounder in a model of language development and use and therefore the practice of nonverbal IQ matching may be both unwarranted and deleterious to the research mission. Within the clinical setting, this greater measurement error will obviously mean that there is greater misdiagnosis. Clearly, among a group of children with SLI, there will be a greater rate of false positives. This means that these cases will be treated unnecessarily and that these cases can also appear as instances of positive responses to intervention when in fact they are not. This latter issue is why it is necessary to include placebo or no treatment control groups in intervention studies.

The analysis above shows that some differences between SLI and NLI are the outgrowth of the correlational nature of language and performance IQ. For one thing, this results in quantitative differences in the severity of language impairment. We still need to consider whether these two groups differ with respect to qualitative properties of language. Early in this project we examined this question using the test scores obtained during kindergarten (Tomblin & Zhang, 1999). We reported that other than severity, we found no evidence for a qualitative difference between children with SLI and children with NLI. In fact, these findings are not at all surprising given that we now know that the test measures reflect one dimension and therefore we should not expect to see profile differences. Our principal component analysis of the full set of language measures obtained during the school years did reveal some evidence of dimensionality, particularly when we added the measures from connected discourse. Therefore, these principal component scores will allow for variations in profile and thus we should inspect these.

Recall that in our analysis of the language measures in second grade we found evidence of four principal components. We labeled these Content/Form, Verbosity, Utterance Complexity/Fluency, Social Communication. Factor scores that represent each of these principal components can be generated, and we can compare the scores for children classified as SLI or NLI in kindergarten, as shown in the upper panel of Figure 4.4. This comparison asks whether the profiles of communication for these two groups differ with respect to overall level differences between the SLI and NLI groups (general severity differences)

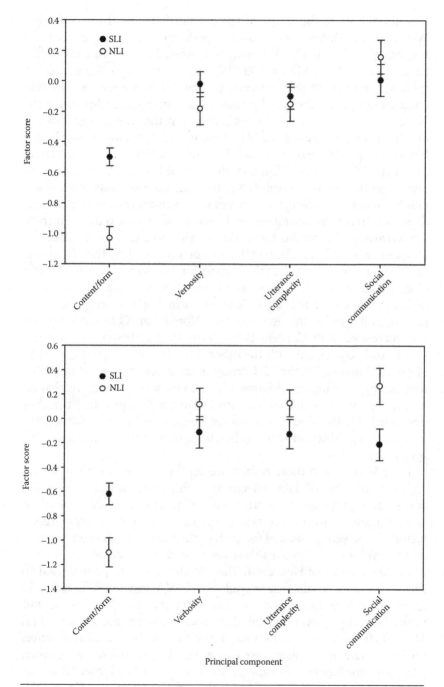

Figure 4.4 Principal component profiles of children with NLI and SLI at second (upper panel) and eighth grades.

and differences in the shape of the profiles between the two groups. We tested for differences in overall performance levels between the two groups using MANOVA. This test showed that there were differences, $F(1, 214) = 4.65$, $p = 0.03$. We can trace the difference using follow-up univariate tests for each variable. Here we see that the NLI children have had substantially poorer Content/Form abilities than the SLI children, $F(1,214) = 32.70$, $p < 0.0001$, but that the two groups did not differ on Verbosity, $F(1,214) = 1.64$, $p < 0.2$, Utterance Complexity/Fluency, $F(1,214) = 0.14$, $p = 0.71$, or Social Communication, $F(1,214) = 0.97$, $p = 0.32$. The fact that the SLI and NLI groups were poorer on the Content/Form factor than the others attests to the independence of these four dimensions of communication and the fact that these children were diagnosed as LI based on poor Content/Form in kindergarten. The reason the children with NLI are poorer than the children with SLI on Content/Form but not on the other factors is likely due to the influence of the correlation between nonverbal IQ and Content/Form. If this is true, we should expect to see nonverbal IQ differentially correlated with Content/Form but not with the other factors, and, in fact, this was the case. Nonverbal IQ in second grade was correlated with Content/Form ($r = 0.54$, $p < 0.0001$), but was not significantly correlated with the other three factors. Thus, this pattern of poorer language in the NLI group is again just a by-product of the fact that by allowing the children with NLI to have lower nonverbal IQ scores they are also able to have lower language scores than the children with SLI. This does not, however, suggest that these children have a qualitatively different form of language impairment other than this severity difference.

In order to see if these results are replicable, we can move to the eighth grade wave of data collection. At this point, several of our discourse and pragmatic measures were different from those used in second grade; however, the factor structure was quite similar. Again, factor scores were generated for each of the four principal components and the SLI and NLI groups were contrasted. These results are shown in the lower panel of Figure 4.4. The overall results are quite similar to those at second grade. An overall MANOVA test for differences in levels of performance across the four principal components did not result in a significant overall difference between the groups, $F(1, 118) = 0.10$, $p = 0.76$. Despite this failure to find an overall difference, the univariate tests again revealed a significant difference between groups for the Content/Form variable, $F(1, 118) = 11.34$, $p = 0.003$, with the SLI children being less severe than the NLI group. Unlike the second grade results, the children with NLI had somewhat better social communication than the children with SLI, $F(1, 118) = 5.87$, $p < 0.02$. The effect size for this difference was quite small ($R^2 = 0.05$). The fact that the NLI children were lower on Content/Form but higher on Social Communication no doubt resulted in their overall level as being similar to the SLI group. We did not find any support for a difference between the groups with respect to the shape of profile. Thus, at both age groups, the two groups have very similar profiles. The principal difference in profile is concentrated in the Content/Form and this is very likely to be due to the correlation that exists between nonverbal IQ and this aspect of language.

CONCLUSIONS ON COMMON SUBTYPES

Within this section, we examined the data gathered from this study to see if there was support for the presence of two forms of subtypes of LI where LI was formed by classifying children according to performance on measures of understanding and producing words and sentences. Although it is common to distinguish between children with predominately expressive versus expressive-receptive patterns of deficit, we found that this distinction is not at all reliable. The same problem arose when we looked at the subtypes of LI based on the presence or absence of a discrepancy between tested language and nonverbal IQ. In this case, the classification of the children with discrepancies (SLI) had very low reliability due to the large amount of error in the discrepancy scores. Furthermore, we found little evidence for a qualitative difference in language profiles between the NLI and SLI groups. Some suggestive evidence of poorer social communication abilities in children with SLI did appear. Why children with SLI would be less capable on the social communication skills represented by the Children's Communication Checklist is unclear. Overall, the data support the skepticism voiced by several researchers (Cole et al., 1990; Lahey, 1990; Plante, 1998) in the last 20 years regarding the value of this distinction. The evidence we have examined concerns various measures of language. In Chapter 5 we can return to this question with respect to measures of cognitive performance.

THE ADOLESCENT YEARS

Beginning in the 1970s and continuing to the present, a number of longitudinal studies have been conducted of adolescents or young adults who were identified as having language disorders during their preschool or early school years (e.g., Aram, Ekelman, & Nation, 1984;

Beitchman, Wilson, Brownlie, Walters, & Lancee, 1996; Conti-Ramsden, 2007; Hall & Tomblin, 1978; Johnson et al., 1999; King, Jones, & Lasky, 1982; Lewis & Freebairn, 1992; Snowling, Bishop, & Stothard, 2000; Stothard et al., 1998; Tomblin, Freese, & Records, 1992). The studies were designed to determine if language disorders persist beyond childhood, to identify factors that predict persistence or recovery, and to understand the nature of any lingering impairments. Collectively, the findings showed that early language disorders often persist, particularly when they are severe, and when nonverbal cognition is impaired. The findings also showed that early language disorders often manifest themselves as poor academic achievement in spoken and written domains (listening, speaking, reading, and writing in school) during adolescence and adulthood.

In the past, persistent language disorders in adolescents were identified primarily through standardized testing that targeted key areas such as the understanding of words, sentences, and paragraphs; the ability to follow spoken directions involving complex syntax; and accuracy in repeating long and complex sentences (e.g., Aram et al., 1984; Beitchman et al., 1996; Johnson et al., 1999; Stothard et al., 1998). Examples of standardized tests that were used in those studies to identify language deficits include the Peabody Picture Vocabulary Test – Revised (Dunn & Dunn, 1981), the Test of Adolescent/Adult Language – 3 (Hammill, Brown, Larsen, & Wiederholdt, 1994), and the Clinical Evaluation of Language Fundamentals – Revised (Semel, Wiig, & Secord, 1986).

Standardized tests are a valuable tool for documenting the existence of language disorders in adolescents. However, they provide little information about how a speaker actually uses language when attempting to communicate in natural settings. To obtain this type of functional information, it is necessary to elicit and analyze language samples. When elicited from adolescents, language samples can provide substantial insight into a speaker's strengths and weaknesses in areas such as the ability to access subordinate clauses and to produce complex sentences with multiple levels of embedding that communicate meaning in a clear and informative manner.

This section of the chapter discusses spoken language development at eighth grade (mean age = 13;11; range = 12;10–15;5) and again at 10th grade (mean age = 15;10; range = 14;6–17;5), reporting the performance of participants from the Iowa Project who had been identified in kindergarten as having typical language development (TLD), specific language impairment (SLI), or nonspecific language impairment (NLI). At eighth grade, there were 254 adolescents with TLD,

106 with SLI, and 84 with NLI (Nippold, Mansfield, Billow, & Tomblin, 2008). At 10th grade, there were 247 adolescents with TLD, 102 with SLI, and 77 with NLI (Nippold, Mansfield, Billow, & Tomblin, 2009). At both points in time, language development was examined using standardized measures and language sampling tasks, targeting syntax, the structural foundation of language.

STANDARDIZED TESTING

At 8th and 10th grades, syntactic development was examined using two subtests from the Clinical Evaluation of Language Fundamentals, Third Edition (CELF-III; Semel, Wiig, & Secord, 1995). These subtests were Concepts and Directions, a measure of receptive syntax, and Recalling Sentences, a measure of expressive syntax. Standard scores from the subtests were averaged to form a composite of syntactic development (SYN). Additionally, at eighth grade only, a measure of nonverbal cognition was obtained by administering to each adolescent the Block Design and Picture Completion subtests of the Wechsler Intelligence Scale for Children, Third Edition (Wechsler, 1991). Scaled scores from these subtests were averaged, yielding a performance IQ (PIQ).

As shown in Figure 4.5, the findings indicated that for SYN, the TLD group outperformed the SLI and NLI groups, and the SLI group outperformed the NLI group at both grade levels. Similarly, for PIQ, the TLD group outperformed the SLI and NLI groups, and the SLI

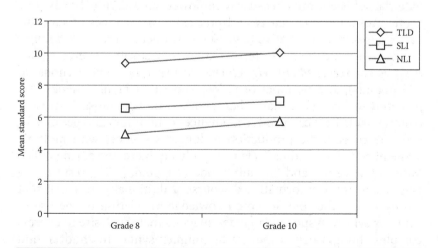

Figure 4.5 Syntactic development at 8th and 10th grades (TLD > SLI, NLI; SLI > NLI, at both grades).

group outperformed the NLI group. It was also found that at eighth grade, SYN and PIQ were closely associated with one another ($r = 0.54$, $p < 0.0001$), indicating that adolescents with stronger syntactic development also had stronger nonverbal cognition.

These findings are consistent with the view that adolescents with TLD, SLI, or NLI fall on a continuum of strengths and weaknesses, and that those with SLI and NLI differ from each other in the degree of impairment, with limitations affecting not only language but also nonverbal cognition. Although the classic definition of SLI assumes that language is the only deficit area (Stark & Tallal, 1981), the findings showed that nonverbal cognition was also affected, with the TLD group outperforming the SLI group. This is consistent with other studies of children with SLI that have reported a pattern of lower-than-expected performance on nonverbal cognitive measures (e.g., Johnston, 1982; Johnston & Ellis-Weismer, 1983; Johnston & Ramstad, 1983; Nippold, Erskine, & Freed, 1988; Restrepo, Swisher, Plante, & Vance, 1992; Swisher, Plante, & Lowell, 1994; also see Leonard, 1998, and Johnston, 2006). This indicates that adolescents with SLI have limitations not only in language development but also in nonverbal cognitive development. However, their weaknesses in nonverbal cognition are less severe than those of adolescents with NLI.

LANGUAGE SAMPLING TASKS

Language samples were elicited and analyzed for syntactic development. The ability to produce complex sentences containing subordinate clauses is essential because it empowers an individual to express subtle meanings with clarity and precision. Major types of subordinate clauses include relative (e.g., The new linebacker, *who's a senior this year*, should help the team march to victory), adverbial (e.g., *Although he recorded only eight tackles last year*, he's a powerhouse at 245 pounds), and nominal (e.g., We know that *he has tremendous potential* to become a state champion). Although most 5-year-old children with TLD can produce sentences containing all types of subordinate clauses, the production of longer sentences with multiple and embedded subordinate clauses gradually increases during childhood, adolescence, and into adulthood (Nippold, 2007), resulting in denser and more informative discourse. Additionally, research that has examined the role of topic knowledge in relation to the use of complex syntax in spoken language suggests that the desire to express complex thought drives the use of complex syntax in children and adolescents (Nippold, 2009).

EIGHTH GRADE

At eighth grade, language samples were elicited in two genres – conversational and expository. Previous research had shown that expository tasks are more likely to elicit complex syntax than conversational tasks in speakers with TLD (Nippold, Hesketh, Duthie, & Mansfield, 2005). In conversational discourse, speakers take turns commenting, asking questions, and otherwise supporting each other's contribution to the dialogue, which often focuses on familiar, well-known topics. In contrast, expository discourse is a monologue where the speaker, in an effort to inform the listener, bears most of the communicative burden. The greater cognitive demands of the expository genre compared to the conversational genre require the speaker to employ a higher level of syntactic complexity to express complex thoughts efficiently (Nippold, 2009). Nevertheless, both genres are important to adolescents. Through conversations, they build peer relationships by sharing opinions, feelings, and concerns, and through explanations, they demonstrate to teachers their understanding of complex topics that are discussed at school in classes such as history, biology, and economics.

To elicit the language samples, trained examiners interviewed each adolescent at school. The interview began with a general conversation (CON) about common topics such as school, family, and pets. To encourage conversation, the examiner asked questions and made comments (e.g., "How is school going these days? I've heard your school has a new library. Have you checked out any books yet?"). Once an adolescent expressed interest in a topic, the examiner responded positively by asking additional questions, commenting further, nodding, smiling, and listening attentively to encourage conversation.

After the conversation had ended, the examiner elicited a sample of expository discourse using the Favorite Game or Sport (FGS) task (Nippold et al., 2005). The examiner began by asking the adolescent to name a favorite game or sport. Once an activity had been chosen, the examiner asked a series of questions about it, following a script that prompted the adolescent to explain certain details such as how to play the game or sport; to describe the goals, rules, and number of players; to explain how to win the activity; and to describe some key strategies that every good player should know.

TENTH GRADE

At 10th grade, the Peer Conflict Resolution (PCR) task (Nippold, Mansfield, & Billow, 2007) was employed to elicit a sample of spoken discourse. This task consisted of two scenarios that involved conflicts between young people, one in a school situation ("The Science Fair") and one in a work situation ("The Fast-Food Restaurant"). The examiner presented each scenario, one at a time. The scenario was read aloud to the adolescent, who was asked to retell it in as much detail as possible. For the Science Fair scenario, the story involved a teacher who had assigned a group of students to work on a project together, to design an airplane that could actually fly. However, one of the students in the group refused to help with the project and let the others do all of the work. This bothered one of the group members considerably. For the Fast-Food scenario, two young people worked together at a restaurant, sharing the duties of working the grill (a more desirable task) and taking out the garbage (a less desirable task). One night, the worker whose turn it was to take out the garbage claimed to have a sore arm, and asked the other worker to switch jobs for the evening. However, the individual who had planned to work the grill was reluctant to give up an opportunity to perform a preferred activity. For the two scenarios, male names were used with male participants, and female names were used with female participants. The names were John and Bob or Debbie and Melanie for the Science Fair scenario, and Mike and Peter or Jane and Kathy for the Fast-Food Restaurant scenario. This adjustment in the task was an effort to increase the participants' interest in the story and their ability to relate to the characters.

After the adolescent retold the scenario, the examiner asked a series of questions. The questions were designed to prompt the adolescent to discuss the nature of the conflict and how it might be resolved, and to speculate on what might happen if it were handled that way and how the characters then might feel, thereby producing a sample of expository discourse.

TRANSCRIPTION, CODING, AND ANALYSIS

Each sample (CON, FGS, and PCR) was transcribed into its own SALT file (Miller & Chapman, 2003), segmented into C-units (communication units), and coded for main and subordinate clauses. A C-unit consists of a main clause and optionally may contain one or more subordinate clauses. The sentence, *Mike enjoys flipping burgers even though it gets hot in the kitchen*, is a 12-word C-unit that consists of a main clause (*Mike enjoys flipping burgers*) and one adverbial clause (*even though it gets hot in the kitchen*) that is linked to the main clause. Any utterances that were less than a C-unit in that they did not contain a subject or a predicate (i.e., fragments) were placed within parentheses and excluded from analyses. All mazes (e.g., false starts, repetitions) were also parenthesized and ignored during data analysis. All C-units were examined for the use of three types of subordinate clause: relative, adverbial, and nominal. Only clauses that contained finite verbs were coded – a procedure that had been employed in previous research using these same tasks (Nippold et al., 2005, 2007). After each sample had been coded for main and subordinate clauses, clausal density was determined by summing the total number of main and subordinate clauses and dividing this number by the total number of C-units produced. The total number of C-units served as a measure of language productivity, and mean length of C-unit (MLCU) and clausal density served as measures of syntactic complexity.

RESULTS

At eighth grade, the findings indicated that the conversational task (CON) elicited a greater number of C-units than did the expository task (FGS) for all three groups. However, MLCU, clausal density, and the use of relative, nominal and adverbial clauses – measures of syntactic complexity – were greater during the FGS task than the CON task for all three groups. Although the groups did not differ in syntactic complexity on the CON, on the FGS, the TLD group outperformed the SLI and NLI groups on MLCU, and the TLD group outperformed the NLI group on relative clause use. Thus, only the FGS task was effective in revealing syntactic weaknesses in the SLI and NLI groups. Figure 4.6 illustrates the differences between genres and groups for MLCU, a general index of syntactic development.

Despite the statistically significant group differences, however, there were individual exceptions, where, for example, some adolescents in the SLI or NLI groups performed as well as adolescents in the TLD group, and some adolescents in the TLD group showed poor use of syntax on the FGS. This suggests that the way in which an adolescent performs on a discourse task cannot always be predicted from group membership.

Nevertheless, it is useful to examine the performance of adolescents in the study who were clear representatives of their diagnostic groups. Table 4.3 shows excerpts from the language samples of three eighth grade boys talking about football on the FGS. Each boy is answering the same question posed by the examiner. Inspection of these excerpts indicates that Speaker #1, a boy with TLD, produces longer utterances that contain a greater number and variety of subordinate clauses than does Speaker #2, a boy with SLI, or Speaker #3, a boy with NLI, whose use of language is particularly weak. Overall, it is apparent that Speaker

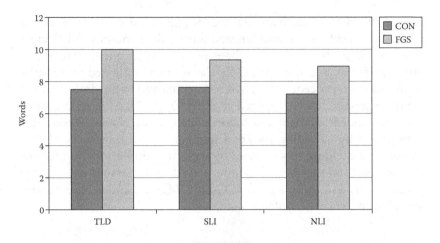

Figure 4.6 At eighth grade, Mean Length of C-Unit (MLCU) was greater on the expository (FGS) task than on the conversational (CON) task for all three groups, and only the expository task revealed differences between the groups (TLD > SLI, NLI).

#1 communicates in a clearer and more informative manner than Speaker #2 or #3, and that the degree of communicative competence declines with each successive speaker (i.e., TLD > SLI > NLI). Moreover, informal analysis of the content of Speaker #1's discourse suggests that he may be more knowledgeable about football than Speaker #2 or Speaker #3. The possibility of a pattern in which greater syntactic complexity is associated with richer content (e.g., Speaker #1) and where simpler syntax is associated with simpler content (e.g., Speaker #3) in expository discourse should be examined in future research with adolescents having TLD, SLI, and NLI.

At 10th grade, the findings indicated that the TLD group outperformed the SLI and NLI groups on MLCU, clausal density, and the use of nominal clauses, and that the TLD group outperformed the NLI group on the use of relative clauses. Thus, the PCR task was effective in revealing weaknesses in syntactic complexity in the SLI and NLI groups. Figure 4.7 illustrates the differences between groups for MLCU. Once again, however, there were individual exceptions where some adolescents performed in ways that were inconsistent with their diagnostic groups, suggesting that each adolescent's performance should be examined carefully before making assumptions.

Nevertheless, as with the eighth grade study, it is informative to examine the performance of adolescents who represent their diagnostic groups unambiguously. Table 4.4 shows excerpts from the language samples of three 10th grade boys discussing the Science Fair scenario

Table 4.3 Examples of three eighth grade boys answering the same question about football during the FGS task. Each boy's reply has been segmented into C-units and coded for main and subordinate clauses

Examiner:

Now I would like you to tell me what a player should do in order to *win* the game of football. In order words, what are some key strategies that every good player should know?

Speaker #1: Boy with TLD, age 14;2

Make [MC] sure your teammates know [NOM] the play. And don't argue [MC] with your teammates. Because if you're arguing [ADV] with a lineman, the lineman could let [MC] the guy get by and you could get [MC] drilled. So your linemen are [MC] a big part of the game. You want [MC] your linemen in all of your plays. You want [MC] your linemen to feel good about themselves and their job because it doesn't seem [ADV] like they do [NOM] a lot. They just block [MC] the guy. But if nobody was [ADV] there, the running backs would get [MC] nowhere. And it helps [MC] to have a good lineman, and a good running back that can block [REL], and a halfback that can block [REL], and receivers that can catch [REL] and know [REL] their routes well, and just a team that doesn't fight [REL] and argue [REL] about everything. If you mess [ADV] up, then just do [MC] better next time or try [MC] harder.

Speaker #2: Boy with SLI, age 14;1

You have [MC] to wear pads because when you're hit [ADV], it hurts [ADV]. They have [MC] to work together and get the ball down the field. You pass [MC] the ball. And you run [MC] the ball so you can get [ADV] to the end zone to score. You have [MC] to know how to kick. Because if you get [ADV] to the fourth down, you have [MC] to punt the ball away if you're [ADV] not ready to make it.

Speaker #3: Boy with NLI, age 13;9

You should be [MC] a team player. Like motivate [MC] your team to win, not to fight. Have [MC] good sportsmanship. Don't criticize [MC] or put [MC] down other teammates. Be [MC] kind to other teammates. Work [MC] as a team. Encourage [MC] other people. Be [MC] kind to your coaches.

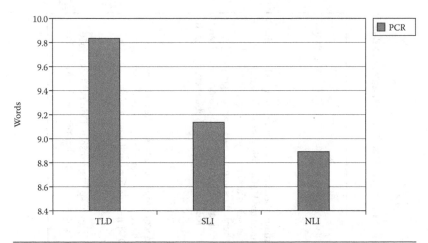

Figure 4.7 At 10th grade, the groups continued to differ on Mean Length of C-Unit (MLCU) using the expository Peer Conflict Resolution (PCR) task (TLD > SLI, NLI).

during the PCR task. Inspection of these excerpts indicates that Speaker #4, a boy with TLD, produces longer and denser utterances that contain a greater number and variety of subordinate clauses than Speaker #5, a boy with SLI, or Speaker #6, a boy with NLI. Once again, the degree of communicative competence declines with each successive speaker (TLD > SLI > NLI). When viewed in relation to the 8th grade findings, the 10th grade findings reveal a pattern of stability in the use of complex syntax in expository discourse.

Each boy's response to the last question ("How do you think they both will feel?") is particularly interesting. For example, in addition to producing greater syntactic complexity, Speaker #4 expresses greater insight into the perspectives of the two main characters, the nature of their feelings, and the conditionality of their reactions, and offers a greater number of reasons for his own views, fueling the need to use complex syntax. Unfortunately, Speaker #5 and Speaker #6 have responded more simplistically to the question, offering fewer details and insights.

Similar patterns can be seen in Table 4.5, which presents excerpts from the samples of three 10th grade girls discussing the Fast-Food Restaurant scenario during the PCR task. Again, the speaker with TLD (#7) employs greater syntactic complexity than the speaker with SLI (#8) or the speaker with NLI (#9); moreover, Speaker #7 shows greater insight into the nature of the conflict between the two workers, the resolution, and feelings of the people involved. In contrast, the responses of Speaker #8 and Speaker #9 are shorter and seem to reflect a more simplistic understanding of the conflict and its possible resolution and outcome.

Table 4.4 Examples of three 10th grade boys answering the same set of questions concerning the Science Fair Scenario during the PCR task. Each boy's replies have been segmented into C-units and coded for main and subordinate clauses

---

Speaker #4: Boy with TLD, age 15;9

Examiner:
What is the problem here?

Boy:
Bob didn't do [MC] any work. He let [MC] the other three do all the work.

Examiner:
Why is that a problem?

Boy:
Because if it's [ADV] a group experience, they all should share [MC] the work.

Examiner:
What is a good way for John to deal with Bob?

Boy:
Well, he could approach [MC] Bob and say [MC], "Hey, if you want [ADV] to get any credit, you have [MC] to do some work," and have [MC] the other two guys back him up or something like that. He could approach [MC] the teacher and say [MC], "Hey, Bob's not doing [NOM] any work."

Examiner:
What do you think will happen?

Boy:
If he approaches [ADV] the teacher, I think [MC] he'd probably get [NOM] the best result because the teacher could tell [ADV] Bob, "If you don't do [ADV] anything on this project like if you don't help [ADV] the other three boys, then you're gonna fail [NOM] the project and I'll drop [NOM] you from my class." Or if John approaches [ADV] Bob, Bob might change [MC]. Who knows [MC]. I doubt [MC] it. But he might [MC].

Examiner:
How do you think they both will feel?

continued

Table 4.4 Continued

Boy:

Well, I don't think [MC] Bob would be [NOM] too happy if John approached [ADV] the teacher because he'd be [ADV] forced to do something. But I think [MC] John would be [NOM] happy because Bob would finally be [ADV] putting in the amount of work that he's [REL] supposed to be putting in. And if John approaches [ADV] Bob, Bob might be [MC] kind of upset because John's kind of singling [ADV] him out. But John should be singling [MC] him out because he's not doing [ADV] anything. And I think [MC] the fact that John is approaching [REL] Bob might make [NOM] him feel a little bit happier because he's trying [ADV] to get Bob to actually go out and do the work that he's [REL] supposed to be doing.

Speaker #5: Boy with SLI, age 16;4

Examiner:
What is the problem here?

Boy:
Bob doesn't wanna [MC] work. And he makes [MC] everybody else mad.

Examiner:
Why is that a problem?

Boy:
Because you gotta have [MC] everybody working, not just like one or two.

Examiner:
What is a good way for John to deal with Bob?

Boy:
Just go [MC] up to him and tell [MC] him the problem. Just tell him [MC] he needs [NOM] to work too.

Examiner:
What do you think will happen?

Boy:
Either he'll wanna [MC] work so he gets [ADV] the credit. Or if not, he'll probably quit [MC].

Examiner:
How do you think they both will feel?

Boy:
John would probably feel [MC] better. And Bob would probably feel [MC] kinda mad or something.

Speaker #6: Boy with NLI, age 16;0

Examiner:
What is the problem here?

Boy:
Bob doesn't do [MC] his job.

Examiner:
Why is that a problem?

Boy:
Because John was getting [MC] angry over it.

Examiner:
What is a good way for John to deal with Bob?

Boy:
Tell [MC] him to do his job.

Examiner:
What do you think will happen?

Boy:
The problem will be [MC] solved.

Examiner:
How do you think they both will feel?

Boy:
Better, and so they can get [MC] the job done.

Table 4.5 Examples of three 10th grade girls answering the same set of questions concerning the Fast-Food Scenario during the PCR task. Each girl's replies have been segmented into C-units and coded for main and subordinate clauses

Speaker #7: Girl with TLD, age 15;9

Examiner:
What is the problem here?

Girl:
Kathy can't find [MC] anybody to do her job since she hurt [ADV] her arm.

Examiner:
Why is that a problem?

Girl:
Because the garbage needs [MC] to be taken out. And she's [MC] not able to do it in her physical state that she's [REL] in.

Examiner:
What is a good way for Jane to deal with Kathy?

Girl:
I'd just help [MC] her even if it means [ADV] sacrificing something that you really wanna [REL] do. Just to help somebody out is [MC] better. Or if there's [ADV] somebody else who'd be [REL] able to, that'd be [MC] another option.

Examiner:
What do you think will happen?

Girl:
I think [MC] she'd feel [NOM] good if she helped [ADV] Kathy since they're [ADV] friends. It would all work [MC] out really.

Examiner:
How do you think they both will feel?

Girl:
Kathy will probably be [MC] very thankful that Jane helped [NOM] her because she couldn't do [ADV] that. And Jane may be [MC] a little sad that she doesn't get [NOM] to work on the grill. But there'll be [MC] plenty of other times when she will get [REL] to work on the grill.

Speaker #8: Girl with SLI, age 15;8

Examiner:
What is the problem here?

Girl:
It was [MC] Jane's part. And Kathy didn't wanna [MC] do it. And she wanted [MC] to keep her part.

Examiner:
Why is that a problem?

Girl:
Because that's [MC] her part that she had [REL] for the day. So that's [MC] what she wanted [REL] to do.

Examiner:
What is a good way for Jane to deal with Kathy?

Girl:
Tell [MC] her, "ask [NOM] somebody else" because that's [ADV] her part and she don't wanna [ADV] trade. Or just help [MC] her out with the garbage. And go [MC] back to it.

Examiner:
What do you think will happen?

Girl:
Kathy might be [MC] a little upset because she wanted [ADV] to do the grilling instead of doing the garbage because her arm hurt [ADV].

Examiner:
How do you think they both will feel?

Girl:
Mad probably. But it's [MC] a job. So they have [MC] to stick with it.

Speaker #9: Girl with NLI, age 15;11

Examiner:
What is the problem here?

continued

Table 4.5 Continued

Girl:
Jane won't switch [MC] with Kathy.

Examiner:
Why is that a problem?

Girl:
Because Jane likes [MC] working on the grill.

Examiner:
What is a good way for Jane to deal with Kathy?

Girl:
Switch [MC] jobs with her and be [MC] nice.

Examiner:
What do you think will happen?

Girl:
Then Kathy will be [MC] happy. And her arm won't hurt [MC].

Examiner:
How do you think they both will feel?

Girl:
Good.

These observations support the need for future research to examine the relationship between topic knowledge and the use of complex syntax in adolescents with typical and impaired language development. Such a study could be quite informative given that both the SLI and NLI groups had obtained lower scores on the formal, standardized measures of syntax and nonverbal cognition than the TLD group.

SUMMARY

The studies discussed in this section of the chapter (Nippold et al., 2008, 2009) indicate that adolescents with a history of SLI or NLI, diagnosed in kindergarten, continued to show deficits in syntactic development, as measured by standardized testing and spoken language samples elicited in the expository genre. Although exceptions were observed where some adolescents in each group – TLD, SLI, and NLI – performed differently from the majority of participants in their diagnostic category, in general, the findings indicate that patterns of language strengths or weaknesses identified in kindergarten tend to persist through adolescence. Future research is necessary to determine if high-quality intervention delivered to children during the early school-age years can resolve the language deficits, preventing a pattern of continued impairment.

In terms of clinical implications, the findings suggest that both standardized measures and language samples can effectively identify communicative strengths and weaknesses. However, it is emphasized that in the Iowa Project, language samples elicited in the conversational genre did not reveal differences between groups, possibly because the subject matter (e.g., daily activities, pets, and friends) did not provide a sufficient amount of cognitive stimulation to support the need to use complex syntax. Thus, it is suggested that language samples be elicited in the expository genre in order to reveal aspects of syntactic development and communicative competence that could be addressed during language intervention. Further, to support adolescents' use of complex spoken language, intervention activities should incorporate efforts to build the adolescent's knowledge base concerning the topic of discussion. This could be especially beneficial if the intervention activities are tied into the adolescent's curriculum in core subject areas such as history, biology, or economics.

REFERENCES

American Psychiatric Association. (2000). *Diagnostic and statistical manual of mental disorders* (4th rev. ed.) Washington, DC: Author.

Aram, D. M., Ekelman, B. L., & Nation, J. E. (1984). Preschoolers with language disorders: 10 years later. *Journal of Speech and Hearing Research, 27,* 232–244.

Aram, D. M., & Nation, J. (1980). Preschool language disorders and subsequent language and academic difficulties. *Journal of Communication Disorders, 13,* 159–170.

Baker, L., & Cantwell, D. P. (1987). A prospective psychiatric follow-up of children with speech/language disorders. *Journal of the American Academy of Child & Adolescent Psychiatry, 26,* 546–553.

Beitchman, J. H., Wilson, B., Brownlie, E. B., Walters, H., & Lancee, W. (1996). Long-term consistency in speech/language profiles: I. Developmental and academic outcomes. *Journal of the American Academy of Child & Adolescent Psychiatry, 35*(6), 804–814.

Bishop, D. V. M., & Edmundson, A. (1987a). Language-impaired 4-year-olds: Distinguishing transient from persistent impairment. *Journal of Speech and Hearing Disorders, 52,* 156–173.

Bishop, D. V. M., & Edmundson, A. (1987b). Specific language impairment as a maturational lag: Evidence from longitudinal data on language and motor development. *Developmental Medicine & Child Neurology, 29,* 442–459.

Cole, K. N., Dale, P. S., & Mills, P. E. (1990). Defining language delay in young children by cognitive referencing: Are we saying more than we know? *Applied Psycholinguistics, 11,* 291–302.

Cole, K. N., Schwartz, I., Notari, A., Dale, P., & Mills, P. (1995). Examination of the stability of two methods of defining specific language impairment. *Applied Psycholinguistics, 16,* 103–123.

Conti-Ramsden, G. (2007, April). *Heterogeneity of specific language impairment (SLI): Outcomes in adolescence.* Lecture presented at the Afasic 4th International Symposium, University of Warwick, England.

Conti-Ramsden, G., & Botting, N. (1999). Classification of children with specific language impairment: Longitudinal considerations. *Journal of Speech, Language, and Hearing Research, 42,* 1195–1204.

Conti-Ramsden, G., Crutchley, A., & Botting, N. (1997). The extent to which psychometric tests differentiate subgroups of children with SLI. *Journal of Speech, Language, and Hearing Research, 40,* 765–777.

Dunn, L. M., & Dunn, L. M. (1981). *Peabody Picture Vocabulary Test, revised.* Circle Pines, MN: American Guidance Service.

Eisenson, J. (1972). *Aphasia in children.* New York: Harper & Row.

Fletcher, J. M., Francis, D. J., Rourke, B. P., Shaywitz, S. E., & Shaywitz, B. A. (1992). The validity of discrepancy-based definitions of reading disabilities. *Journal of Learning Disabilities, 25,* 555–561, 573.

Francis, D. J., Fletcher, J. M., Shaywitz, B. A., Shaywitz, S. E., & Rourke, B. P. (1996). Defining learning and language disabilities: Conceptual and psychometric issues with the use of IQ tests. *Language, Speech, and Hearing Services in Schools, 27*, 132–143.

Hall, P. K., & Tomblin, J. B. (1978). A follow-up study of children with articulation and language disorders. *Journal of Speech and Hearing Disorders, 43*, 227–241.

Hammill, D., Brown, V., Larsen, S., & Wiederholt, J. (1994). *Test of Adolescent/Adult Language* (3rd ed.). Austin, TX: Pro-Ed.

Johnson, C. J., Beitchman, J. H., Young, A., Escobar, M., Atkinson, L., Wilson, B., et al. (1999). Fourteen-year follow-up of children with and without speech-language impairments: Speech/language stability and outcomes. *Journal of Speech, Language, and Hearing Research, 42*, 744–760.

Johnston, J. R. (1982). Interpreting the Leiter IQ: Performance profiles of young normal and language-disordered children. *Journal of Speech and Hearing Research, 25*, 291–296.

Johnston, J. R. (2006). *Thinking about child language: Research to practice.* Eau Claire, WI: Thinking Publications.

Johnston, J. R., & Ellis-Weismer, S. (1983). Mental rotation abilities in language-disordered children. *Journal of Speech and Hearing Research, 26*, 397–403.

Johnston, J. R., & Ramstad, V. (1983). Cognitive development in preadolescent language impaired children. *British Journal of Disorders of Communication, 18*, 49–55.

Jorm, A. F., Share, D. L., MacLean, R., & Matthews, R. (1986). Cognitive factors at school entry predictive of specific reading retardation and general reading backwardness: A research note. *Journal of Child Psychology and Psychiatry and Allied Disciplines, 27*, 45–54.

King, R. R., Jones, C., & Lasky, E. (1982). In retrospect: A fifteen-year follow-up report of speech-language-disordered children. *Language, Speech, and Hearing Services in Schools, 13*, 24–32.

Lahey, M. (1990). Who shall be called language disordered? Some reflections and one perspective. *Journal of Speech and Hearing Disorders, 55*, 612–620.

Leonard, L. B. (1998). *Children with specific language impairment.* Cambridge, MA: MIT Press.

Lewis, B. A., & Freebairn, L. (1992). Residual effects of preschool phonology disorders in grade school, adolescence, and adulthood. *Journal of Speech and Hearing Research, 35*, 819–831.

Miller, J. F., & Chapman, R. (2003). *SALT: Systematic Analysis of Language Transcripts* [computer software]. Madison: University of Wisconsin-Madison, Waisman Center, Language Analysis Laboratory.

Myklebust, H. R. (1954). *Auditory disorders in children: A manual for differential diagnosis.* New York: Grune & Stratton.

Nippold, M. A. (2007). *Later language development: School-age children, adolescents, and young adults* (3rd ed.). Austin, TX: Pro-Ed.

Nippold, M. A. (2009). School-age children talk about chess: Does knowledge drive syntactic complexity? *Journal of Speech, Language, and Hearing Research, 52,* 856–871.

Nippold, M. A., Erskine, B. J., & Freed, D. B. (1988). Proportional and functional analogical reasoning in normal and language-impaired children. *Journal of Speech and Hearing Disorders, 53,* 440–448.

Nippold, M. A., Hesketh, L. J., Duthie, J. K., & Mansfield, T. C. (2005). Conversational versus expository discourse: A study of syntactic development in children, adolescents, and adults. *Journal of Speech, Language, and Hearing Research, 48,* 1048–1064.

Nippold, M. A., Mansfield, T. C., & Billow, J. L. (2007). Peer conflict explanations in children, adolescents, and adults: Examining the development of complex syntax. *American Journal of Speech-Language Pathology, 16,* 1–10.

Nippold, M. A., Mansfield, T. C., Billow, J. L., & Tomblin, J. B. (2008). Expository discourse in adolescents with language impairments: Examining syntactic development. *American Journal of Speech-Language Pathology, 17,* 356–366.

Nippold, M. A., Mansfield, T. C., Billow, J. L., & Tomblin, J. B. (2009). Syntactic development in adolescents with a history of language impairments: A follow-up investigation. *American Journal of Speech-Language Pathology, 18,* 241–251.

Plante, E. (1998). Criteria for SLI: The Stark and Tallal legacy and beyond. *Journal of Speech, Language, and Hearing Research, 41,* 951–957.

Rapin, I. (1996). Practitioner review: Developmental language disorders – A clinical update. *Journal of Child Psychology and Psychiatry, 37,* 643–655.

Rapin, I., & Allen, D. (1983). Developmental language disorders: Nosologic considerations. In U. Kirk (Ed.), *Neuropsychology of language, reading and spelling.* New York: Academic Press.

Rapin, I., Allen, D. A., Aram, D., Dunn, D., Fein, D., Morris, R., et al. (1996). Classification issues. In I. Rapin (Ed.), *Preschool children with inadequate communication* (pp. 190–228). London: MacKeith Press.

Restrepo, M. A., Swisher, L., Plante, E., & Vance, R. (1992). Relations among verbal and nonverbal cognitive skills in normal language and specifically language-impaired children. *Journal of Communication Disorders, 25,* 205–219.

Rice, M. L., Wexler, K., & Hershberger, S. (1998). Tense over time: The longitudinal course of tense acquisition in children with specific language impairment. *Journal of Speech, Language, and Hearing Research, 41,* 1412–1431.

Scarborough, H. S., & Dobrich, W. (1990). Development of children with early language delay. *Journal of Speech & Hearing Research, 33,* 70–83.

Semel, E., Wiig, E. H., & Secord, W. A. (1986). *Clinical evaluation of language fundamentals, revised.* San Antonio, TX: Psychological Corporation.

Semel, E., Wiig, E. H., & Secord, W. A. (1995). *Clinical evaluation of language fundamentals* (3rd ed.). San Antonio, TX: Psychological Corporation.

Shaywitz, B. A., Fletcher, J. M., Holahan, J. M., & Shaywitz, S. E. (1992). Discrepancy compared to low achievement definitions of reading disability: Results from the Connecticut Longitudinal Study. *Journal of Learning Disabilities, 25,* 639–648.

Shepard, L. (1980). An evaluation of the regression discrepancy method for identifying children with learning disabilities. *Journal of Special Education, 14,* 79–81.

Silva, P. A. (1987). Epidemiology, longitudinal course and some associated factors: An update. In W. Yule & M. Rutter (Eds.), *Language development and disorders* (pp. 1–15). Oxford: Blackwell Scientific Publications Ltd.

Silva, P. A., McGee, R., & Williams, S. (1983). Developmental language delay from three to seven years and its significance for low intelligence and reading difficulties at age seven. *Developmental Medicine & Child Neurology, 25,* 783–793.

Snowling, M., Bishop, D. V. M., & Stothard, S. E. (2000). Is preschool language impairment a risk factor for dyslexia in adolescence? *Journal of Child Psychology and Psychiatry, 41*(5), 587–600.

Stark, R., Bernstein, L., Condino, R., Bender, M., Tallal, P., & Catts, H. (1984). Four-year follow-up study of language impaired children. *Annals of Dyslexia, 34,* 49–68.

Stark, R., & Tallal, P. (1981). Selection of children with specific language deficits. *Journal of Speech and Hearing Disorders, 46,* 114–122.

Stark, R. E., & Tallal, P. (1988). *Language, speech, and reading disorders in children.* Boston: Little, Brown and Co.

Stothard, S. E., Snowling, M. J., Bishop, D. V. M., Chipchase, B. B., & Kaplan, C. A. (1998). Language-impaired preschoolers: A follow-up into adolescence. *Journal of Speech Language and Hearing Research, 41,* 407–418.

Swisher, L., Plante, E., & Lowell, S. (1994). Nonlinguistic deficits of children with language disorders complicate the interpretation of their nonverbal IQ scores. *Language, Speech, and Hearing Services in Schools, 25,* 235–240.

Tager-Flusberg, H., & Cooper, J. (1999). Present and future possibilities for defining a phenotype for specific language impairment. *Journal of Speech, Language, and Hearing Research, 42,* 1275–1278.

Tomblin, J. B., Freese, P. R., & Records, N. L. (1992). Diagnosing specific language impairment in adults for the purpose of pedigree analysis. *Journal of Speech and Hearing Research, 35,* 832–843.

Tomblin, J. B., & Zhang, X. (1999). Are children with SLI a unique group of language learners? In H. Tager-Flusberg (Ed.), *Neurodevelopmental disorders: Contributions to a New Framework from the Cognitive Neurosciences* (pp. 361–382). Cambridge, MA: MIT Press.

Tomblin, J. B., Zhang, X., Buckwalter, P., & O'Brien, M. (2003). The stability of primary language impairment: Four years after kindergarten diagnosis. *Journal of Speech-Language-Hearing Research, 46,* 1283–1296.

Wechsler, D. (1991). *Wechsler Intelligence Scale for Children* (3rd ed.). San Antonio, TX: Psychological Corporation.

5

THE ROLE OF PROCESSING IN CHILDREN AND ADOLESCENTS WITH LANGUAGE IMPAIRMENT

**Laurence B. Leonard, Susan Ellis Weismer,
Christine Weber-Fox, and Carol A. Miller**

INTRODUCTION

Much of the literature on children with language impairments has been devoted to the description of these children's difficulties with details of language content and form. In this chapter, we explore the possibility that these children's language problems are exacerbated by – or perhaps even caused by – limitations in their ability to process the information that is needed to acquire language adequately. Language itself may not be the problem; rather, the problem may rest with the children's difficulty accessing language from the input and retaining it with sufficient fidelity to make use of it in language comprehension and production.

For example, one of the fundamental abilities exhibited by children is that of associating a label with a referent object or action. However, to make use of this association, children must be able to retain the phonological sequence that makes up this label. Without adequate retention, the word will not become part of the child's lexicon. It could also be the case that children are able to hypothesize the grammatical function of morphemes such as *is* and *are*, but if they cannot keep up with the continuous speech stream, these morphemes may flow by without being adequately processed. As a result, the children may need many more encounters with these morphemes before they can hypothesize their grammatical function and incorporate them into their grammars.

Our focus on such processing factors is hardly new; systematic research on this topic began over 30 years ago, and our own research benefited greatly from this earlier work. Informative reviews of the processing abilities and weaknesses of children with language impairment can be found in Ellis Weismer and Thordardottir (2002), Gillam, Montgomery, and Gillam (2008), and Graf Estes, Evans, and Else-Quest (2007), among others.

PROCESSING SPEED AND WORKING MEMORY

The notion that processing factors play a role in the problems of children and adolescents with language impairment is essentially a statement that the amount of material to be integrated and stored and the time available for performing these mental operations are crucial factors, apart from the nature of the material itself (Bishop, 1992). Kail and Salthouse (1994) noted that processing ability can be considered from the perspective of *time, space,* and *energy*. Time is relevant because information must be processed quickly enough to avoid decay or interference from additional information that immediately follows. Space refers to the computational region of memory; there must be sufficient work space to complete the task successfully. From the standpoint of energy, there must be sufficient fuel to perform the task; difficulties arise if the available energy is expended before the task is completed.

In the literature on processing abilities, a focus on time is usually referred to as "processing speed," whereas a focus on either space or energy is referred to as "processing capacity." The tasks used to tap processing capacity are often tasks of "working memory," that is, the system employed to store small amounts of information for a short period while keeping it available for mental manipulation. In this chapter, we emphasize both processing speed and working memory. The two are not unrelated, of course – faster speed can translate into faster rehearsal, which can benefit the amount of information that can be retained. However, apart from the differences in tasks used to measure processing speed and working memory, there is also evidence, reviewed later in this chapter, that suggests the two are separable.

Advantages of the Iowa Project for the Study of Processing Speed and Working Memory

Several design features of the Iowa Project afforded us the opportunity to ask questions that often cannot even be approached in traditional laboratory studies. First, the children participating in the project were part of a large epidemiological study with the aim of determining the prevalence of specific language impairment (SLI). Thus, the children were sought out in their communities rather than being referred by professionals. Most studies of children with language impairments use clinically referred samples of children. It is quite possible that the presence of processing limitations in children with language impairments is more common when children are referred than when children are identified in their communities because children with multiple deficits are more likely to come to the attention of professionals. By studying the processing abilities of the children who participated in the Iowa Project, we could perhaps obtain a more representative picture of the degree to which processing limitations are at play in children's language impairments.

Another design advantage of the Iowa Project was the inclusion of children with language impairments who did not meet the conventional criteria for SLI. These children's nonlinguistic IQ scores fell below normal limits, though were not sufficiently low to warrant a diagnosis of intellectual disability. The participation of these children with "nonspecific language impairment" (NLI) allowed us to ask whether children with SLI and those with NLI constitute distinct diagnostic groups or instead should be viewed as part of a continuum, at least until new methods of research can prove otherwise.

The longitudinal nature of the Iowa Project represented yet another advantage to the study of processing limitations in children with language impairments. The stability of processing measures over time is not well understood in this population. It is assumed that processing speed and working memory constitute rather fundamental abilities or traits. Changes, of course, occur with development. For example, response time becomes faster across childhood and through adolescence (Kail, 1991). However, it is assumed that children who are relatively slow, or those with limitations in working memory, will not change their standing relative to their peers when tested at a later point. The Iowa Project enabled us to test this assumption.

SPEED OF PROCESSING

The first evidence that children with SLI process information relatively slowly appeared over 45 years ago, when Anderson (1965) reported that children meeting the SLI criteria named pictures more slowly than their typically developing peers. Over the years, slower response times (RTs) on the part of children with SLI were also reported for word monitoring (Stark & Montgomery, 1995), judgments of grammaticality

(Wulfeck & Bates, 1995), and other linguistic tasks. Such findings may not have been surprising given that slow RTs can reflect limited proficiency with the language material. More surprising, however, were findings that children with SLI were slower than their typically developing peers on tasks of a nonlinguistic nature, such as mental rotation (Johnston & Ellis Weismer, 1983) and moving pegs on a board (Bishop, 1990). Given the age-appropriate nonverbal IQ scores of children with SLI, slower processing speed on nonlinguistic tasks would not ordinarily be expected.

THE GENERALIZED SLOWING HYPOTHESIS

Given earlier findings that nonlinguistic as well as linguistic processing may be relatively slow in children with SLI, Kail (1994) proposed a method for testing the hypothesis of "generalized slowing" in these children. The hypothesis was that children with SLI respond more slowly than typically developing peers by a constant proportion on all processing tasks. The assumption is that any task involves several cognitive processes (e.g., perceiving a stimulus, interpreting it, executing a response), and children with SLI are slow in completing each process. The number and type of cognitive processes required will vary from task to task, rendering some tasks faster to complete than others. In absolute terms, RT differences between children with SLI and typically developing peers will be greater for tasks that require more time to complete. However, they will be slower than their typically developing peers by a constant proportion.

Kail (1994) tested his hypothesis by analyzing the RT data from previous studies on children with SLI and same-age typically developing children. The tasks used in these studies varied in nature and in time required to completion. For example, one of the tasks that resulted in very short RTs required the children to name pictures that served to complete sentences that were embedded in stories. The context provided by the sentence and story were highly consistent with the name of the picture (e.g., *We can walk to the main road and then we can wait for the* [picture of bus]). A task that resulted in much slower RTs was one in which the children had to judge whether particular digits had just appeared on a list that was two to four digits in length. When Kail examined the RTs of the children with SLI across the different tasks as a function of the RTs of the typically developing children, he found that the slope of the function reflected an approximately 30% slowing on the part of the children with SLI, with 96% of the variance accounted for by this proportional model. Similar findings were subsequently reported by Windsor and Hwang (1999) in their analysis of data from separate studies. They found that the children with SLI were approximately 21% slower than the typically developing group.

Miller, Kail, Leonard, and Tomblin (2001) tested the generalized slowing hypothesis using as participants 71 9-year-olds from the Iowa Project. One advantage of this work is that the same children participated in 10 different tasks, designed to cover a range of linguistic and nonlinguistic activities. The tasks included simple motor RT tasks such as tapping a computer key as quickly as possible for 5 seconds and nonverbal cognitive tasks such as finding a nonsense figure in an array that matched a target nonsense figure. Linguistic tasks required judgments based on phonological, lexical, or grammatical characteristics of the stimuli. For example, the children had to judge whether the name of a picture (e.g., a picture of a clock) began with the same consonant as a spoken word (e.g., *clown*) presented immediately after the picture. Grammatical information was tapped in a task requiring the children to judge whether a spoken sentence such as *The girl is being chased by the cat* matched the events depicted in a drawing. In all of these tasks, RT was the measure of interest. In keeping with the response time literature, RTs were calculated only for correct responses.

Along with children with SLI (N = 29) and typically developing peers (N = 29), Miller et al. (2001) included 19 children with NLI. Initially, all tasks were included in the same analysis. When the RTs of the SLI and NLI groups were regressed on those for the children with typical development, the proportional model explained 97% and 94% of the variance for the SLI and NLI groups, respectively. The children with SLI were approximately 14% slower than the typically developing (TLD) children; the children with NLI were approximately 28% slower.

Similar results obtained when Miller et al. (2001) divided the tasks according to whether they involved the linguistic or nonlinguistic domain. The linguistic and nonlinguistic domains were then subdivided. The linguistic tasks were divided according to their phonological, lexical, or grammatical nature; the nonlinguistic tasks were divided according to whether they required little more than a motor response, or instead required cognitive judgments. For the tasks from two particular sub-areas – the lexical tasks from the linguistic domain and the motor tasks from the nonlinguistic domain – the slopes for the SLI group did not fall outside the 95% confidence interval for the typically developing group. These findings suggested that the slowing seen in children with SLI may not be as broad-based as the generalized slowing hypothesis would predict. For the children with NLI, in contrast, all sub-areas showed comparable slowing relative to typically developing peers.

It also appears that not all children with SLI or NLI exhibit significant slowing. Miller et al. (2001) found that 8 of the 29 children with SLI and 4 of the 19 children with NLI had slopes that fell within the 95% confidence interval based on the typically developing children's RTs.

STABILITY OF SLOWING

A subsequent investigation by Miller et al. (2006) allowed additional questions to be asked about the RTs of children with SLI and NLI. First, they asked whether differences in slowing were still apparent when the children in the Iowa Project reached 14 years of age. In addition, they asked whether the children's RTs at 9 years of age could predict RTs at age 14. The tasks were the same as used in the earlier Miller et al. (2001) study, and the same three groups (SLI N = 20, NLI N = 15, TLD N = 31) participated. Not surprisingly, the RTs of all three groups were faster at 14 years of age than at age 9; this finding is in keeping with studies that show faster RTs with increasing age through adolescence (Kail, 1991). When the data were analyzed across all tasks in the same manner as in Miller et al. (2001), similar results were seen; the children with SLI were approximately 20% slower than the typically developing children whereas the children with NLI were approximately 26% slower.

Miller et al. (2006) also divided the tasks into motor, cognitive, and language domains to determine whether slowing might have been domain-specific. Both the SLI and NLI group were slower than their typically developing peers in all three domains. However, as many as seven participants in the SLI group and as many as five participants in the NLI group (depending upon the domain) did not show a degree of slowing that fell outside the 95% confidence intervals of the typically developing group.

When all 10 tasks were considered together, the age 9 RTs for both the SLI and NLI group were significantly correlated with the age 14 RTs. When the tasks were divided according to domain, the correlations between age 9 and age 14 were significant for each of the domains, motor, cognitive, and language, for the children with SLI. However, for the children with NLI, only the correlations for the motor and language domains were significant.

Together, the findings suggest that RTs continue to be relatively slow for children with SLI and those with NLI as they reach 14 years of age. For these groups, RTs at 9 years are related to their later RTs when all tasks are considered together, and for most domains when these are considered separately.

HOW DIFFERENT ARE NLI AND SLI GROUPS?

The study of SLI has had a long history, though many early studies escape notice because children with this impairment have been given a variety of other clinical labels. These include "congenital aphasia," "developmental dysphasia," "delayed language," and "developmental language disorder," among others. The children described in many of these earlier studies appeared to have striking dissociations between their language abilities and their nonverbal intelligence. However, as is true in any field, the assessment instruments available to investigators in these early studies were limited or lacking altogether. As a result, we cannot be certain of the degree of dissociation between linguistic and nonlinguistic skills in these children.

Eventually, of course, assessment tools came into greater use, and formal criteria were proposed for SLI. These criteria included the requirement of a nonverbal IQ score of at least 85 – representing a score no more than 1 standard deviation below the mean. Once the nonverbal IQ criterion began to be applied widely, it became apparent that some children with very obvious language impairments scored below the 85 cut-off, yet were clearly above the level suggestive of clinical categories such as mild intellectual disability. In fact, these are the children referred to as those with NLI in this volume.

The evidence that children with NLI differ in some qualitative way from children with SLI has been called into question in recent years. For example, children with NLI appear to show linguistic profiles that are very similar to those of children with SLI (Tomblin & Zhang, 1999). In addition, children with NLI appear to benefit from language treatment to the same degree as children with SLI (Cole, Dale, & Mills, 1990; Fey, Long, & Cleave, 1994).

These observations certainly invite the question of whether, on processing tasks, children with NLI and SLI will prove to be different in either their degree of speed/accuracy or in their pattern of performance across tasks. The studies by Miller et al. (2001, 2006) allowed for this type of comparison with regard to speed of processing. As noted earlier, NLI as well as SLI groups participated in these studies, with RTs obtained across a variety of linguistic and nonlinguistic tasks. When tested at 9 years of age, the children with NLI were slower than the children with SLI as well as the same-age typically developing peers. In addition, their slowing seemed to be broader in scope than the slowing exhibited by the children with SLI. These findings might have been expected given that the children were assigned to the NLI group based on relatively low nonverbal IQ scores as well as language test scores.

However, the findings from the later Miller et al. (2006) study complicate this interpretation somewhat. At 14 years of age, the NLI group (26% slower than the typically developing group) was not significantly slower than the SLI group (20% slower than the typically developing group). On the other hand, the SLI and NLI groups differed somewhat in the correlations among the RTs for the three domains of motor, cognitive, and language. For the children with SLI, RTs for each of these domains were significantly correlated with each other. However, for the children with NLI, RTs for the motor and cognitive domains proved unrelated, as did the RTs for the motor and language domains. Furthermore, for the NLI group, there was no relationship between RTs on the cognitive tasks at 9 years of age and RTs on the same cognitive tasks at 14 years of age. In contrast, the RTs of the SLI group at 9 and 14 years were significantly related for each of the domains. Further inspection of the data revealed that it was the NLI group and not the SLI group that showed the strongest evidence of domain differences. This is rather paradoxical given that, according to the selection criteria, the children with SLI showed higher scores on nonverbal IQ tests than on language tests, whereas the children with NLI had low scores in both nonverbal IQ and on language measures. Thus, a "flat" profile should be more likely to be seen in the data from the NLI group than the SLI group.

Future research is needed to determine whether these differences between SLI and NLI groups are replicable and meaningful, or whether they reflect, in part, a certain imprecision inherent in RT tasks. Another complicating factor is that, from age 9 to 14, some of the children's test profiles warranted placing them in a diagnostic category that differed from the one to which they were assigned at the younger age. For example, two of the children in the NLI group at age 9 were reclassified as SLI at 14 years of age, whereas four of the children in the SLI group at 9 years of age were reclassified NLI at the later testing point. With this type of shifting in classification – in both directions – it is not surprising that some of the data evade easy interpretation.

Any conclusions from these findings must remain tentative. However, the nature of the differences seen between children with SLI and children with NLI does not provide strong evidence that they constitute distinct groups.

WORKING MEMORY

The working memory abilities of children with SLI have been examined in many earlier studies. The verbal memory tasks have included recalling lists of words, recalling lists of digits, responding to the semantic or grammatical accuracy of sets of sentences while also recalling the last word of each sentence, and repeating nonwords of increasing syllable length. In addition, nonverbal memory tasks have been employed, such as recalling the location at which a particular visual stimulus appeared on a computer screen. The evidence for weaknesses in a range of verbal memory tasks is quite strong (e.g., Dollaghan & Campbell, 1998; Ellis Weismer, Evans, & Hesketh, 1999; Gathercole & Baddeley, 1990; Graf Estes et al., 2007; Gray, 2004; Hoffman & Gillam, 2004; Kirchner & Klatsky, 1985; Mainela-Arnold & Evans, 2005; Montgomery, 1995, 2000; Montgomery & Evans, 2009). Nonverbal spatial memory, too, appears to be relatively weak (Bavin, Wilson, Maruff, & Sleeman, 2005; Hoffman & Gillam, 2004), though this finding is not universal (Archibald & Gathercole, 2006).

The Iowa Project afforded the opportunity to pursue similar questions with the SLI and NLI groups. Ellis Weismer et al. (2000) examined phonological short-term memory performance through a nonword repetition task administered to the children when they were in the second grade. The SLI and NLI children were significantly less accurate than their typically developing same-age peers. These investigators also determined the degree to which this measure could accurately classify children as typically developing or as language impaired (either SLI or NLI). Using likelihood ratios, Ellis Weismer et al. found that the nonword repetition task was somewhat successful in classifying the children into these groups; however, when "typically developing" and "language impaired" were defined in terms of whether the children were receiving language intervention, the classification accuracy of the nonword repetition task was even higher.

Ellis Weismer and Thordardottir (2002) reported a study that examined the interplay between processing capacity and nonverbal cognition in elementary school-age children with and without language impairment. Performance was assessed on three tasks that tapped working memory capacity. One task measured dual-processing during sentence comprehension. In this task, children responded to sentences such as *Put the white square on the red circle* and *Touch the big boat and the little shoe* in either competing or non-competing conditions. In the competing condition, two sentences were presented simultaneously (one in a male voice, one in a female voice) and the children had to respond first to the sentence designated as primary (e.g., by putting the white square on the red circle) and then to the sentence designated as secondary (e.g., by touching the big boat and the little shoe). A second working memory task provided a measure of listening span. The children heard short sentences (e.g., *Sugar is sweet*) and had to judge each as true or false. However, the children also had to remember the last word in each sentence. After several sentences had been presented, the children had to recall the list of sentence-final words. The third task used by Ellis Weismer and Thordardottir involved nonword repetition, in which the children were asked to repeat nonwords (e.g., *doif*) that ranged from one to four syllables in length. Although each of the measures focused on verbal working memory, these tasks also included controls for the contribution of extant language knowledge.

Group comparisons indicated that children with SLI, as well as those with NLI, performed significantly worse than grade-level peers on all three tasks. Hierarchical multiple regression analysis revealed that nonverbal cognition and verbal working memory predicted concurrent language abilities. After the contribution of nonverbal cognition was accounted for, the three measures of verbal working memory capacity added significant unique variance in language scores. These results support the claim that verbal working memory capacity is associated with school-age children's language abilities. Further, the findings indicate that children with language impairment, whether defined narrowly or more broadly in terms of cognitive level, demonstrate limitations in verbal working memory.

Ellis Weismer (2006) presented data from the same population when the children had reached the 8th and then the 10th grade. At both grade levels, the SLI and NLI groups earned lower scores than their typically developing peers on a nonword repetition task, two tasks requiring the children to respond to sentences and also to remember the last word in each sentence, a standardized auditory memory task, and a nonlinguistic spatial working memory task. The same pattern of results was observed across each of the verbal working memory measures such that the SLI and NLI groups performed at similar (reduced) levels of accuracy. Performance on the spatial working memory task appeared to be related to both low language and low cognitive abilities, as the NLI group scored significantly worse than the SLI group on this measure. Deficits on the nonlinguistic working memory task suggest a domain-general processing deficit. However, some have argued that difficulties on verbal working memory measures simply reflect poor linguistic knowledge and that these constructs are not separable (MacDonald & Christiansen, 2002; Mainela-Arnold & Evans, 2005). In order to assess this claim, Ellis Weismer employed a confirmatory factor analysis using the eighth grade data. Verbal working memory and language were highly correlated for children with and without language impairment; however, these two factors were statistically distinguishable for both groups of children.

Karasinski and Ellis Weismer (2010b) investigated longitudinal predictors of language and verbal working memory in children participating in the Iowa Project. A battery of language and verbal working memory assessments was administered in the 2nd and 10th grades. For the purposes of this study, participants were assigned to three diagnostic groups – normal language, current language impairment (SLI or NLI) at 10th grade, and history of language impairment that had resolved at 10th grade. Regression analyses revealed that second grade verbal working memory predicted both verbal working memory and language at 10th grade for all groups. Second grade language scores were predictive of both areas of ability in 10th grade for the normal language group, but did not predict both areas for the language impairment groups. Results suggest that the developmental relationship between language and verbal working memory may differ for children with typical language development compared to those with prior or current language impairment.

THE RELATIONSHIP BETWEEN PROCESSING SPEED AND WORKING MEMORY

A fundamental relationship exists between speed of processing and working memory. As noted earlier, faster speed can promote faster rehearsal, which could increase the amount of information that is retained. In addition, attention, which is assumed to be essential for performing timed tasks, has also been found to play an important role in working memory (Cowan, 1999). It seems that brain mechanisms that control attention might also be those that refresh representations in working memory (Jonides, Lacey, & Nee, 2005). In studies of language impairment, too, there seem to be demonstrable links. In a study that employed functional magnetic resonance imaging (fMRI), Ellis Weismer, Plante, Jones, and Tomblin (2005) found differences between adolescents with language impairment and typically developing peers in regions associated with both attention and memory.

In spite of the clear overlap between speed of processing and working memory, they are separable. For example, when children with language impairment are matched with typically developing children on measures of working memory, they may nevertheless respond more slowly on tasks involving language processing (Gillam & Ellis Weismer, 1997).

The Iowa Project permitted an examination of the relationship between processing speed and working memory given that, at particular ages, the participants were administered both types of tasks. Using the pooled SLI, NLI, and typically developing data obtained when the participants were 14 years of age, Leonard et al. (2007) examined the relationship between speed and working memory by asking whether these two processes function in a manner that allows them to be considered a single processing factor. These investigators also asked whether linguistic and nonlinguistic processing function in a similar manner. The tasks employed by Miller et al. (2001, 2006) were used for the speed of processing measures. These were subdivided into motor, nonlinguistic cognitive, and linguistic tasks. For working memory, the children's performance on a nonword repetition task, an auditory working memory task, and two listening span tasks were used to assess verbal working memory. A spatial working memory task was used to assess nonverbal working memory.

Using confirmatory factor analysis, Leonard et al. (2007) found that the models that proved satisfactory treated processing speed and working memory as separate factors. In one model, separate motor speed, cognitive speed, and linguistic speed were factors, along with separate verbal and nonverbal working memory factors. In a second satisfactory model, a general speed factor was used, with the same separation of verbal and nonverbal working memory as in the first model.

Both models accounted for the data quite well, suggesting that processing speed and working memory are not interchangeable measures of processing. Furthermore, nonlinguistic speed (motor, cognitive) and nonverbal working memory functioned as dimensions that were separable from the corresponding linguistic speed and verbal working memory abilities.

THE ROLE OF PROCESSING FACTORS IN LANGUAGE IMPAIRMENT

The findings reviewed here reveal substantial evidence that children with SLI and NLI are more limited than same-age typically developing peers in their processing ability. When these children are considered as a group, it is clear that they are slower in processing both linguistic and nonlinguistic information, and are more limited in their verbal and nonverbal working memory.

Given findings such as these, the next logical step is to ask whether deficits in processing ability are related to the language impairment itself. Several earlier studies have examined this issue.

Early proposals of a likely connection between phonological short-term memory and lexical learning (e.g., Gathercole & Baddeley, 1990) have not been evaluated extensively. However, Gray (2004) found relatively little support for this relationship in a study of novel word learning by preschoolers with SLI. This finding suggests that a phonological short-term memory limitation might not be sufficient to lead to a lexical deficit. Findings concerning the relationship between phonological short-term memory and sentence comprehension have been mixed. In some cases, phonological short-term memory performance is correlated with complex sentence comprehension (e.g., Montgomery, 1995), whereas in other studies, it is correlated with simple sentence comprehension but not with complex sentence comprehension (Montgomery & Evans, 2009).

Other studies have employed a working memory task in which children must answer questions about a set of sentences while retaining the last word of each sentence for subsequent recall. Ellis Weismer (1996) reported a relationship between performance on this type of task and production of newly learned novel morphemes in a group of children with SLI. Similar working memory tasks have been studied in relation to sentence comprehension. Thus far, the strongest results in the SLI literature are those that show a relationship between working memory performance and the comprehension of complex sentences (Montgomery & Evans, 2009). This type of listening span task has also been found to be associated with comprehension of implicit information in discourse processing. As part of the Iowa Project, adolescents' ability to link distant information across several sentences in a spoken narrative in order to construct inferences was examined (Karasinski & Ellis Weismer, 2010a). Regression analyses indicated that verbal working memory predicted unique variance in distant inference accuracy beyond that accounted for by measures of language and nonverbal cognition.

The Iowa Project data have also been applied to address the issue of the relationship between processing and language ability. Recall that in the Leonard et al. (2007) study these investigators found that two models met the criteria for successfully characterizing the processing speed and working memory data obtained from the 14-year-old children. They then applied latent variable regression analysis to determine the degree to which each of these satisfactory models could predict the children's scores on a composite language ability measure obtained at the same age. The composite score was based on the children's performance on tests of vocabulary, syntax, and narrative comprehension and production. Leonard et al. found that each model explained a substantial and statistically significant amount of the variance (62%) in the children's composite language test scores. In both models, nonlinguistic (or general) speed and verbal working memory emerged as significant factors, with verbal working memory playing an especially important role.

What are we to make of these and earlier findings of a relationship between processing measures and language ability? We discuss here the alternative roles that processing factors may play.

PROCESSING LIMITATIONS AS A CAUSE OF LANGUAGE IMPAIRMENT

There are many obstacles to clear before one could reasonably conclude that language impairment is caused by processing limitations. One of these obstacles is the difficulty in relating particular processing deficits to particular patterns of impaired language production or comprehension. Of course, one can see how, in principle, processing deficits could play a causal role. For example, phonological short-term memory must be sufficiently robust to ensure that the phonological representation of a newly encountered word is retained long enough for it to be stored with a likely meaning. Poor phonological short-term memory is likely to require multiple encounters with the word to ensure adequate retention, resulting in a limited vocabulary (Baddeley, Gathercole, & Papagno, 1998).

According to some proposals, the number of vocabulary words in a child's lexicon predicts the child's level of grammatical development (e.g., Marchman & Bates, 1994), or may even determine when a biologically driven grammatical analysis device is set in motion (Locke, 1994). However, memory limitations could also have a more focused effect. For example, sentences in the input such as *The girl who chased the boy is tall* might well prove difficult, leading the child to conclude that the boy, rather than the girl, is tall because information earlier in the sentence was not properly retained.

Difficulty processing adult input sentences could also contribute to errors in tense/agreement morphology. For example, in an input utterance such as *The dad sees the cat eating*, children might fail to understand that the nonfinite clause, *the cat eating*, is permissible only if tense/agreement information appears elsewhere (earlier) in the sentence. Without this understanding, children might assume that meaningful propositions such as *The cat eating* can serve as an alternative to other sentences heard in the input, such as *The cat's eating*. As a result, children might go through a period of using both forms until these details are eventually learned. In the meantime, if the children's ability to create novel utterances is not severely impaired, they might well generate new utterances using either sentence frame (The N Verbing, The N is Verbing) as the basis. For example, an utterance created by the child might take the form of either *The bird hopping* or *The bird's hopping*.

Limitations in working memory might also lead to cases of "syntactic encapsulation" described by Just and Carpenter (1992). These authors proposed that working memory limitations can tax syntactic computations to the point where nonsyntactic information is not retained. For example, in a sentence such as *The mom knows that the boys played cards at the beach*, a child's judgment about the appropriateness of *the boys played cards* as opposed to *the boys·play cards* cannot be made within the syntax itself, because both are locally grammatical. Instead, this type of judgment depends on the child's retention of the temporal relationship between the events in the two clauses.

PROCESSING LIMITATIONS EXACERBATING A LANGUAGE IMPAIRMENT

It could also be the case that a child's language impairment has a different cause, but the presence of processing limitations makes an already difficult language learning process even more arduous. Even among individuals with typical language skills, there are elements of language that place severe demands on processing. This is clear from our difficulty in understanding grammatical sentences such as *The dog that the horse that the man bought stepped on was quite friendly*. For children with processing limitations, it probably does not take sentences with embedded clauses before limits to processing capacity are reached.

Processing limitations might well lead to an underestimation of children's language abilities during formal language assessment. Tests of children's language comprehension require attention to detail, the storage and rehearsal of information, and other online processes in addition to knowledge of language. Tests of language production, too, have processing demands. Sentence completion tasks require that the child pay attention to and retain the lexical items and the syntactic frame in the examiner's carrier phrase in order to provide the correct response. Sentence repetition tasks require the child to retain an entire sentence in order to repeat it. A child with a language impairment might possess the linguistic knowledge that particular test items are designed to assess, yet respond incorrectly to these items because processing limitations prevent the child from exhibiting that knowledge.

If processing limitations serve as obstacles to children's language production and comprehension in the moment, it is likely that these limitations will have also adversely affected the children's language learning over the course of their lives, even if the language impairment has another source. Children's accumulation of language knowledge depends on adequate processing of the input. Processing limitations could cause words and syntactic structures appearing in the speech stream to be incompletely processed. The result would be a protracted development of these language details because children would need to encounter these details many more times than typically developing children before they could fully process them and incorporate them into their linguistic system.

It is also possible that processing limitations at a younger age might become less pronounced with age but nevertheless have had a slowing effect on the development of language knowledge because of the prime (critical) period during which the limitations were in effect. Both processing speed and working memory increase with age, but the acquisition of particular types of language knowledge might be constrained to particular maturational periods (Locke, 1994). If this is the case, a child tested at a later age might show symptoms of the language impairment but not the processing limitation. Longitudinal studies will be necessary to assess the feasibility of this possibility.

Although much research remains to be done before we can understand the precise role that processing limitations play in language impairment, there is at this point sufficient evidence to consider processing factors when planning for clinical assessment and intervention. Recall that in the Leonard et al. (2007) investigation, processing measures contributed significantly to the prediction of language test scores. Such a finding is particularly noteworthy considering that the processing measures required the children to respond quickly to, or retain in working memory, material that they already knew, whereas language tests are at least intended to be measures of what children know or don't know about language.

This finding suggests that clinicians must be especially careful in planning an assessment of children's knowledge of particular details of language. If an accurate gauge of knowledge is the goal, the material probably needs to be presented in a manner that keeps processing demands to a minimum. An alternative course of action would be to assess children's knowledge of language details in a range of contexts that vary systematically in the demands they place on children's processing skills. The results of such an assessment might indicate the conditions under which intervention should begin. Emphasis could be placed on helping the child learn the function or meaning of the language detail in cases where the child showed no understanding even when processing demands were minimal. For cases in which a child demonstrated understanding when demands were low, intervention might focus on assisting the child in recognizing or producing the language detail when processing demands are somewhat greater.

ONLINE BEHAVIORAL MEASURES OF SENTENCE PROCESSING

Speed of processing is a factor that has been put to good use in studies of sentence comprehension in children with SLI. In particular, this measure can provide insight into the nature of children's understanding as a sentence unfolds. Such online sentence processing holds an advantage over offline sentence comprehension because the latter necessarily involves a delayed response on the part of the child, which, in turn, could introduce factors unrelated to the child's understanding of the sentence. Some of the early online sentence processing studies involving children with SLI made use of word monitoring. In this task, children are told to listen for a particular word (the target) that might appear in a sentence, and to press a button or computer key when they detect the word. Questions about the sentences are also asked to ensure that the child is processing the sentence. Target words appear in several different positions in the sentence and the children's RTs are measured. Montgomery, Scudder, and Moore (1990) and Montgomery (2000a) found that children with SLI are slower than same-age peers at responding to the target word, but, like typically developing children, their RTs are faster when the target word appears later in the sentence. These findings suggest slower sentence processing by children with SLI but not a different type of processing from typically developing peers.

Montgomery and Leonard (1998) used an adaptation of the word monitoring procedure to examine sensitivity to grammatical details during sentence processing by children with SLI. Specifically, for some of the sentences, the word immediately preceding the target word was missing an obligatory inflection (e.g., *She always gets up early and eat breakfast*, where *breakfast* is the target word). Detection of the error causes a brief distraction, which results in a slower response to the target word than when no grammatical error appears in the sentence. Montgomery and Leonard found that children with SLI, like their typically developing peers, were slower to respond to the target word when the missing inflection was syllabic (the progressive inflection *-ing*) but showed no slowing effect – suggesting a failure to detect the omission – when the missing inflection was consonantal (the third person singular *-s* or past tense *-ed*).

Sixteen-year-olds from the Iowa Project participated in a similar study conducted by Leonard, Miller, and Finneran (2009). These investigators asked whether adolescents with SLI or NLI would show a subtle weakness in their sensitivity to omissions of inflections that mark tense (e.g., *We went home and bake cookies with our mother*), relative to omissions of inflections unrelated to tense (e.g., *I put a nail in my neighbor wall to hang his painting*) or commission errors involving tense-related inflections (e.g., *I want to buy and wrapped my presents before the holidays*). Same-age peers showed the predicted slow RTs to all types of errors relative to equivalent grammatical sentences. However, the adolescents with SLI and NLI showed slowing only for non-tense-related omissions and for tense-related commission errors. When tense-related inflections were omitted, no slowing occurred. Leonard et al. proposed that this pattern of performance might constitute subtle, residual effects of an early stage of development when children with SLI and NLI sometimes omit tense-related inflections in particular, but only rarely produce such inflections in inappropriate contexts.

ELECTROPHYSIOLOGICAL MEASURES OF PROCESSING

Tone Processing. Previous studies of younger children with SLI employing measures of event-related brain potentials (ERPs) have indicated that online neural indices mediating processing of brief or rapidly changing auditory stimuli often function atypically, both at the level of the brainstem (e.g., Basu, Krishnan, & Weber-Fox, 2010; Wible, Nicol, & Kraus, 2004) and for longer latency cortical potentials (e.g., McArthur & Bishop, 2004a, 2004b; McArthur, Atkinson, & Ellis, 2009; Neville, Coffey, Holcomb, & Tallal, 1993). In a study of adolescents from the Iowa Project, Weber-Fox, Leonard, Hampton Wray, and Tomblin (2010) examined whether the participants with SLI would exhibit atypical neural activity for rapid auditory tone processing. Fifteen adolescents with SLI and 15 with TLD participated; each group ranged in age from 14 to 18 years. All participants met strict criteria for displaying consistent diagnoses (SLI or TLD) across kindergarten, second, fourth, and eighth grades. The two groups were matched according to nonverbal IQ in addition to age.

Brief tonal stimuli (1000 Hz Standard and 2000 Hz Target tones) with a short (200 ms) and long (1000 ms) interstimulus interval (ISI) were presented in an oddball paradigm in which target tones occurred on 20% of the trials. Participants were asked to press a button as quickly as possible when they detected a target tone.

There was considerable heterogeneity in the group with SLI and not all adolescents with SLI functioned in an atypical manner, either in their behavioral or electrophysiological measures. However, as a group, the adolescents with SLI performed with significantly reduced accuracy and a tendency for longer reaction times in detecting the target tones. The simple brief tonal stimuli presented with a 200 ms ISI elicited reduced N100 amplitudes to target tones over right hemisphere anterior regions in a significant number of adolescents with SLI. The reduced amplitude of this early cortical potential may indicate a less robust perceptual representation of the brief auditory signal. No group differences in N100 amplitude were found when the tones were presented with a longer (1000 ms) ISI. In addition, the later occurring cognitive potential, the P300 elicited by target tones, was reduced in amplitude in the adolescents with SLI. The P300 is thought to reflect the summation of cognitive events including focusing on novel information and updating working memory (e.g., Knight & Nakada, 1998; Polich & Kok, 1995). In summary, the findings from the tone processing study indicated that reduced efficiency in nonlinguistic auditory processing in adolescents with SLI is more vulnerable to rapid rates of presentation (200 ms ISI) indexed by reduced accuracy, a tendency for longer RTs, reduced N100 amplitude over right anterior sites, and reduced amplitude P300.

Sentence Processing. Electrophysiological studies of sentence processing in SLI have shown that younger children with SLI display atypical ERPs for closed-class (function) words (Neville et al., 1993; Shafer, Schwartz, Morr, Kessler, & Kurtzberg, 2000), syntactic dependencies (Fonteneau & van der Lely, 2008), and semantic integration (Neville et al., 1993; Sabisch, Hahne, Glass, von Suchodoletz, & Friederici, 2006). Electrophysiological measures of sentence processing were also employed in the Weber-Fox et al. (2010) study of tone processing with adolescents from the Iowa Project. The sentence stimuli focused on processing of verbs as the critical comparison across conditions and allowed for examining both morphosyntactic and semantic constraints. Converging evidence (Leonard, 1998) indicates that the well-known problem with verb-related morphology (e.g., third person singular -s verb inflections) in children with SLI may not be limited to the formal grammatical functions of the morphemes but may reflect a broader problem with how verbs combine with other elements in the sentence. Like nouns, verbs convey conceptual meaning, but in addition, they provide relational information for integrating grammatical inflections and argument structures across the sentence (Hirsh-Pasek & Golinkoff, 2006; Langacker, 1987). And, verb processing has been found to engage distinctive neural activations compared to nouns as indexed by measures of ERPs and fMRI in both children and adults (Federmeier, Segal, Lombrozo, & Kutas, 2000; Weber-Fox et al., 2006; Yokoyama et al., 2006).

The adolescents from the Iowa Project in the Weber-Fox et al. (2010) study listened to sentences such as *Every day, the horses gallop to the top of the hill*. ERPs elicited by verb-agreement violations were measured for sentences such as *Every day, the horses gallops to the top of the hill*. For examining processes mediating lexical access and integration for reduced semantic expectation, ERPs elicited by sentences such as *Every day, the horses sing to the top of the hill* were measured. Compared to their typically developing peers, many adolescents with SLI displayed reduced behavioral accuracy for detecting verb-agreement violations. In addition, the P600 elicited by verb-agreement violations was less robust in the group of adolescents with SLI compared to their peers. The P600 is thought to index post-lexical syntactic repair/re-analysis processes (e.g., Osterhout & Holcomb, 1992; Osterhout & Mobley, 1995). Thus, although overt language production errors no longer characterize SLI during adolescence, the results indicate that ERPs elicited by morphosyntactic aspects of language processing are atypical in many adolescents with SLI. On the other hand, it was noted that P600 amplitudes elicited in some of the adolescents with SLI fell within the range of those that were elicited in their typically developing peers. Overall, the findings are consistent with behavioral measures indicating continued (but more subtle) deficits with tense/agreement morphosyntax in many adolescents with SLI (Leonard et al., 2009).

Compared to their typically functioning peers, the adolescents with SLI in the Iowa Project also performed with less accuracy for processing verbs with reduced semantic expectation in the sentence processing task. It is possible that the difficulty of the task was increased relative to a previous study that utilized highly primed, frank semantic anomalies on nouns (Neville et al., 1993). In contrast, the unexpected verbs in the Iowa Project study were not necessarily anomalous at the point of the verb in the sentence (e.g., one could imagine a cartoon horse singing). Also, unlike the previous study by Neville and colleagues (1993), the participants in the Iowa study had to simultaneously monitor for both verb-agreement and semantic violations, which may have increased the meta-linguistic demands on the participants. These behavioral findings for semantic processing in adolescents from the Iowa Project are consistent with the idea that semantic representations for verbs may be weaker in SLI (Sabisch et al., 2006). The ERP measures, however, did not yield group differences for the amplitude of the N400 elicited by the unexpected verbs. The N400 is thought to index ease of lexical access and integration (e.g., Kutas & Hillyard, 1980; Federmeier et al., 2000). In the previous ERP study by Neville et al. (1993), children with SLI displayed a larger N400 amplitude over posterior electrode sites for frank semantic anomalies (in which the control nouns had high cloze probability) compared to their typically developing peers. In addition, written, rather than auditorily presented sentences were employed. It is possible that differences in specific characteristics of the stimulus sentences may have contributed to the subtle differences in ERP findings for the Iowa Project study.

The participation of the same group of adolescents from the Iowa Project in both the tone processing and sentence processing studies of Weber-Fox et al. (2010) made it possible to examine the relationship between performance and ERPs elicited in the two types of tasks. It could be hypothesized that fundamental abilities in auditory processing might directly contribute to abilities in morphosyntactic processing. However, evidence from twin studies suggests that the relationship between auditory processing and language ability may be less direct (Bishop et al., 1999). Thus, the observed relationships between deficits in these two areas may be due to their relatively high degree of comorbidity in the SLI population. Our findings for the subgroup of adolescents from the Iowa Project indicated that behavioral performance in processing tones with a short ISI correlated with behavioral performance in detecting verb-agreement violations in the SLI group, but not the typically developing group. However, electrophysiological indices for processing tones with a short ISI correlated with those for verb-agreement violations in the typically developing group, but correlations only approached significance for the SLI group. Even the significant correlations were modest, however, suggesting that the integrity of neural functions for auditory processing may account for only a small proportion of the variance in morphosyntactic processing in some adolescents.

SUMMARY

In this chapter we have reviewed the evidence for processing limitations in children and adolescents with SLI and NLI who participated in the Iowa Project. Both speed of processing and working memory measures have been considered. At a group level, it is clear that children and adolescents with SLI and NLI process information more slowly than same-age typically developing peers, and their working memory, likewise, is more limited. Processing limitations are not confined to linguistic tasks; they are seen as well when non-linguistic processing is evaluated. These limitations are seen at both younger and older ages, and are related to language ability, though they are not necessarily the direct cause of language impairment. Although speed of processing appears to be related to language ability, verbal working memory, especially, seems important in this relationship.

The sentence processing abilities of adolescents with SLI and NLI are clearly not at the level of their peers, whether assessed by RT or by electrophysiological measures. Processing of grammatical details seems quite vulnerable, especially when sensitivity to grammatical agreement is the focus.

Children and adolescents with NLI often process information more slowly and less accurately than their counterparts carrying the designation of SLI, but evidence for a diagnostic distinction between these two groups is not compelling. Even though the low language test scores of individuals with NLI are (by definition) accompanied by relatively low scores on nonverbal IQ tests, their performance profile across linguistic and nonlinguistic processing tasks do not diverge greatly from the profiles seen for individuals with SLI.

Over the years of the Iowa Project, we have employed a wide variety of processing tasks with the participants, and have endeavored to determine how performance on these tasks might explain a piece of the larger puzzle of language impairment. We are not certain that the processing limitations observed in SLI and NLI are the direct source of the language impairment. However, we are quite firm in our belief that, whatever the original source of the language impairment, these processing limitations render more difficult the children's intake and interpretation of linguistic material. For this reason, the processing limitations of children with SLI and NLI must remain an important focus of future investigations and should be considered in any clinical assessment and treatment plan for these children.

REFERENCES

Anderson, J. (1965). Initiatory delay in congenital aphasoid conditions. *Cerebral Palsy Journal, 26,* 9–12.

Archibald, L., & Gathercole, S. (2006). Visuospatial immediate memory in specific language impairment. *Journal of Speech, Language, and Hearing Research, 49,* 265–277.

Baddeley, A., Gathercole, S., & Papagno, C. (1998). The phonological loop as a language learning device. *Psychological Review, 105,* 158–173.

Basu, M., Krishnan, A., & Weber-Fox., C. (2010). Brainstem correlates of temporal auditory processing in children with specific language impairment. *Developmental Science, 13,* 77–91.

Bavin, E., Wilson, P., Maruff, P., & Sleeman, F. (2005). Spatio-visual memory of children with specific language impairment: Evidence for generalized processing problems. *International Journal of Language & Communication Disorders, 40,* 319–332.

Bishop, D. V. M. (1990). Handedness, clumsiness and developmental language disorders. *Neuropsychologia, 28,* 681–690.

Bishop, D. V. M. (1992). The underlying nature of specific language impairment. *Journal of Child Psychology and Psychiatry, 33,* 3–66.

Bishop, D. V. M., Bishop, S. J., Bright, P., James, C., Delaney, T., & Tallal, P. (1999). Different origin of auditory and phonological problems in children with language impairment: Evidence from a twin study. *Journal of Speech, Language, and Hearing Research, 42,* 155–168.

Cole, K., Dale, P., & Mills, P. (1990). Defining language delay in young children by cognitive referencing: Are we saying more than we know? *Applied Psycholinguistics, 11,* 291–302.

Cowan, N. (1999). Embedded-processes model of working memory. In A. Miyake & P. Shah (Eds.), *Models of working memory: Mechanisms of active maintenance and executive control* (pp. 62–101). Cambridge: Cambridge University Press.

Dollaghan, C., & Campbell, T. (1998). Nonword repetition and child language impairment. *Journal of Speech, Language, and Hearing Research, 41,* 1136–1146.

Ellis Weismer, S. (1996). Capacity limitations in working memory: The impact on lexical and morphological learning by children with language impairment. *Topics in Language Disorders, 17,* 33–44.

Ellis Weismer, S. (2006). *Examining the role of processing limitations in specific language impairment.* Invited keynote lecture, Symposium on Research in Child Language Disorders, Madison, WI.

Ellis Weismer, S., Evans, J., & Hesketh, L. (1999). An examination of verbal working memory capacity in children with specific language impairment. *Journal of Speech, Language, and Hearing Research, 42,* 1249–1260.

Ellis Weismer, S., Plante, E., Jones, M., & Tomblin, J. B. (2005). A functional magnetic resonance imaging investigation of verbal working memory in adolescents with specific language impairment. *Journal of Speech, Language, and Hearing Research, 48*, 405–425.

Ellis Weismer, S., & Thordardottir, E. T. (2002). Cognition and language. In P. Accardo, A. Capute, & B. Rogers (Eds.), *Disorders of language development* (pp. 21–37). Timonium, MD: York Press.

Ellis Weismer, S., Tomblin, J. B., Zhang, X., Buckwalter, P., Chynoweth, J. G., & Jones, M. (2000). Nonword repetition performance in school-age children with and without language impairment. *Journal of Speech, Language, and Hearing Research, 43*, 865–878.

Federmeier, K. D., Segal, J. B., Lombrozo, T., & Kutas, M. (2000). Brain responses to nouns, verbs, and class-ambiguous words in context. *Brain, 123*, 2552–2566.

Fey, M., Long, S., & Cleave, P. (1994). Reconsideration of IQ criteria in the definition of specific language impairment. In R. Watkins & M. Rice (Eds.), *Specific language impairments in children* (pp. 161–178). Baltimore: Paul H. Brookes.

Fonteneau, E., & van der Lely, H. K. J. (2008). Electrical brain responses in language-impaired children reveal grammar-specific deficits. *PLoS ONE 3*, e1832.

Gathercole, S., & Baddeley, A. (1990). Phonological memory deficits in language disordered children: Is there a causal connection? *Journal of Memory and Language, 29*, 336–360.

Gillam, R., & Ellis Weismer, S. (1997, November). *Capacity limitations, activation, and working memory in specific language impairment.* Paper presented at the Annual Convention of the American Speech-Language-Hearing Association, Boston.

Gillam, R., Montgomery, J., & Gillam, S. (2008). Attention and memory in child language disorders. In R. Schwartz (Ed.), *Handbook of child language disorders.* New York: Psychology Press.

Graf Estes, K., Evans, J., & Else-Quest, N. (2007). Differences in the nonword repetition performance of children with and without specific language impairment: A meta-analysis. *Journal of Speech, Language, and Hearing Research, 50*, 177–195.

Gray, S. (2004). The relationship between phonological memory, receptive vocabulary, and fast mapping in young children with specific language impairment. *Journal of Speech, Language, and Hearing Research, 49*, 955–969.

Hirsh-Pasek, K., & Golinkoff, R. M. (2006). *Action meets word: How children learn verbs.* New York: Oxford University Press.

Hoffman, L., & Gillam, R. (2004). Verbal and spatial information processing constraints in children with specific language impairment. *Journal of Speech, Language, and Hearing Research, 47*, 114–125.

Johnston, J., & Ellis Weismer, S. (1983). Mental rotation abilities in language-disordered children. *Journal of Speech and Hearing Research, 26,* 397–403.

Jonides, J., Lacey, S., & Nee, D. (2005). Processing of working memory in mind and brain. *Current Directions in Psychological Science, 14,* 2–5.

Just, M., & Carpenter, P. (1992). A capacity theory of comprehension: Individual differences in working memory. *Psychological Review, 98,* 122–149.

Kail, R. (1991). Processing time declines exponentially during childhood and adolescence. *Developmental Psychology, 27,* 259–266.

Kail, R. (1994). A method for studying the generalized slowing hypothesis in children with specific language impairment. *Journal of Speech and Hearing Research, 37,* 418–421.

Kail, R., & Salthouse, T. (1994). Processing speed as a mental capacity. *Acta Psychologica, 86,* 199–225.

Karasinski, C., & Ellis Weismer, S. (2010a). Comprehension of inferences in discourse processing by adolescents with and without language impairment. *Journal of Speech, Language, and Hearing Research, 53,* 1268–1279.

Karasinski, C., & Ellis Weismer, S. (2010b, June). *Predictors of language and verbal working memory in tenth grade.* Poster presented at the Symposium on Research for Child Language Disorders, Madison, WI.

Kirchner, D., & Klatsky, R. (1985). Verbal rehearsal and memory in language-disordered children. *Journal of Speech and Hearing Research, 28,* 556–565.

Knight, R. T., & Nakada, T. (1998). Cortico-limbic circuits and novelty: A review of EEG and blood flow data. *Reviews in the Neurosciences, 9,* 57–70.

Kutas, M., & Hillyard, S. A. (1980). Reading between the lines: Event-related brain potentials during natural sentence processing. *Brain and Language, 11,* 354–373.

Leonard, L. B. (1998). *Children with specific language impairment.* Cambridge, MA: MIT Press.

Leonard, L. B., Ellis Weismer, S., Miller, C. A., Francis, D. J., Tomblin, J. B., & Kail, R. (2007). Speed of processing, working memory, and language impairment in children. *Journal of Speech, Language, and Hearing Research, 50,* 408–428.

Leonard, L. B., Miller, C. A., & Finneran, D. (2009). Grammatical morpheme effects on sentence processing by school-aged adolescents with specific language impairment. *Language and Cognitive Processes, 24,* 450–478.

Locke, J. (1994). Gradual emergence of developmental language disorders. *Journal of Speech and Hearing Research, 37,* 608–616.

MacDonald, M. C., & Christiansen, M. H. (2002). Reassessing working memory: Comment on Just & Carpenter (1992) and Waters & Caplan (1996). *Psychological Review, 109,* 35–54.

Mainela-Arnold, E., & Evans, J. (2005). Beyond capacity limitations: Determinants of word-recall performance on verbal working memory span tasks in children with SLI. *Journal of Speech, Language, and Hearing Research, 48*, 897–909.

Marchman, V., & Bates, E. (1994). Continuity in lexical and morphological development: A test of the continuity hypothesis. *Journal of Child Language, 21*, 339–366.

McArthur, G. M., Atkinson, C. M., & Ellis, D. (2009). Atypical brain responses to sounds in children with specific language and reading impairments. *Developmental Science, 12*, 768–783.

McArthur, G. M., & Bishop, D. V. M. (2004). Which people with specific language impairment have auditory processing deficits? *Cognitive Neurophysiology, 21*, 79–94.

McArthur, G. M., & Bishop, D. V. M. (2005). Speech and non-speech processing by people with specific language impairment: A behavioral and electrophysiological study. *Brain and Language, 94*, 260–273.

Miller, C. A., Kail, R., Leonard, L. B., & Tomblin, J. B. (2001). Speed of processing in children with specific language impairment. *Journal of Speech, Language, and Hearing Research, 44*, 416–433.

Miller, C. A., Leonard, L. B., Kail, R., Zhang, X., Tomblin, J. B., & Francis, D. J. (2006). Response time in 14-year-olds with language impairment. *Journal of Speech, Language, and Hearing Research, 49*, 712–728.

Montgomery, J. (1995). Sentence comprehension in children with specific language impairment: The role of phonological working memory. *Journal of Speech, Language, and Hearing Research, 38*, 187–199.

Montgomery, J. (2000a). Relation of working memory to off-line and real-time sentence processing in children with specific language impairment. *Applied Psycholinguistics, 21*, 117–148.

Montgomery, J. (2000b). Verbal working memory in sentence comprehension in children with specific language impairment. *Journal of Speech, Language, and Hearing Research, 43*, 293–308.

Montgomery, J., & Evans, J. (2009). Complex sentence comprehension and working memory in children with specific language impairment. *Journal of Speech, Language, and Hearing Research, 52*, 269–288.

Montgomery, J., & Leonard, L. B. (1998). Real-time inflectional processing by children with specific language impairment. *Journal of Speech, Language, and Hearing Research, 41*, 1432–1443.

Montgomery, J., Scudder, R., & Moore, C. (1990). Language-impaired children's real-time comprehension of spoken language. *Applied Psycholinguistics, 11*, 273–290.

Neville, H. J., Coffey, S. A., Holcomb, P. J., & Tallal, P. (1993). The neurobiology of sensory and language processing in language-impaired children. *Journal of Cognitive Neuroscience, 5*, 235–253.

Osterhout, L., & Holcomb, P. J. (1992). Event-related brain potentials elicited by syntactic anomaly. *Journal of Memory and Language, 31*, 2–22.

Osterhout, L., & Mobley, L. A. (1995). Event-related brain potentials elicited by failure to agree. *Journal of Memory and Language, 34*, 739–773.

Polich, J., & Kok, A. (1995). Cognitive and biological determinants of P300: An integrative review. *Biological Psychology, 41*, 113–146.

Sabisch, B., Hahne, A., Glass, E., von Suchodoletz, W., & Friederici, A. D. (2006). Lexical-semantic processes in children with specific language impairment. *NeuroReport, 17*, 1511–1514.

Shafer, V. L., Schwartz, R. G., Morr, M. L., Kessler, K. L., & Kurtzberg, D. (2000). Deviant neurophysiological asymmetry in children with language impairment. *NeuroReport, 11*, 3715–3718.

Stark, R., & Montgomery, J. (1995). Sentence processing in language-impaired children under conditions of filtering and time compression. *Applied Psycholinguistics, 16*, 137–154.

Tomblin, J. B., & Zhang, X. (1999). Language patterns and etiology in children with specific language impairment. In H. Tager-Flusberg (Ed.), *Neurodevelopmental disorders* (pp. 361–382). Cambridge, MA: MIT Press.

Weber-Fox, C., Hart, L. J., Spruill, III, J. (2006). Effects of grammatical categories on children's visual language processing: Evidence from event-related brain potentials. *Brain and Language, 98*, 26–39.

Weber-Fox, C., Leonard, L. B., Hampton Wray, A., & Tomblin, J. B. (2010). Electrophysiological correlates of rapid auditory and linguistic processing in adolescents with specific language impairment. *Brain and Language, 115*, 162–181.

Wible, B., Nicol, T., & Kraus, N. (2004). Atypical brainstem representation of onset and formant structure of speech sounds in children with language-based learning problems. *Biological Psychology, 67*, 299–317.

Windsor, J., & Hwang, M. (1999). Testing the generalized slowing hypothesis in specific language impairment. *Journal of Speech, Language, and Hearing Research, 42*, 1205–1218.

Windsor, J., Milbrath, R. L., Carney, E. J., & Rakowski, S. E. (2001). General slowing in language impairment: Methodological considerations in testing the hypothesis. *Journal of Speech, Language, and Hearing Research, 44*, 446–461.

Wulfeck, B., & Bates, E. (1995). *Grammatical sensitivity in children with language impairment* (Technical Report CND-9512). San Diego: Center for Research in Language, University of California.

Yokoyama, S., Miyamoto, T., Riera, J., Kim, J., Akitsuki, Y., Iwata, K., et al. (2006). Cortical mechanisms involved in the processing of verbs: An fMRI study. *Journal of Cognitive Neuroscience, 18*, 1304–1313.

6

THE RELATIONSHIP BETWEEN
LANGUAGE AND READING ABILITIES

Hugh W. Catts, Marc E. Fey, Susan Ellis Weismer, and Mindy Sittner Bridges

Research over the last 30 years has documented a strong relationship between oral and written language abilities/disabilities (Brady & Shankweiler, 1991; NICHD Early Child Care Research Network, 2005; Vellutino, Scanlon, Small, & Tanzman, 1991). This relationship, however, is complex and still not fully understood. The Iowa Project provided us with a unique opportunity to examine this relationship across a wide age range and a variety of language and reading measures. In this chapter, we review the results of our work and what these findings tell us about the relationship between oral and written language abilities/disabilities. In addressing our results, we divide our discussion into work that has investigated (a) the relationship between emerging language abilities and subsequent reading achievement, (b) the language abilities of poor readers, and (c) the reading outcomes of children with language impairments.

THE ASSESSMENT OF WRITTEN LANGUAGE

Before discussing the results of our research, it is important to place these results in the context of the measures that we used. In Chapter 2, our battery of written language measures was summarized. As shown in Table 2.7, measures of written language were administered to children in second, fourth, eighth, and tenth grades. These measures assessed word recognition and reading comprehension.

Word Recognition. Two subtests from the Woodcock Reading Mastery Tests – Revised (WRMT-R; Woodcock, 1987) and a subtest from the Gray Oral Reading Test–3 (GORT-3; Wiederholt, & Bryant, 1992) were used to assess word recognition. The Word Identification subtest from the WRMT-R measured participants' ability to accurately pronounce printed English words ranging from high to low frequency of occurrence. The Word Attack subtest assessed participants' ability to read pronounceable nonwords varying in complexity. In the GORT-3, participants read aloud short passages, and word reading accuracy was assessed.

Reading Comprehension. The Passage Comprehension subtest of the WRMT-R and the comprehension standard score from the GORT-3 were used to assess reading comprehension across grades. The Passage Comprehension subtest uses a cloze procedure in which participants read short passages aloud and provided a missing word. For the GORT-3, participants read aloud a short passage and answered multiple-choice questions concerning the passage. In second and fourth grades, participants were also administered the Reading Comprehension subtest of the Diagnostic Achievement Battery–2 (DAB-2; Newcomer, 1990). This subtest was not appropriate for eighth and tenth grades and was replaced by the reading comprehension component of the Qualitative Reading Inventory – Second Edition (QRI-2; Leslie & Caldwell, 1995). For both of the latter measures, participants read short passages and answered open-ended questions.

Our battery of tests also included several additional measures that have specific relevance to the study of written language. These included measures of letter identification, phonological awareness, and rapid naming, each of which was administered to children in kindergarten.

Letter Identification. The Letter Identification subtest of the WRMT-R was administered to assess children's ability to name letters of the alphabet that are presented in various fonts.

Phonological Awareness. Phonological awareness was assessed by a syllable/phoneme deletion task (Catts, 1993), which was an adaptation of Rosner's Auditory Analysis Test (Rosner & Simon, 1971). In this task, participants were required to delete a syllable or, in some cases, a phoneme of a word and say the remaining sound sequence.

Rapid Naming. The Rapid Automatized Naming of Animals (RAN:A, Catts, 1993) task was also administered. In this task, participants rapidly named a series of colored animals presented on an 8.5" × 11" chart. The 24 stimulus items used in the naming task consisted of three animals (cow, pig, horse) randomly displayed in one of three color-filled drawings (black, blue, red). The total duration to name all stimulus items (e.g., "red pig," "blue cow," "black horse") was measured with a stopwatch and recorded.

RELATIONSHIP BETWEEN EMERGING LANGUAGE ABILITIES AND SUBSEQUENT READING ACHIEVEMENT

At the time we began the Iowa longitudinal study, most of the attention on the language basis of reading was focused on phonological processing (Brady & Shankweiler, 1991; Catts, 1989; Wagner & Torgesen, 1987). Phonological processing refers to the perception, storage, retrieval, and awareness of speech sounds. Numerous studies had shown a strong link between phonological processing and reading achievement, especially word reading abilities (Bradley & Bryant, 1985; Torgesen, Wagner, & Rashotte, 1997a, 1997b). Despite the growing evidence of the relationship between phonological processing and reading achievement, few studies had considered this relationship in the context of other language abilities.

In one of our initial studies (Catts, Fey, Tomblin, & Zhang, 1999), we examined the relationship between phonological processing and oral language abilities in kindergarten and reading achievement in second grade. Hierarchical multiple regression analyses were carried out with 604 participants from the Iowa study. In these analyses, measures of phonological awareness and rapid naming were used to assess phonological processing, and measures of vocabulary, grammar, and narration were combined to form an index of oral language abilities.[1] Consistent with previous research, our results showed that phonological processing was a robust predictor of reading achievement. Our kindergarten measures of phonological awareness and rapid naming accounted for 41% of the variance in second grade reading comprehension and 38% of variance in second grade word recognition. However, we also found that the contributions of kindergarten oral language abilities to second grade reading achievement were as great or greater than that observed for phonological processing. Our overall regression model accounted for 54.5% of the variance in reading comprehension. When we decomposed the total explained variance, the largest portion (35%) was shared by phonological processing and oral language skills, demonstrating a shared relation between these skills and reading comprehension. Of the remaining 19.2% of the variance accounted for by our model, oral language abilities contributed 13.8% unique variance, leaving 5.4% for phonological processing. Oral language abilities also proved to be a good predictor of word recognition. Our overall model accounted for 42.9% of the variance in word recognition. When our composite measure of oral language was entered first in the regression analysis, it accounted for 33.2% of the variance in word recognition. Much of this variance was shared with phonological processing (27.9%), but oral language did explain 5.1% of the variance in word recognition over and above phonological processing. Although this was less than what was found for reading comprehension, it suggests that language factors other than phonological processing play a role in word recognition. This finding should not be surprising. Children with larger vocabularies or more advanced syntax or morphology should learn to recognize words more quickly than children with smaller vocabularies or less advanced grammars. For example, one of the processes by which this could occur is contextual facilitation. Children with good language skills have been shown to be better than those with poor language skills in recognizing words in context (Nation & Snowling, 1998). The ability to recognize unfamiliar or partially decoded words in context could, in turn, lead to more fully developed representations of printed words.

The Iowa Project also afforded us the opportunity to examine the long-term relationship between kindergarten language abilities and reading achievement. We expected that this relationship might change across grades. First, we predicted that the amount of variance accounted for by kindergarten predictors might decrease somewhat in later grades due to the longer interval between prediction and outcome. However, we expected that we would continue to find that oral language abilities made a unique contribution to reading achievement. Furthermore, there was reason to believe that the unique contribution of oral language might increase in later grades. As children progress through school, the texts they encounter become linguistically more complex. That is, texts progressively include more low frequency and multi-morphemic words as well as more grammatically complex sentences. As such, we expected that individual differences in oral language abilities in kindergarten might explain *relatively* more variance in reading achievement in later grades than would measures of phonological processing. To examine this issue, we investigated the overall and relative contributions of oral language and phonological processing in kindergarten to reading achievement in eighth grade and compared these results to the results above for second grade. We again used hierarchical multiple regression analyses.

Our results showed that kindergarten measures of oral language and phonological awareness did account for less overall variance in eighth grade than second grade reading achievement. However, this difference was surprisingly small for reading comprehension. Overall, the kindergarten predictors explained 49.2% of the variance in eighth grade reading comprehension compared to 54.5% in second grade.

When we decomposed this total explained variance in eighth grade, the largest portion (30.3%) was shared by phonological processing and oral language. Of the remaining 18.8% of the variance accounted for by our model, oral language abilities contributed 15.8% unique variance, leaving 3.1% for phonological processing. Thus, oral language abilities accounted for slightly more unique variance in reading comprehension at eighth grade than second grade.

Further analyses showed that our kindergarten model accounted for much less variance in word recognition in eighth grade than in second grade. In fact, this model explained only about 25% of the variance in word recognition as compared to about 43% explained by the second grade model. Thus, it appears that variables other than those we measured in kindergarten account for much of the variance in word reading abilities in eighth grade. As for our other prediction, we failed to find that oral language accounted for any more unique variance in eighth grade than second. Most of the unique variance (12.4%) was explained by phonological processing (9.6%) with oral language explaining only a small percentage of the unique variance (2.8%).

KINDERGARTEN PREDICTION OF READING DISABILITIES

Our work on the relationship between oral language and reading achievement not only has theoretical implications, but also has implications for educational practice. Specifically, the above findings suggested that the language abilities of kindergarten children might be used in combination with other variables in the identification of children at risk for reading disabilities. Emerging research indicated that if children at risk for reading difficulties could be identified early, their reading outcomes could be significantly improved with appropriate intervention (Snow, Burns, & Griffin, 1998). Therefore, in a further study (Catts, Fey, Zhang, & Tomblin, 2001), we specifically addressed the early identification of reading disabilities. In our study, we used logistic regression analyses to determine what combination of language and other variables in kindergarten children provided the best prediction of reading outcomes in second grade. Rather than use composite scores for oral language and phonological processing, we considered each of the measures individually that made up our composite scores. We also included mother's education and a measure of children's early literacy knowledge (letter identification). For reading outcome, we divided our participants into those with good or poor reading comprehension in second grade. We used the 16th percentile as a cut-score to classify children as good and poor readers.

Our results showed that a combination of five variables could predict reading outcome in second grade with a high degree of accuracy. We found that letter identification was the best kindergarten predictor, followed closely by sentence imitation. Mother's education, phonological awareness, and rapid naming also were included in our prediction model. Note that the only predictor variable that was included in our earlier composite measure of oral language was sentence imitation. It is likely, however, that this variable and others in the model had considerable overlap with other measures in the oral language composite in predicting outcomes in second grade reading comprehension. In fact, we know from the analyses in Chapter 3 that all the measures of language in kindergarten were reflecting a single dimension and sentence imitation was a good single measure of this dimension.

More recently, we considered how our prediction model might change when examining reading outcomes at a later grade. Specifically, Adlof, Catts, and Lee (2010) used a modified best-subsets variable-selection technique to examine kindergarten predictors of second versus eighth grade reading achievement. Results for the prediction of second grade reading outcome in this study were similar to those found in our earlier study. Specifically, we found that letter identification and sentence imitation were the best predictors of second grade reading outcome. Measures of mother's education, phonological awareness, and rapid naming also proved to be good secondary predictors. However, a different set of variables were found to be the best predictors of eighth grade reading outcome. This set included phonological awareness, grammatical completion, and nonverbal IQ. The latter two variables failed to make our earlier model. We believe that this finding is due to the existence of quantitatively different poor readers in second versus eighth grades. Evidence from our other work (reviewed below) suggests that in second grade most poor readers have problems in word reading, whereas most poor readers in eighth grade have problems in language and higher-level thinking. Others have also found that earlier measures of grammatical skills provide a unique prediction of reading outcome in later grades (Botting, Simkin, & Conti-Ramsden, 2006). Finally, the finding that our kindergarten measure of phonological awareness was among the best predictors of eighth grade reading outcome was surprising. Phonological awareness is generally thought to be most closely related to word reading ability, which has been shown to play less of a role in later reading comprehension. One possible explanation is that the meta-linguistic nature of the phono-logical awareness measure in kindergarten overlapped with other higher-level cognitive processes which were related to reading com-prehension in later grades.

LANGUAGE ABILITIES OF POOR READERS

The Iowa Project longitudinal data set also provided us with an excel-lent opportunity to examine the early language abilities of poor readers. In our initial study (Catts et al., 1999), we documented the nature of these abilities in second grade poor readers. In this study, we identified 183 children from our sample who performed at least 1 standard deviation below the weighted mean on our composite measure of reading comprehension in second grade. We then investi-gated the kindergarten language abilities of these poor readers. Specifi-cally, we examined what proportion of poor readers had deficits in phonological processing and/or oral language in kindergarten. A deficit in a given area was defined as performance of at least 1 standard deviation below the weighted mean of our sample. Our results showed that many of our poor readers had deficits in both phonological processing and oral language abilities (37.2%). Only a small percentage (14.3%) had deficits in phonological processing alone. Furthermore, this percentage was below the percentage of poor readers who had def-icits in oral language alone (21.9%). Finally, we considered what per-centage of poor readers had deficits in various components of oral language in kindergarten. Our results showed that 56% of poor readers had a deficit in grammar, 39.3% had a deficit in vocabulary, and 44.4% had a deficit in narration. Taken together, the results of this study clearly demonstrated that poor readers in second grade had a history of a wide range of language deficits in kindergarten.

CLASSIFYING POOR READERS BASED ON THE SIMPLE VIEW OF READING

In another line of research, we used the Simple View of Reading (Gough & Tunmer, 1986) to identify subgroups of poor readers across school grades. The Simple View of Reading proposes that reading comprehension comprises two primary components: word recognition and linguistic comprehension. Simply stated, the word recognition component translates print into linguistic information, and the com-prehension component makes sense of this linguistic information. Because the linguistic component plays a major role in oral language comprehension, a measure of listening comprehension is most often used to assess this component.

Numerous studies have shown that word recognition and listening comprehension are relatively independent of each other (particularly at the lower end of performance), but highly correlated with reading comprehension (Hoover & Gough, 1990; Stanovich, Cunningham, & Freeman, 1984). Furthermore, studies employing multiple regression analyses have shown that when these components are combined, they account for a large proportion of the variance in reading comprehension (Aaron, Joshi, & Williams, 1999; de Jong & van der Leij, 2002).

The Simple View also predicts the occurrence of subgroups of poor readers who differ in their relative strengths and/or weaknesses in word recognition and listening comprehension. Some poor readers have deficits in word recognition, but relatively good listening comprehension. These poor readers are commonly referred to as having dyslexia (Lyon, Shaywitz, & Shaywitz, 2003). A second subgroup is predicted to have poor listening comprehension and relatively good word recognition. Children in this subgroup may be said to have a specific comprehension deficit. A third subgroup is predicted to have problems in both word recognition and listening comprehension. We have used the term mixed reading disability to indicate that this subgroup has a combination of deficits (Catts & Kamhi, 2005).

Catts, Hogan, and Adlof (2005) used the Simple View of Reading to subgroup poor readers from the Iowa Longitudinal study. In this investigation, we identified poor readers from our sample of 527 children who had a complete data set through eighth grade. Again, a child was identified as a poor reader at a given grade if he/she performed at least 1 standard deviation below the weighted mean on the composite measure of reading comprehension at that grade. Based on this criterion, 150, 140, and 154 students were identified as poor readers in second, fourth, and eighth grades, respectively. We then used students' performance in word recognition (word reading composite score) and listening comprehension (receptive language composite score) at a given grade to subgroup poor readers at that grade. Our findings showed that in second grade, 32.3% of poor readers could be classified as having dyslexia, 36.3% as having a mixed reading disability, and 16.3% as having a specific comprehension deficit.[2] The pattern of performance changed in fourth and eighth grades. The prevalence of poor readers classified as having dyslexia decreased to 22.3% in fourth grade and to 13.3% at eighth grade. Even more noteworthy, the percentage of poor readers with a specific comprehension deficit nearly doubled in fourth (31.0%) and eighth grades (30.1%). The mixed subgroup remained essentially the same across fourth (32.9%) and eighth grades (33.0%).

For the most part, the change in the prevalence of the dyslexic and specific comprehension deficit subgroups from one grade to the next was not the result of poor readers shifting in subgroup placement. In fact, children in these subgroups were quite stable in their word recognition/listening comprehension profiles. For example, 83% of the children in the dyslexic subgroup in second grade showed a dyslexic or dyslexic-like (i.e., borderline cases that were within 0.25 SD of the cutoff) profile in fourth grade and 67% showed this pattern in eighth grade. The reduction in the percentage of poor readers who were dyslexic across grades was more a reflection of the fact that children who showed this profile were less likely to qualify as a poor reader (i.e., have poor reading comprehension) in the later grades. For example, whereas the majority of second grade poor readers with dyslexia continued to show a similar profile in eighth grade, less than a third of these children were classified as poor readers at that time. A similar explanation can account, in part, for the large increase in children with a specific comprehension deficit from second to fourth/eighth grades. Our results showed that approximately 77% of poor readers who were in the specific comprehension deficit subgroup in fourth/eighth grades showed the same or similar profile of word recognition/listening comprehension abilities in second grade. However, less than half of these children met the criterion for a poor reader at that time. The fact that these children were not identified as poor readers until fourth/eighth grades suggests that they might fit the category of late-emerging poor readers discussed by Leach, Scarborough, and Rescorla (1996) as well as others (Badian, 1999; Lipka, Lesaux, & Siegel, 2006). The latter children often get off to a good start in the early school grades, only to fall behind in later grades.

LATE-EMERGING POOR READERS

In a recent study (Catts, Compton, Tomblin, & Bridges, 2012), we used the Iowa data set to more directly investigate the prevalence and nature of late-emerging poor readers. In this study, we employed latent transition analyses to explore intra-individual change across grades in latent variables representing word reading and reading comprehension (e.g., Bollen & Curran, 2006; Duncan, Duncan, & Strycker, 2006). We first classified children as good or poor readers on the basis of word reading or reading comprehension scores at second, fourth, eighth, or tenth grades. Four reading classes were possible at each grade. These were good readers, poor readers with deficits in word reading, poor readers with deficits in comprehension, or poor readers with deficits in both areas. Latent transition analysis was then used to identify children who changed class from one grade to another.

With the latent transition model we used, a total of 512 different latent change classes were possible (two classes representing children who moved or stayed in a class from one grade to the next $\times 4^4$ [four possible reading classes at each of four grades]). Only 26 of the 512 possible classes (5%) were represented in the data, and these classes could further be reduced to five general classes. Using weighted analyses, we estimated that the largest percentage of children (67.9%) were in a class representing good readers across grades. Another 16.8% of children showed deficits in either word reading or comprehension in second grade, and for the most part, had problems that were persistent across grades. The remaining 15.3% of the children fell into one of three late-emerging poor reader classes (late-emerging poor readers – comprehension [7.0%], late-emerging poor readers – word reading [4.8%], or late-emerging poor readers – comprehension and word reading [1.6%]). Our results further showed that the vast majority of transitions took place between second and fourth grades, with far fewer occurring between fourth and eighth grades, and a negligible number occurring between eighth and tenth grades. In addition, children changing classes from one grade to the next were not simply those moving from one side of a cut-score to the other, but rather ones making a sizeable change in reading scores (> 0.3 SD on average). Further results indicated that late-emerging poor readers often had a history of language and/or nonverbal cognitive impairments in kindergarten. Subtypes of poor readers also differed in their profiles of language, early literacy, and nonverbal cognitive abilities in kindergarten.

These results thus suggest that a large proportion of poor readers may have late-emerging reading disabilities. Such problems have received little attention in terms of identification and remediation and warrant further investigation to improve reading outcomes for all children.

READING OUTCOMES OF CHILDREN WITH SPECIFIC LANGUAGE IMPAIRMENTS

One of our primary aims in the Iowa Longitudinal study was the investigation of the reading and writing outcomes of children with specific language impairment (SLI). Previous research had shown that these children were at an increased risk for reading and writing difficulties across the school grades (Bishop & Adams, 1990; Catts, 1993; Menyuk et al., 1991). In our first study (Catts, Fey, Tomblin & Zhang, 2002), we compared the reading outcomes in second and fourth grades of children with language impairments to those with typical language development. Children with language impairments in our sample were subgrouped into those with specific (SLI) and nonspecific language impairment (NLI) based on their performance on tests of nonverbal cognitive abilities (see Chapter 2). In one set of analyses, the reading outcomes of these subgroups were examined in terms of the percentage who showed a reading disability at each grade. As was the case in our other studies, a reading disability was defined as performance at least 1 standard deviation below the weighted mean on our composite measure of reading comprehension. Figure 6.1 shows that 67.0% of children with NLI met the criterion for a reading disability in second grade and 63.7% of these children met the criterion in fourth grade. Children with SLI demonstrated corresponding rates of 41.8% and 35.9%. Thus, compared to typical children (also shown in Figure 6.1), children with NLI were about 7–8 times more likely to have a reading disability and those with SLI were about 4–5 times more likely. Again, though some children with LI (especially those with SLI) did not meet our definition for reading disability in second or fourth grades, most had below-average reading achievement scores. This pattern of performance is illustrated by the reading achievement distributional data displayed in Figure 6.2. These data show that only 13 children with SLI and 3 children with NLI scored above the mean (i.e., z-score > 0) in

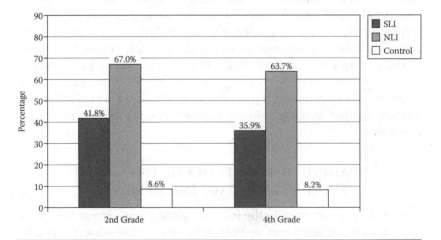

Figure 6.1 Percentage of children in each group meeting the criterion for reading disability in second and fourth grades.

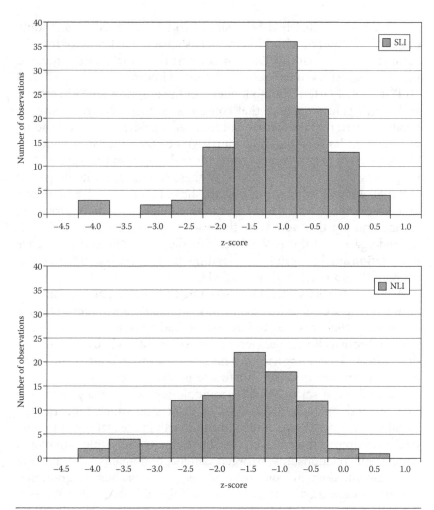

Figure 6.2 Reading achievement distribution for second grade reading comprehension in children with SLI and NLI.

second grade reading achievement. (Although they are not displayed here, similar distributions characterized reading comprehension in fourth grade.)

We also investigated the variables related to reading outcomes in children with language impairments. The above differences between the outcomes of SLI and NLI subgroups suggested that kindergarten nonverbal cognitive abilities were related to subsequent reading achievement. This relationship also held when the severity of the language impairment (also related to reading outcome) was controlled.

Another variable that had been shown to be correlated with reading outcome in children with LI is the persistence of the language impairment (Bishop & Adams, 1990). To examine this variable, we compared the reading achievement scores of those children with LI (SLI and NLI) in kindergarten who no longer met the criterion for LI in second and fourth grades to those that continued to meet the criterion. Our results showed that the former children had significantly better reading outcomes in both second and fourth grades than the latter children. This pattern of results was the same for children from the SLI and NLI subgroups. Another interpretation of these results is that kindergarten children with LI who continued to show LI in second and fourth grades were those with true LI and those LI children who improved in second and fourth grades were those who were falsely identified as LI in kindergarten. If this is the case, it further strengthens the evidence of a relationship between LI and reading disorder (RD) and the significance of LI as an early indicator of RD.

Although the above results concerning the concurrent relationships between language abilities and reading outcomes are important, they are limited when it comes to forecasting reading outcomes in children with LI. From a clinical perspective, we would like to know which children with LI in kindergarten are most likely to have poor versus good reading outcomes in second or fourth grades. To examine this issue, we carried out a set of stepwise multiple regression analyses. In the first of these analyses, we sought to determine which kindergarten variables were predictive of second and fourth grade reading outcomes in the children with LI. Given the above results indicating differential concurrent relationships between language domains and reading achievement, domain composite scores (i.e., vocabulary, grammar, narrative) were used in these analyses. Table 6.1 shows that the best kindergarten predictor of reading outcomes was letter identification. This variable explained 24.7% and 13.4% of the variance in second and fourth grade reading comprehension scores, respectively. Letter identification also accounted for 27.3% and 19.5% of the variability in second and fourth grade word recognition scores respectively. Among the remaining variables, grammar composite, nonverbal IQ, rapid naming, and phonological awareness accounted for unique variance in the various measures of reading achievement.

Because our longitudinal study followed children through the tenth grade, we were also able to compare the long-term reading achievement growth trajectories of children with LI to those of children with typical language abilities. In this study (Catts, Bridges, Little, & Tomblin, 2008), children with SLI and NLI were combined into one

Table 6.1 Multiple regression of kindergarten predictors on to subsequent word recognition and reading comprehension in second and fourth grade

Order of Kindergarten Predictors	R2	R2 change	Partial Correlations
Second Grade Reading Comprehension			
1 Letter Identification	0.247		0.376
2 Grammar Composite	0.312	0.065**	0.195
3 Nonverbal IQ	0.347	0.036**	0.201
4 Rapid Naming	0.367	0.020**	-0.179
Second Grade Word Recognition			
1 Letter Identification	0.273		0.395
2 Phonological awareness	0.315	0.042**	0.185
3 Rapid Naming	0.343	0.027**	0.190
4 Nonverbal IQ	0.361	0.019*	0.160
Fourth Grade Reading Comprehension			
1 Letter Identification	0.134		0.225
2 Nonverbal IQ	0.196	0.062**	0.173
3 Rapid Naming	0.218	0.022*	-0.131
4 Phonological awareness	0.238	0.020*	0.134
Fourth Grade Word Recognition			
1 Letter Identification	0.195		0.305
2 Nonverbal IQ	0.244	0.049**	0.155
3 Rapid Naming	0.270	0.027**	-0.156
4 Grammar Composite	0.287	0.016*	0.119

Notes:

$*p < 0.05$, $**p < 0.01$.

Long-term reading outcomes of children with LI.

group with LI. We also combined children with normal language and good and poor nonverbal abilities into the typical language group (TL).

The reading achievement growth trajectories of children with LI could take several forms when compared to those of children with TL. Children with LI could show lower initial reading achievement but parallel growth over the school years. This has been referred to as a deficit model of reading growth (Francis, Shaywitz, Stuebing, Shaywitz, & Fletcher, 1996). Alternatively, children with LI could demonstrate lower initial reading achievement but accelerated growth, which would allow them to catch up to their typical language peers during the later school years. This pattern is known as a developmental lag or delayed pattern of reading growth (Francis et al., 1996). Finally, children with LI could get off to a slow start in reading achievement, as well as demonstrate slower growth. This would lead to a widening of the gap in reading achievement between them and their TL peers. The latter pattern is characteristic of what some have called the "Matthew effect" (Stanovich, 1986) and others have referred to as a cumulative trajectory model of achievement (Leppänen, Niemi, Aunola, & Nurmi, 2004).

We used latent growth curve analysis to compare the pattern of reading growth in reading comprehension and word recognition from second to tenth grades of children with LI and TL. Growth models for both aspects of reading achievement showed that children with LI had a significantly lower intercept in second grade than children with TL. Such a finding is evidence of early reading problems in children with LI and is consistent with the results reported by Catts et al. (2002) above. Whereas groups differed significantly in reading achievement intercepts, there were no significant differences in the shape of their growth trajectories. For word recognition and reading comprehension, both groups showed initial high acceleration followed by slower growth between fourth and eighth/tenth grades (see Figures 6.3 and 6.4).[3]

Our results concerning group differences in intercept but similarities in slope of reading achievement growth trajectories support a deficit model of reading achievement in children with LI. These children showed lower initial reading abilities and failed to catch up with their typical language peers over the span of this investigation. In addition, group differences did not increase across grades, and thus there was no evidence of a Matthew effect in reading achievement. Again, our findings are compatible with Francis et al. (1996) who reported a deficit model for poor readers. Whereas poor readers in their study were not identified on the basis of problems in language

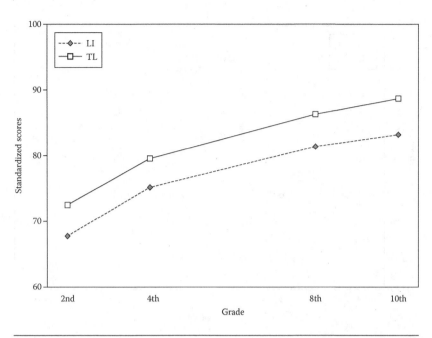

Figure 6.3 Growth in word recognition in children with language impairments (LI) and typical language (TL).

development, these children showed lower initial reading scores, but growth trajectories similar to those of good readers. This pattern of significant intercept but no slope differences is the same as the growth curve analysis for oral language.

Finally, when the composite measure of nonverbal cognitive abilities was added as a covariate into the model, it was found to be related to intercept but not shape of the reading achievement trajectories. These results indicated that children with low nonverbal cognitive abilities (in both groups) generally had lower initial reading achievement than those with normal nonverbal cognitive abilities but showed no differences in the growth of reading achievement over the school grades. These findings are in line with the results of other studies that have found that children with LI and low nonverbal IQ have poorer reading outcomes than those with normal nonverbal IQ (Aram, Ekelman, & Nation, 1984; Bishop & Adams, 1990; Snowling, Bishop, & Stothard, 2000). However, our results are contrary to those of Snowling and colleagues who found a tendency for children with lower nonverbal cognitive abilities to show slower growth in word reading than those with normal abilities.

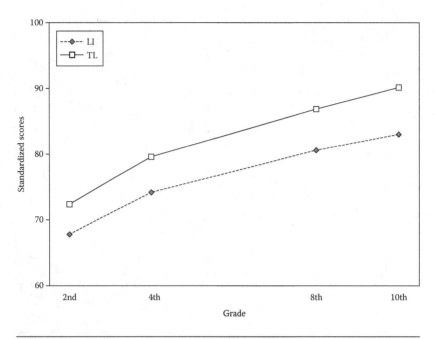

Figure 6.4 Growth in reading comprehension in children with language impairments (LI) and typical language (TL).

SUMMARY

The results of our work add to a growing body of research concerning the relationship between oral and written language abilities/disabilities. As part of the Iowa Project, we showed that oral language abilities, as measured by tests of vocabulary, grammar, and narration, explained considerable variance in both word recognition and reading comprehension across the school years. In all cases examined, oral language accounted for significant variance over and above phonological processing, the language construct that had been most closely linked to reading achievement. We were also able to use kindergarten measures of oral language, phonological processing, and other factors to predict reading outcomes in the short (second grade) and long (eighth grade) term.

Our work further demonstrated that poor readers displayed a wide range of language deficits, including problems in phonological processing, vocabulary, grammar, and narration. We also showed that poor readers could be subgrouped according to the Simple View of Reading and that the relative prevalence of these subgroups changed across grades. Our data also provided evidence of the nature and prevalence of late-emerging poor readers. Finally, other results documented that children with LI were at a high risk for subsequent reading disabilities. Our findings showed that for most of these children, reading problems were apparent in the early school grades and continued to be present at the same relative degree throughout the school years. It was not the case that these children eventually caught up or got significantly worse (e.g., the Matthew effect). This was the same result that we found for oral language differences between the groups with impaired and typical language development (see Chapter 4).

Our results have implications for the identification and remediation of reading disabilities. Our findings provide direct evidence of the need to include language measures in screening for reading disabilities. Such measures may be important for identifying early- as well as late-emerging poor readers. In addition, the presence of a developmental language impairment should be considered a possible early indicator of a reading disability. Children with such an impairment should be provided with early intervention that includes literacy goals and assessment of progress in literacy. Our results also indirectly suggest that remediation efforts will need to include work on both phonological awareness and oral language. Currently, there is considerable research on how to improve children's phonological awareness and subsequent word reading skills. More work is necessary to gain similar knowledge concerning oral language intervention and its impact on reading achievement. Finally, given the language basis of many reading disabilities, it is critical that those with expertise in language play a role in identification and remediation.

NOTES

1. It is acknowledged that some aspects of phonological processing (e.g., rapid naming) are "oral." Similarly, the oral language abilities we tested in this study have phonological components. However, these two aspects of language are theoretically distinct and have been shown to represent different abilities in factor analyses (Tomblin, Zhang, Weiss, Catts, & Ellis Weismer, 2004).

2. Because the Iowa Longitudinal data set included a greater number of children with language and/or cognitive deficits, we used weighted analyses to calculate the percentage of poor readers in each of the Simple View subgroups. These weighted percentages are our best estimates of the prevalence of each of the subgroups in a more representative sample.

3. In Figures 6.3 and 6.4, the constructs of word recognition and reading comprehension were standardized to have to a common metric (M = 80, SD = 10) across the span of second to tenth grades. This transformation allowed us to keep the integrity of any between-group or across-grade differences but place the variables on a common, and therefore comparable, metric. Because monotonic transformations such as this do not change the relative individual differences standings of the children either within time or across time, the developmental change patterns and associations are not artifactually altered. Our choice of 80 as the centering mean level and 10 as the standard deviation metric is arbitrary because there is no "standard" metric for all variables in the analyses.

REFERENCES

Aaron, P. G., Joshi, M., & Williams, A. K. (1999). Not all reading disabilities are alike. *Journal of Learning Disabilities, 32,* 120–138.

Adlof, S., Catts, H., & Lee, J. (2010). Kindergarten prediction of second vs. eighth grade reading comprehension impairments. *Journal of Learning Disabilities, 43,* 332–345.

Aram, D. M., Ekelman, B. L., & Nation, J. E. (1984). Preschoolers with language disorders: 10 years later. *Journal of Speech and Hearing Research, 27,* 232–244.

Badian, N. A. (1999). Reading disability defined as a discrepancy between listening and reading comprehension: A longitudinal study of stability, gender differences, and prevalence. *Journal of Learning Disabilities, 32,* 138–148.

Bishop, D. V., & Adams, C. (1990). A prospective study of the relationship between specific language impairment, phonological disorders and reading retardation. *Journal of Child Psychology and Psychiatry, 31,* 1027–1050.

Bollen, K. A., & Curran, P. J. (2006). *Latent curve models: A structural equation perspective.* Hoboken, NJ: John Wiley & Sons.

Botting, N., Simkin, Z., & Conti-Ramsden, G. (2006). Associated reading skills in children with a history of Specific Language Impairment (SLI). *Reading and Writing, 19,* 77–98.

Bradley, L., & Bryant, P. E. (1985). *Rhyme and reason in reading and spelling.* Ann Arbor, MI: University of Michigan Press.

Brady, S., & Shankweiler, D. (Eds.). (1991). *Phonological processes in literacy: A tribute to Isabelle Liberman.* Hillsdale, NJ: LEA Publishers.

Catts, H. W. (1989). Defining dyslexia as a developmental language disorder. *Annals of Dyslexia, 39,* 50–64.

Catts, H. W. (1993). The relationship between speech-language impairments and reading disabilities. *Journal of Speech and Hearing Research, 36,* 948–958.

Catts, H. W., Bridges, M. S., Little, T., & Tomblin, J. B. (2008). Reading achievement growth in children with language impairments. *Journal of Speech Language, and Hearing Research, 51*, 1569–1579.

Catts, H. W., Compton, D., Tomblin, J. B., & Bridges, M. S. (2012). Prevalence and nature of late-emerging poor readers. *Journal of Educational Psychology, 104*, 166–181.

Catts, H. W., Fey, M. E., Tomblin, J. B., & Zhang, X. (2002). A longitudinal investigation of reading outcomes in children with language impairments. *Journal of Speech, Language, and Hearing Research, 45*, 1142–1157.

Catts, H. W., Fey, M., Zhang, X., & Tomblin, J. B. (1999). Language basis of reading and reading disabilities: Evidence from a longitudinal study. *Scientific Studies of Reading, 3*, 331–361.

Catts, H. W., Fey, M. E., Zhang, X., & Tomblin, J. B. (2001). Estimating the risk of future reading difficulties in kindergarten children: A research-based model and its clinical implementation. *Language, Speech, and Hearing Services in Schools, 32*, 38–50.

Catts, H. W., Hogan, T., & Adlof, S. (2005). Developmental changes in reading and reading disabilities. In H. Catts & A. Kamhi (Eds.), *Connections between language and reading disabilities*. Mahwah, NJ: Erlbaum.

Catts, H. W., & Kamhi, A. G., (2005). *Language and reading disabilities*. Boston: Allyn & Bacon.

de Jong, P. F., & van der Leij, A. (2002). Effects of phonological abilities and linguistic comprehension on the development of reading. *Scientific Studies of Reading, 6*, 51–77.

Denckla, M. B., & Rudel, R. G. (1976). Rapid automatized naming (RAN): Dyslexia differentiated from other learning disabilities. *Neuropsychologia, 14*, 471–479.

Duncan, T. E., Duncan, S. C., & Strycker, L. A. (2006). *An introduction to latent variable growth curve modeling: Concepts, issues, and application.* Mahwah, NJ: Erlbaum.

Francis, D. J., Shaywitz, S. E., Stuebing, K. K., Shaywitz, B. A., & Fletcher, J. M. (1996). Developmental lag versus deficit models of reading disability: A longitudinal, individual growth curves analysis. *Journal of Educational Psychology, 88*, 3–17.

Gough, P. B., & Tunmer, W. E. (1986). Decoding, reading, and reading disability. *Remedial and Special Education, 7*, 6–10.

Hoover, W. A., & Gough, P. B. (1990). The simple view of reading. *Reading and Writing: An Interdisciplinary Journal, 2*, 127–160.

Leach, J. M., Scarborough, H. S., & Rescorla, L. (2003). Late-emerging reading disabilities. *Journal of Educational Psychology, 95*, 211–224.

Leppänen, U., Niemi, P., Aunola, K., & Nurmi, J. E. (2004). Development of reading skills among preschool and primary school pupils. *Reading Research Quarterly, 39*, 72–93.

Leslie, L., & Caldwell, J. (1995). *Qualitative Reading Inventory* (2nd ed.). New York: HarperCollins.

Lipka, O., Lesaux, N. K., & Siegel, L. S. (2006). Retrospective analyses of the reading development of Grade 4 students with reading disabilities: Risk status and profiles over 5 years. *Journal of Learning Disabilities, 39,* 105–131.

Lyon, G. R., Shaywitz, S. E., & Shaywitz, B. A. (2003). A definition of dyslexia. *Annals of Dyslexia, 53,* 1–14.

Menyuk, P., Chesnick, M., Liebergott, J. W., Korngold, B., D'Agostino, R., & Belanger, A. (1991). Predicting reading problems in at-risk children. *Journal of Speech and Hearing Research, 34,* 893–903.

Nation, K., & Snowling, M. J. (1998). Individual differences in contextual facilitation: Evidence from dyslexia and poor reading comprehension. *Child Development, 69,* 996–1011.

Newcomer, P. (1990). *Diagnostic Achievement Battery* (2nd ed.). Austin, TX: Pro-Ed.

NICHD Early Child Care Research Network. (2005). Pathways to reading: The role of oral language in the transition to reading. *Developmental Psychology, 4,* 428–442.

Rosner, J., & Simon, D. (1971). The Auditory Analysis Test: An initial report. *Journal of Learning Disabilities, 4,* 40–48.

Scarborough, H. S. (1998). Early identification of children at risk for reading disabilities: Phonological awareness and some other promising predictors. In B. K. Shapiro, P. J. Accardo, & A. J. Capute (Eds.), *Specific reading disability: A view of the spectrum* (pp. 75–119). Timonium, MD: York Press.

Snow, C. E., Burns, M. S., & Griffin, P. (Eds.). (1998). *Preventing reading difficulties in young children.* Washington, DC: National Academy Press.

Snowling, M., Bishop, D. V. M., & Stothard, S. E. (2000). Is preschool language impairment a risk factor for dyslexia in adolescence? *Journal of Child Psychology and Psychiatry, 41,* 587–600.

Stanovich, K. E. (1986). Matthew effects in reading: Some consequences of individual differences in the acquisition of literacy. *Reading Research Quarterly, 21,* 360–406.

Stanovich, K. E., Cunningham, A. E., & Freeman, D. J. (1984). Intelligence, cognitive skills and early reading progress. *Reading Research Quarterly, 19,* 278–303.

Tomblin, J. B., Zhang, X., Weiss, A., Catts, H., & Ellis Weismer, S. (2004). Dimensions of individual differences in communication skills among primary grade children. In M. L. Rice & S. F. Warren (Eds.), *Developmental language disorders: From phenotypes to etiologies.* Mahwah, NJ: Lawrence Erlbaum Associates.

Torgesen, J. K., Wagner, R. K., & Rashotte, C. A. (1997a). Approaches to the prevention and remediation of phonologically based reading disabilities.

In B. Blachman (Ed.), *Foundations of reading acquisition and dyslexia: Implications for early intervention* (pp. 287–304). Mahwah, NJ: Lawrence Erlbaum Associates.

Torgesen, J. K., Wagner, R. K., & Rashotte, C. A. (1997b). Prevention and remediation of severe reading disabilities: Keeping the end in mind. *Scientific Studies of Reading, 1,* 217–234.

Vellutino, F. R., Scanlon, D. M., Small, S. G., & Tanzman, M. S. (1991). The linguistic basis of reading ability: Converting written to oral language. *Text, 11,* 99–133.

Wagner, R. K., & Torgesen, J. K. (1987). The nature of phonological processing and its causal role in the acquisition of reading skills. *Psychological Bulletin, 101,* 192–212.

Wiederholt, J., & Bryant, B. (1992). *Gray Oral Reading Test* (3rd ed.). Austin, TX: Pro-Ed.

Wolf, M., & Obregon, M. (1991). Early naming deficits, developmental dyslexia, and specific deficit hypothesis. *Brain and Language, 42,* 219–247.

Woodcock, R. (1987). *Woodcock Reading Mastery Tests, revised.* Circle Pines, MN: American Guidance Service.

7

EDUCATIONAL AND PSYCHOSOCIAL OUTCOMES OF LANGUAGE IMPAIRMENT IN KINDERGARTEN

J. Bruce Tomblin

In Chapter 1, I argued that, in my view, the reason we assign the term "impairment" to a certain domain of individual differences in language development is that we believe that these individual differences will have important consequences in the lives of these children. In this regard, children with these poor language abilities face greater risk for poor outcomes than we believe is tolerable. In the previous chapter, we have already seen that the successful development of reading is clearly threatened by poor listening and speaking skills present at school entry that persist through the school years. Within this chapter, we will examine whether, in addition to reading, other domains of development are also threatened by poor language. Furthermore, we will attempt to develop empirical evidence that can be used to estimate this risk of poor performance across the important domains of childhood outcome.

This approach should be clinically useful in that it places the meaning of language impairment squarely in the domain of health and well-being. In doing so, it also introduces the challenge of establishing which outcomes should be viewed as important to health and well-being. Given that these concepts are based on cultural values, we need some guidance as to what outcomes are important in the current U.S. culture. Fortunately, as described in Chapter 1, researchers studying outcomes in risk populations can provide us with a useful framework concerning valued outcomes where these are viewed as "competence." We noted in Chapter 1 that competence can be viewed as "adaptation success in the developmental tasks expected of individuals of a given age in a particular cultural and historical context" (Masten et al., 1999). This statement emphasizes that competences will vary across development, and this has been incorporated into the notion of salient developmental tasks that represent those skills and behaviors that are socially defined to be the important accomplishments for an individual at his/her developmental level. In the preschool years, language development clearly represents a salient developmental task. Within the elementary school years, several competences have been identified, specifically: successful academic performance, development of appropriate conduct, prosocial behaviors, and the establishment of friendships. The period of adolescence retains the premium on academic performance, along with the establishment of close and stable friendships, continued appropriate behavioral conduct, and the achievement of a sense of psychological well-being (Roisman, Masten, Coatsworth, & Tellegen, 2004). This framework was shown in Figure 1.2 in Chapter 1. Using this framework in this chapter, we seek to determine if and when poor language in early childhood places children at risk for compromised competence during the school years. We will organize these competences into two general domains of academic achievement and psychosocial outcomes. Within each of these domains, we will examine indicators of competences within the elementary grades, focusing on fourth grade, and adolescence, focusing on 10th grade.

ACADEMIC OUTCOMES

There is a well-established literature showing that reading and literacy outcomes in children with poor language are substantially depressed. Because reading and writing are probably the seminal aspects of academic progress, there remains little doubt that spoken language abilities and these concomitant reading difficulties will have a strong bearing on general academic success. The learning environment of the classroom is multifaceted and varied across grades (Nelson, 1984). During the early grades, much of the curriculum is conveyed via spoken language, thus requiring reasonable receptive language skills, and the children's learning is reflected via their use of spoken language. As was noted in Chapter 6, reading and writing at this point place demands on the core skills of word recognition and orthographic production. By the middle grades, however, the student must use both oral and written language to master the curriculum, and reading and writing become more intimately associated with speaking and listening. For the child with poor language abilities, access to the curriculum is constrained across grades, but in fact may become more limited as the curriculum places more demands on language and in particular decontextualized and complex language. From this viewpoint and from our existing knowledge of the greater reading difficulties of our cohort of children with poor language (both SLI and NLI) in this study, we might hypothesize that their academic achievement will suffer because of their reading difficulties, but additionally because of the effect of language on classroom listening.

Prior Studies of Academic Outcomes

Concerns about the academic performance of children with poor language abilities were voiced in the 1960s by pioneers such as Johnson and Myklebust (1967) and McGinnis (1963). By the 1970s, stronger data-based evidence began to appear. For instance, de Ajuriaguerra (1976) described 17 children with dysphasia who had been first described in 1965. Very few of these children were reported to be progressing through regular education and most required special services. Subsequently, Hall and Tomblin (1978) reported poorer academic achievement measured on a classroom administered achievement test (Iowa Tests of Basic Skills) for a group of children with both language and speech sound disorders when compared with a group of children with just speech sound disorders. These academic difficulties extended through the school years, and parental reports indicated differences in fewer post-secondary attendance patterns associated with poor language. These observations of academic difficulty were then further shown in longitudinal studies of children with language impairment (Aram, Ekelman, & Nation, 1984; Bishop & Adams, 1990; Catts, 1993; Silva, Williams, & McGee, 1987; Stark et al., 1984; Stark & Tallal, 1988).

Academic Outcomes of the Iowa Longitudinal Sample

During the longitudinal study, we collected a variety of measures and indicators of academic achievement and academic difficulty. In Chapter 6, we provided extensive documentation of the reading problems associated with the language status of the children in our study. Here, we will report on measures and indicators of academic performance that go beyond reading. A difficulty we face is that the dominant means of measuring academic performance is via tests that involve reading. However, we did obtain indicators of academic performance that were at least somewhat removed from the direct effects of reading.

Specifically these indicators are group administered standardized achievement tests, grade retention prior to eighth grade, and teacher report of classroom performance.

Standardized Achievement Testing. Currently, a common way to measure educational attainment is the use of group administered standardized achievement tests. In the United States, these tests are often used as indicators of the performance of schools themselves. In the state of Iowa, there is a long tradition of standardized achievement tests concerning school performance beginning as early as 1929 (Peterson, 1983) when E. E. Lindquist developed the Iowa Tests of Basic Skills (ITBS) for grades 3 through 8 (Hoover, Dunbar, & Frisbie, 2001) and the Iowa Tests of Educational Development for high school (ITED; Feldt, Forsyth, Ansley, & Alnot, 1994).

These tests were not required by the state at the time of this study, and therefore not all of the students attended schools that administered the tests. However, we were able to obtain test results from many of these children when they were in either third ($N = 264$) or fourth grades ($N = 204$). At these two grade levels, the content of the ITBS is the same and were reported as scores of relative standing for the respective grade. Therefore, these scores were merged such that fourth grade scores were used where available and third grade scores when a fourth grade score was not available.

The ITBS contains several subtests that span the elementary academic curriculum. The subtests selected for this analysis were: Reading Comprehension, Language (Arts), Mathematics, and Social Studies. The content of these tests is summarized in Table 7.1.

The scores on the ITBS are scaled in several different ways; however, because we were combining the scores across two grade levels, we employed the National Curved Equivalent (NCE) scores. These scores are norm referenced to the child's grade with a mean of 50 and a standard deviation of 21. Figure 7.1 displays the average scores and standard deviations for the children who were diagnosed in kindergarten as SLI and NLI along with the typically developing (TLD) controls. We see a very similar profile across the four areas of achievement. A profile analysis using MANOVA confirmed that the profile shapes over the three groups were not different across the four tests ($p > 0.05$).

The MANOVA also showed that there were significant effects of group for the combined set of Reading, Language, Mathematics, and Social Studies, $F(8, 604) = 8.21$, < 0.0001. Follow-up univariate tests showed that the children with SLI and the children with NLI differed from the controls across all four tests, Tukey LSD $p < 0.05$. Furthermore, the SLI and NLI groups only differed from each other on the

Table 7.1 Content of Iowa Tests of Basic Skills (ITBS) subtests.

ITBS subtest	Content Description
Reading Comprehension	Children read passages of varying length and difficulty. At each test level, there is at least one narrative, a poem, and one passage about a science and social studies topic. Comprehension is assessed via questions.
Mathematics	Children are tested on their understanding of fundamental ideas in the areas of number properties and operations, geometry, measurement, algebra, probability and statistics, and estimation involving mental arithmetic, number sense, and various estimation skills such as rounding.
(Written) Language	Students' skills are tested in areas of the conventions of standard written English. The tests constitute a thorough sampling of skills in spelling, capitalization, punctuation, usage, and written expression.
Social Studies	Students are asked to respond to materials such as political cartoons, graphs or charts on social data, timelines, or excerpts from historical texts. The content covers four broad areas: history; geography, economics, government and society.

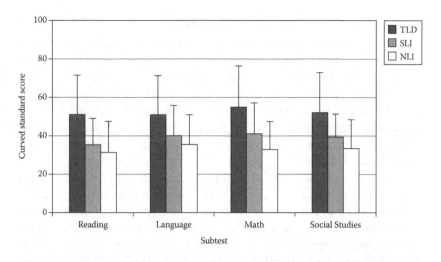

Figure 7.1 Mean and standard deviations (Mean=50) on selected subtests of the Iowa Tests of Basic Skills for children with typical language development (controls), specific language impairment (SLI), and nonspecific language impairment (NLI).

Mathematics subtest, Tukey LSD $p<0.05$. On the Reading, Language, and Social Studies subtests, the SLI and NLI groups were not significantly different ($p<0.05$). Table 7.2 contains the effect sizes of the two subgroups with language impairment contrasted with the control group across these subtests. The magnitude of these values fall within the moderate range of strength using Cohen's nomenclature (Cohen, 1988). Throughout this chapter I will include effect sizes, usually as either eta squared (η^2) or odds ratios, in order that we can consider which areas of development are most at risk due to poor early language. To help make these differences more meaningful, we can also examine the grade equivalent scores these children obtained on the composite score of the ITBS. For those children tested in third grade, the control group had an average grade equivalent score of 3.5 (SD=1.7), whereas the children with SLI had an average score of 2.87 (SD=0.69) and the children with NLI had an average score of 2.50 (SD=0.47). For those children tested in fourth grade, the control children averaged 4.88 (SD=1.41) in contrast with the children with SLI who averaged 3.63 (SD=0.79) and the children with NLI who averaged 3.48 (SD=1.37). Thus, the academic achievement levels for the two groups with poor language averaged around one grade level below the control group and also one year below their grade placement.

Indicators of Academic Status

Parent Report: Grade Retention. The practice of grade retention in response to poor school achievement has been controversial. The debate has been between the merits of retention versus social promotion (Jimerson, 2001). The Center for Mental Health in Schools at UCLA (Center for Mental Health in Schools at UCLA, 2008 Update) estimated that in 2001–2002, 5.5% of children had been retained during the primary grades. The practice of grade retention can vary across school districts and therefore retention rates may not be consistent indicators of school difficulty. In this particular study, we had the advantage that the children with language impairment and the controls were drawn from the same school systems, which should have controlled for variations in this practice among districts. Our data regarding grade retention came from parental report on the *Child Behavior Checklist* (CBCL; Achenbach, 1991a). In this case the parent is asked "Has your child repeated any grades?" This information was gathered at each observation interval. Table 7.3 shows that the rate of retention between kindergarten and eighth grade increased and this pattern of increase seemed more pronounced in the SLI group. In second grade, their level of retention was similar to that of the control group, $X^2(1, N = 501) = 0.03$, $p < 0.86$, and both groups were lower than the NLI group, $X^2(1, N = 600) = 11.70$, $p = 0.0006$. By fourth grade, the SLI group's retention rate was greater than the controls, $X^2(1, N = 472) = 7.62$, $p = 0.006$; and no different than the NLI group $X^2(1, N = 206) = 3.27$, $p = 0.07$. When report of retention at any grade was computed we found significantly elevated rates of retention for the SLI and NLI groups relative to the control groups, $X^2(2, N = 600) = 23.53$, $p < 0.0001$. However, although the rate of retention was greater for the NLI group compared with the SLI group this difference was not statistically significant, $X^2(1, N = 184) = 1.90$, $p = 0.17$.

Table 7.2 Effect sizes ($\eta2$) of the contrast between control group and children with specific language impairment (SLI) or nonspecific language impairment (NLI) in kindergarten on Iowa Tests of Basic Skills scores in third or fourth grade

ITBS Subtests	SLI	NLI
Language Arts	0.07	0.09
Total Reading	0.10	0.11
Total Mathematics	0.08	0.14
Social Studies	0.07	0.10

Table 7.3 Rate of grade retention in the children with specific language impairment (SLI), non-specific language impairment (NLI), and typical language development (TLD) through eighth grade

	2nd Grade	4th Grade	8th Grade	Retained Prior to 8th Grade
TLD	3.70 (378)	3.66 (342)	4.22 (318)	3.71 (328)
SLI	4.07 (123)	10.26 (117)	14.15 (106)	15.09 (106)
NLI	12.12 (99)	19.10 (89)	17.72 (79)	23.08 (78)

These data show that the relative risk for grade retention is 4.06 for children with SLI and 6.22 for the children with NLI. When the continuous measure of composite language obtained in kindergarten was regressed on grade retention at some point prior to eighth grade using logistic regression, we found a significant association, $X^2(1) = 32.35$, $p = 0.0001$. The resulting logistic function is shown in Figure 7.2. This plot shows how as language achievement in kindergarten declines, the probability of being retained at some point during grade school increases. At 2 standard deviations below the mean (z-score = –2), the probability of grade retention is at 0.25 which is over eight times the rate for children with average language ability (4%).

Teacher Rating of Academic Competence. In grades 2 and 4, the teachers were asked to complete the Social Skills Rating System (SSRS; Gresham & Elliott, 1990). This questionnaire asks nine questions regarding the teacher's perception of the child's classroom performance (see Table 7.4).

The content of the questions in the SSRS regarding classroom performance covered indicators of academic performance, motivation, parental support, and general classroom behavior. There was a significant association between language diagnostic status across all the questions; however, the effect sizes were generally quite large for the questions concerning academic performance and more modest for the questions concerning motivation, parental support, and classroom behavior. The SSRS provides a composite norm referenced score for these items. The mean scores for the three groups on this composite are shown in Figure 7.3. We can see that the children with TLD in kindergarten were viewed by their teachers as performing about a third of a standard deviation below the mean for the normative sample both in second and fourth grades. In contrast, the children with SLI and NLI were about 1 standard deviation below the mean. At the second grade, there was a significant difference between the groups, $F(2, 560) = 48.44$, $p < 0.0001$, $\eta^2 = 0.15$. A follow-up Tukey's test showed that the SLI group was perceived significantly better (Mean = 88.03, $p < 0.04$) than the NLI group (Mean = 84.25) although the effect size

Table 7.4 Items concerning classroom performance from the Social Skills Rating System (Gresham & Elliott, 1990) and the effect sizes for diagnostic group effects for each item

	Effect Size ($\eta 2$) for Language Diagnosis	
	2nd Grade	4th Grade
Compared with other children in my classroom, the overall academic performance of this child is	0.12	0.18
In reading, how does this child compare with other students?	0.10	0.18
In mathematics, how does this child compare with other students?	0.13	0.15
In terms of grade-level expectations, this child's skills in reading are:	0.15	0.21
In terms of grade-level expectations, this child's skills in mathematics are:	0.17	0.18
This child's overall motivation to succeed academically is:	0.08	0.10
This child's parental encouragement to succeed academically is:	0.06	0.10
Compared with other children in my classroom this child's intellectual functioning is:	0.13	0.19
Compared with other children in my classroom this child's overall classroom behavior is:	0.03	0.04

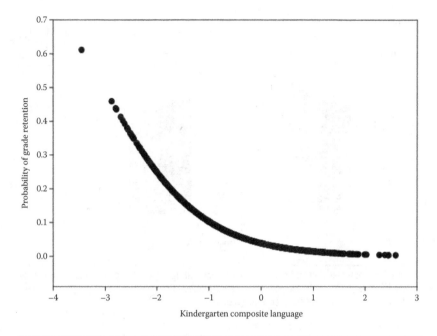

Figure 7.2 The probability of grade retention by eighth grade as a logistic function of kindergarten composite language.

was small ($\eta^2 = 0.04$) and both groups were perceived more poorly than the controls (Mean = 96.6, $p < 0.0001$). In the fourth grade, an overall difference continued, $F(2, 529) = 66.58$, $p < 0.000$, $\eta^2 = 0.20$. Again a Tukey's test showed the controls were perceived significantly better (Mean = 96.6, $p < 0.0001$) than either of the two groups with language impairment; however, now the children with SLI were not significantly (Mean = 86.5, $p < 0.10$) different from the NLI group (Mean = 83.2) with an even smaller effect size ($\eta^2 = 0.02$). These data are consistent with the standardized achievement test results showing a strong relationship between early language status and classroom achievement. The effect sizes, however, are larger for these teacher reports than for the standardized achievement test scores. One possibility is that while the achievement tests reflect a narrower range of skills that are all mediated by an assessment method that depends on reading, the teacher reports reflect a wider perspective of the child's performance. Support for this account was found in a study where we showed that spoken language abilities in kindergarten had a unique effect over and above second grade reading on teacher and parent reports in fourth grade (Tomblin, 2006).

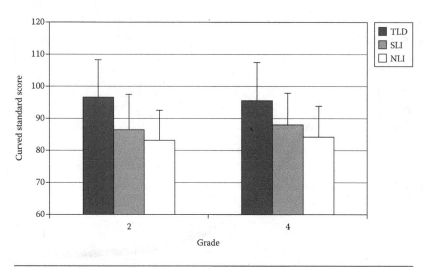

Figure 7.3 Mean and standard deviations for teacher ratings of academic performance in grades 2 and 4 for the children with specific language impairment (SLI), nonspecific language impairment (NLI), and the typically developing controls (TLD).

We can also examine the relationship of language as a continuous trait and these quantitative measures of teachers' perceptions. Table 7.5 provides the correlations between kindergarten composite language and teacher ratings of classroom competence at second and fourth grades, as well as the correlation between teacher rating between second and fourth grade. In all cases the correlations were quite strong, supporting the view that the association of language and classroom performance is continuous. This can be seen in the linear regression of kindergarten language onto the fourth grade teacher rating shown in Figure 7.4. This continuous relationship between a quantitative language measure and a quantitative measure of later school performance is not at all surprising and has two important consequences. First, there is no convenient place to differentiate children whose language skills are going to be a liability from children whose language skills are benign. Even children who had average language skills in kindergarten fared less well later on than the children who were above average. Thus, finding a natural cut-point on this distribution to determine who is likely to perform at unacceptable levels is not going to be easy. Second, though, we can see that intervention such as improved general classroom communication will benefit all children.

Table 7.5 Correlations between kindergarten composite language scores and teacher ratings of academic performance in second and fourth grades and also correlations between teacher ratings at second and fourth grades

	Second Grade Teacher Rating	Fourth Grade Teacher Rating
Kindergarten Language	0.56	0.59
Second Grade Teacher Rating		0.73

Reading Proficiency in Grade 10

The data presented so far show that academic performance across the spectrum of important subject matter is at considerable risk for children with SLI or NLI throughout the elementary school years. We also saw that this relationship between academic performance and academic achievement is largely continuous. This makes it difficult to arrive at outcomes that fall into categories of "good" and "bad" from which we can arrive at guidelines for clinical decision making. In an effort to approach this, we will now turn to adolescence and focus on an academic outcome that is indicative of very limited competence. In

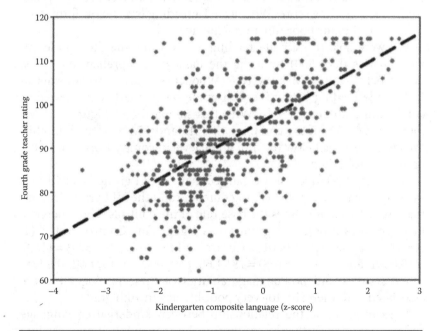

Figure 7.4 A scatter plot of kindergarten composite language ability and fourth grade rating of academic performance based on the Academic Competence Scale of the Social Skills Rating System.

this analysis, we will focus on the reading status of the cohort members at the end of the follow-up period when they were nominally in 10th grade (16 years old). This is a point in time when mandatory school attendance ends and the cohort members were entering early adulthood. The analysis of these 10th grade outcomes will parallel one reported earlier (Tomblin, 2008); however, in that analysis, individuals with nonverbal IQs below 75 (N = 27) were excluded. Since we have not eliminated these participants in the analysis reported in the rest of this volume, we will retain these individuals here as well. In this analysis, we sought to establish whether the youth in our cohort had achieved functional literacy by 10th grade. Functional literacy is a common concept that has a wide range of meanings (Ehringhaus, 1990). The National Adult Literacy Act of 1991 (National Institute for Literacy, 1991) defined functional literacy as the ability to read, write, and speak in English, and compute and solve problems at levels of proficiency necessary to function on the job and in society. Obviously, any simple scheme for distinguishing between inadequate literacy levels and adequate levels is difficult due to the wide range of contexts members of our society may find themselves in. Although controversial, definitions of functional literacy are often characterized by a grade equivalence reading score. We selected a reading level below fifth grade as our criterion for poor functional literacy.

We were able to estimate reading levels below the fifth grade (W score of less than 500) by using the Passage Comprehension of the Woodcock Reading Mastery test (Woodcock, 1998). Adolescents in 10th grade reading below the fifth grade on this test were viewed as approaching illiteracy levels. With this standard (see Figure 7.5), we found that 25.3% of the children with SLI and 55.9% of the NLI children were reading below the fifth grade level in comparison with 6.58% of the control group.

In terms of relative risk we can see that the SLI group is 3.84 times as likely to have this poor reading outcome and the NLI group is more than twice this at 8.9 times the base rate of the controls. The difference in these rates among all groups was significant: Control–SLI $X^2(1, N = 417) = 27.36$, $p < 0.0001$; Control–NLI $X^2(1, N = 389) = 115.8$, $p < 0.0001$; and $X^2(1, N = 168) = 18.71.60$, $p < 0.0001$. Thus, both the language abilities and nonlanguage abilities of these participants were associated with their risk for very poor literacy in 10th grade.

We can examine the relationship between kindergarten language and poor reading further by computing the probability of poor reading in 10th grade, defined as reading below fifth grade, by fitting a logistic regression to these data. This allows us to gain a clearer picture of the

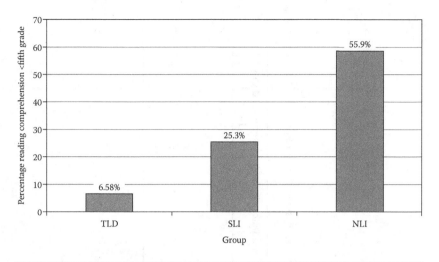

Figure 7.5 The percent of 10th grade adolescents reading below 5th grade level in the group with specific language impairment (SLI), nonspecific language impairment (NLI), and typical language development (TLD).

risk of poorer reading as a continuous function and thus we can see whether our diagnostic cut-off just under −1 standard deviation is reasonable. Figure 7.6 displays this function. We can see that the probability of poor reading is very low for children with above average language abilities. The computed probabilities and the 95% confidence interval for selected values of the composite kindergarten language scores is shown in Table 7.6 and the risk for poor reading for the average child was 4%. This probability increases somewhat as scores decline below the mean. At 1 standard deviation below the mean (16th percentile), this probability reaches 17% and thus at this level the risk has already quadrupled when compared with the average level of risk. By 2 standard deviations below the mean (3rd percentile), it is at 46% and thus is more than 10 times the risk faced by the child with average language ability. I should note that these levels of risk do not include the additional risk that comes from low nonverbal IQ.

Whether a risk of very poor reading is viewed as worrisome depends on our view of the importance of this outcome. If this outcome were life threatening, a quadrupling of the risk faced by the child at −1 standard deviation would very likely be of great concern. Certainly poor reading is not life threatening; however, given the degree to which reading skills near or at levels of illiteracy threaten the quality of life in our current society, it would seem very reasonable to argue that early language skills at or below −1 standard deviation do constitute a

Table 7.6 Probability and confidence intervals of reading ability below 5th grade in adolescents in 10th grade based on their kindergarten composite language ability

Composite Language Z-Score	Predicted Probability of Poor Reading	95% Lower Bound Confidence Interval	95% Upper Bound Confidence Interval
0	0.04	0.03	0.07
–1.0	0.17	0.13	0.21
–1.25	0.22	0.18	0.27
–1.50	0.29	0.24	0.35
–2.00	0.46	0.37	0.54
–2.50	0.64	0.52	0.74

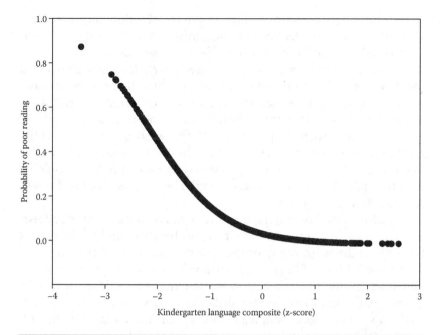

Figure 7.6 The logistic model of kindergarten language composite scores and the probability of poor reading in grade 10 when poor reading was defined as reading comprehension below fifth grade reading level.

very worrisome situation. Given the vital role of reading in our society, an increase of more than three times the risk for something as important as functional literacy would be viewed as substantial indeed.

SUMMARY AND CONCLUSIONS CONCERNING EDUCATIONAL OUTCOMES

We have demonstrated that the children who entered school with poor language ability show very clear evidence of pervasive difficulties in a broad range of academic performance. Earlier, in Chapter 6, we provided an in-depth analysis of the extent and nature of the reading problems found in these children with poor language (e.g., NLI or SLI). Here we showed that these reading difficulties are persistent through 10th grade. Furthermore, these children are at considerable risk for very poor reading abilities in 10th grade, defined by reading levels that are associated with functional illiteracy. The data presented show that academic difficulties are not isolated to reading, but extend across all aspects of the academic curriculum and place these children at risk for negative actions such as grade retention that are overt signs of concern by teachers and administrators. Regardless of what kind of educational outcome we select, we see clear evidence that there is a continuous relationship between early language ability and these later academic outcome indicators. Thus, there is not a clear breakpoint that can be used to establish cut-off values for risk. One solution to this is that interventions could be considered that are graded as well, such that children at the greatest risk receive the greatest amount of intervention, and children at lesser risk receive lower levels of intervention. Alternatively, the data provided could be used to establish a cut-point based on the level of risk that is thought too excessive to be ignored.

In addition to showing the magnitude of risk for academic success, the data show that much of this risk can be attributed to the child's language abilities. In many of the analyses, we showed that the children with NLI and SLI had similar levels of risk for poor academic outcomes. Across the indicators, we saw that the children with NLI usually had somewhat greater difficulties in school; however, this group also had poorer language ability than the children with SLI. Nonverbal cognitive abilities certainly seem to add to the risk of poor academic outcomes; but these data leave little doubt that language ability by itself is clearly a vital skill for children in the classroom both as a vehicle for understanding spoken instruction and for its central role in reading, particularly reading comprehension.

BEHAVIORAL AND PSYCHOSOCIAL OUTCOMES OF CHILDREN WITH LANGUAGE IMPAIRMENT

The research literature concerning the association of psychopathology or behavior disorder (BD) and developmental language impairments including SLI is extensive, and generally consistent, regarding elevated rates of these conditions among children. Aram and her colleagues (1984) followed a clinically served sample of children 10 years after identification and found that 70% of these children presented BD based upon the Child Behavior Checklist (CBCL).

More recently, several studies, using epidemiologic sampling methods, have followed children who were then diagnosed with respect to language impairment. One of the largest studies of this type was conducted in Canada by Beitchman and colleagues (1986, 1987, 1989, 1990, 1996). When this cohort was examined for BD at the time of their initial participation in the study, the researchers found elevated rates of BD for boys and girls with language impairment using teacher report, and among language impaired girls using parent report. Psychiatric examinations of a subsample of these children resulted in 48.7% of the speech-language impaired children having some form of BD, compared with 11.9% of the controls. Recently, Beitchman and his colleagues (1996) reported the results of a 7-year follow-up of these 5-year-old children. Of those children with both speech and language impairments at age 12.5, 57% showed some form of psychiatric condition; those with language only impairment were slightly less affected at 42%, and those with only speech problems were similar to the control group at 26%. Beitchman's work has also shown that the comorbidity of behavior problems is much greater in cases of language impairment than in cases of speech sound disorder.

Two other studies of epidemiological samples have reported similar findings to those of Beitchman. Stevenson and colleagues (1985) reported elevated rates of BD at 8 years of age among a group of children with language delay at 3 years of age. Silva and his colleagues (1984) found significant differences in teacher reported behavior problems in children who had previously been identified as having speech and language problems, but no differences were found for parent reported problems.

These results of community samples are consistent with Cantwell and Baker's (1987) extensive analysis of the psychiatric status of children receiving speech and hearing services. The authors reported that levels of ADHD and anxiety disorders were elevated in these children. However, their analysis did not include a control group. Tallal and her colleagues also examined the behavioral status of a clinically referred sample of children with SLI, and did include a control group. Tallal, Dukette, and Curtis (1989) compared rates of parental report of BD for 4-year-old SLI and control children and found significantly elevated rates among boys with SLI but not among girls. These investigators did not find differences for either boys or girls once language, attention, and motor behaviors were eliminated from their measure of BD. Benasich, Curtiss, and Tallal (1993) examined many of these children when they were 8 years old using the CBCL and the Teacher's Report Form (TRF). Significantly greater rates of BD were endorsed by parents on the CBCL, particularly those associated with hyperactivity for both boys and girls, and social withdrawal for girls, whereas no differences were found on the TRF. When the data from the CBCL and the TRF were combined, rates of ADHD were significantly elevated in the SLI group when compared with the control sample. Camarata, Hughes, and Ruhl (1988) demonstrated a similar relationship between language impairment and behavior disorder when they found elevated rates of language impairment in children referred for psychiatric evaluations.

It is reasonable to conclude that the literature supports a robust association between SLI and BD, particularly those behavior problems involving ADHD, and internalizing disorders such as shyness and anxiety. Despite this robust relationship between language impairment and BD, little is known about the cause of this association. The most common behavioral problem reported in these studies has been ADHD. However, internalizing problems such as anxiety disorder are also reported. Some research has shown that these behavior problems appear to vary with the setting in which the child is observed and in particular are reported by the children's teachers to a greater degree than their parents (Redmond & Rice, 1998). This has been interpreted as evidence that these behavior problems may arise more in the classroom situation than at home and are therefore reactions to classroom stress. Further support for this view arises from data showing that the excess of behavior problems in children with reading disorder (RD) and/or language impairment is found in those children with both conditions (Tomblin, Zhang, & Buckwalter, 2000). Thus, these studies support the notion that LI in conjunction with RD results in the child facing excessive failure, particularly within the classroom, which in turn results in reactive behavior problems. These conclusions, however, fail to explain why behavior problems seem to be reported in preschool children with LI (Beitchman, Nair, Clegg, Ferguson, & Patel, 1986). These findings could be used to argue for an underlying factor such as neurodevelopmental delay that contributes to all these conditions.

Throughout the longitudinal study, we gathered data concerning the psychological and behavioral status of the children in our cohort. These data came primarily from the parents and the teachers, but we were also able to obtain the child's report in 10th grade. As described in Chapter 3, we obtained this information throughout the study, but here we will focus on the data gathered in 4th grade and 10th grade because we have the most extensive data at these two time points and they provide a good sample of the behavioral status of these children in the middle school years, and also around the age of 16, which reveals adolescent outcomes. Most of these data came from two sets of questionnaires, as described in Chapter 2. One set consisted of the Child Behavior Checklist 4/16 (Achenbach, 1991a) and the Teacher's Report Form 4/16 (Achenbach, 1991b) used for children in fourth grade. The revised versions of these scales (CBCL 6/18; TRF 6/18) were again used in 10th grade along with the Youth Self Report (YSR), which is completed by the child (Achenbach & Rescorla, 2001). We also used both the parent and teacher scales of the SSRS in fourth grade. The Achenbach scales provide more information concerning psychopathology, whereas the SSRS provides a richer characterization of positive social behaviors. Thus, the scales can be used in complementary fashion. Finally, we also obtained additional information concerning symptoms of ADHD based on the DSM-IV criteria for ADHD using a questionnaire completed by the teachers in fourth grade.

Fourth Grade Psychosocial Status

The Achenbach scales (CBCL 4/16 and TRF 4/16) provide several scales concerned with psychopathologies. One overall scale represents the child's status with respect to behavior problems in general, and two subscales are concerned with either internalizing problems such as shyness or depression, or externalizing problems such as aggression and rule breaking. Several subscales subsumed under these more global scales are available; to keep things simple we will concentrate on these more global scales. These scales do provide a subscale for ADHD and later we will look at this as a special case. The scores on the CBCL and TRF are provided in the form of T-scores with a mean of 50 and a standard deviation of 10. Higher scores represent a greater degree of impairment. The SSRS provides a summary scale that represents social skills and these scores are reported as standard scores with a mean of 100 and standard deviation of 15, with higher scores representing better social skills. The scores for these three scales reported by the teachers (TRF) and the parents (CBCL) are shown in Figure 7.7 for the children with SLI, NLI, and TLD. The Total Problems scores were significantly different across the three groups of children for both the TRF $F(2, 518) = 21.19$, $\eta^2 = 0.08$, $p < 0.0002$ and CBCL, $F(2, 560) = 9.02$ $\eta^2 = 0.03$, $p = 0.0003$. Also, follow-up post hoc tests showed that in both cases the controls were significantly different from the SLI and the NLI, but these groups were not different from each other ($p > 0.05$).

Similar results were found for both externalizing, $F(2, 518) = 4.62$, $\eta^2 = 0.02$, and internalizing, $F(2,518) = 9.16$, $\eta^2 = 0.03$, $p < 0.0001$, for the TRF and for externalizing, $F(2, 560) = 8.33$, $\eta^2 = 0.03$, $p = 0.0003$ on the CBCL. In these cases, again the SLI and NLI groups did not differ but were different from the control group. An exception was found for the internalizing scale on the CBCL where no group differences were found, $F(2,560) = 2.69$, $\eta^2 = 0.05$, $p = 0.052$. Thus, poor language skills at school entry are associated with poorer psychosocial outcomes by fourth grade. Recall that eta squared values at or below 0.05 are viewed as small, and therefore, although we are finding greater levels of problem behaviors, the effect is not great with the exception of the TRF Total Problems score. With the exception of the TRF Total Problems, these effect sizes are clearly smaller than those reported earlier for academic performance.

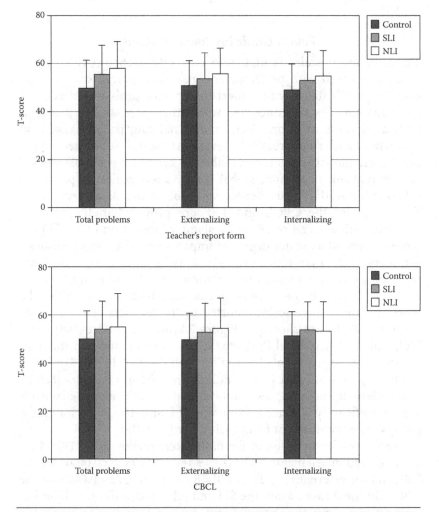

Figure 7.7 T-scores on Teacher's Report Form (upper panel) and Child Behavior Checklist (CBCL; lower panel) for children with typical language development (TLD), specific language impairment (SLI), or nonspecific language impairment (NLI).

ADHD and Language Impairment. The data above suggest a very modest level of risk for behavioral problems in general. As was noted earlier, there has been considerable interest in and evidence for a stronger association between language impairment and ADHD. We have recently noted that most of the research on this topic has used samples of children who were either clinically identified for ADHD or for LI. Clinically identified populations are more likely to have elevated rates of concomitant problems since these will trigger clinical referral. In addition to using clinically identified samples, these prior studies often did not provide for a control group that did not present with the disorder. Recently we have examined the data from the fourth grade assessment with regard to the question of whether ADHD and LI are comorbid (Mueller & Tomblin, 2012).

In this study, we used the DSM-IV diagnostic standards for ADHD, and therefore our analyses included children for whom both the parent CBCL and a teacher DSM-IV questionnaire were available. A risk for ADHD was calculated on the basis of: (1) teacher endorsement of six or more symptoms of Inattention or Hyperactivity/Impulsivity on the subscales of the DSM-IV checklist, or (2) a T-score greater than 60 (<-1 SD) on the CBCL Inattention subscale. Children were then divided into the following groups: (1) children endorsed as ADHD by both parent and teacher report (High Risk for ADHD; HR-ADHD); (2) children endorsed as ADHD by teacher report, but not by parent, or vice versa (moderate risk for ADHD; MR-ADHD); (3) children endorsed as ADHD by neither parent nor teacher (Low Risk for ADHD; LR-ADHD). Our use of the term ADHD risk reflected our acknowledgment that the children had not been diagnosed with ADHD although we were able to show a strong association between our risk assignment and parental report of a diagnostic history of ADHD.

With ADHD status in fourth grade established, we asked whether LI in kindergarten was associated with elevated rates of ADHD in fourth grade. These results revealed that the rates of MR-ADHD and HR-ADHD in children with LI are greater than for controls (49% in the MR-ADHD and 40% HR-ADHD contrasted with 23% and 8% respectively in the TLD group). These rates result in relative risk values of 3.52 for the HR-ADHD group, which was significantly greater than a value of 1 ($z = 5.34$, $p < 0.0001$), which is the value if LI did not influence ADHD. Likewise the RR value was 2.77 for the MR-ADHD ($z = 4.07$, $p < 0.0001$) given an exposure to LI. Thus, children with LI are around three times as likely to have ADHD in fourth grade as children with typical language skills. In the Mueller and Tomblin paper we did not report these rates with regard to the subgroups of SLI and NLI. Here we show in Figure 7.8 that the rates of both MR-ADHD and HR-ADHD are fairly similar for the two groups, and in fact when the rates of MR-ADHD and HR-ADHD were compared in the two groups, we did not find a significant difference $\chi^2(1, N = 115) = 0.07$, $p < 0.0001$. Therefore, we see again that the risk associated with LI seems to be associated with language regardless of nonverbal IQ.

In this analysis we established ADHD using three categories of risk, and therefore our effect size indicators are in the form of relative risk levels. Throughout this chapter we have been examining the relative size of effects, often using eta squared, which requires a continuous trait. We do have quantitative scores concerning ADHD from the CBCL and the TRF, and thus we can use these to gain a sense of the comparable effect size for ADHD. As expected, there was a significant overall difference across the SLI, NLI, and control groups for the Attention scale on the CBCL, $F(2,560) = 20.31$, $p < 0.0001$, $\eta^2 = 0.07$ and on the TRF, $F(2,263) = 13.62$, $p < 0.0001$, $\eta^2 = 0.09$. Both of these effect sizes are in the moderate range, and above the small values obtained for the Total Problems scales and the Internalizing and Externalizing scales. Additionally, these values are within the range found for academic difficulties.

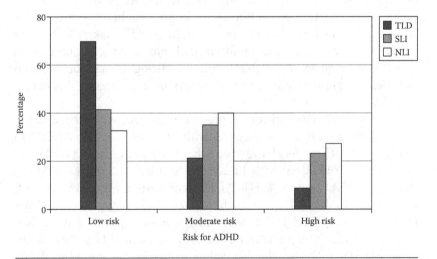

Figure 7.8 Percentage of children with typical language development (TLD), specific language impairment (SLI), and nonspecific language impairment (NLI); showing low, moderate, or high risk of ADHD.

These findings regarding problem behaviors in general and ADHD in particular are in general accord with previous research. They suggest that ADHD is more strongly associated with language status than other forms of behavior problems. The basis for this moderate association is not known. We have argued that it is very possible that both LI and ADHD share common etiologic bases (Muller & Tomblin, 2012). If this notion holds, then we must begin to consider that these two conditions may belong together as a common syndrome or at least within a closely related family of developmental disorders. We also must recognize that ADHD is well known to be associated with poorer educational attainment and reading disorder, which we have shown are strongly associated with LI. This provides clear evidence for a constellation of behavioral and learning problems and should encourage us to seek deeper understanding of the basis of this constellation.

Positive Social Development. The focus above concerned the presence of negative or maladaptive behaviors in children with poor language ability. An alternative way of looking at outcomes in children is to look for the positive behaviors. In order to do this, we asked parents and teachers to complete the Social Skills Rating System (SSRS). This questionnaire primarily asks about the child's social interactions with regard to developmentally expected positive behaviors. It also gathers information on problem behaviors, but we will report here on the positive social skills. Figure 7.9 displays the average social standard scores for each group. The general pattern of these data is becoming familiar. We see that the control subjects were, as expected, quite ordinary with regard to their social skills; whereas the children with SLI and NLI were moderately depressed in this regard. As in many of the analyses, we find that there was a significant overall group effect, $F(2, 560) = 20.80$, $\eta^2 = 0.07$, $p < 0.0001$. This group effect constituted no difference between SLI and NLI ($p > 0.05$), but both groups were different from the controls ($p < 0.0001$).

The effect size in this case is higher than for the problem behaviors other than ADHD. A likely explanation for this is that many of the items in this questionnaire concern social communication behaviors having to do with appropriate conversational initiation, use of greetings, etc. Although the diagnosis of language used in this study was principally based on semantics and grammatical aspects of language, it is very likely that we are seeing weaknesses in pragmatics that are secondary or possibly concomitant with the form and content deficits. Regardless, these data show social vulnerability in children at fourth grade with earlier poor language skills.

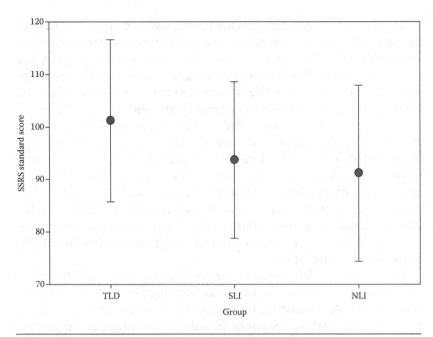

Figure 7.9 Means and standard deviations on the Social Skills Rating System (SSRS) social composite score for children with typical language development (TLD), specific language impairment (SLI), and nonspecific language impairment (NLI).

PSYCHOSOCIAL STATUS AT 16 YEARS

Within the framework of developmental competence there are considerable changes in expectations and roles between children who are 10 years old and usually in fourth grade, and adolescents who are 16 years old and usually in 10th grade. By 16 years of age, adolescents are at the threshold of adulthood and are expected to be more independent and hence also responsible for their behavior. Additionally, by this age their social milieu has changed to involve close relationships with a smaller number of peers. We just saw that these children showed elevated rates of problem behaviors as reported by parents and teachers, and likewise a depressed level of positive social skills as fourth graders. Additionally, we have shown in Chapter 4 that the relative language abilities of these children with early language impairment continue to be poor through the age of 16, and associated with this are substantial deficits in academic performance as reflected by their poor reading by 10th grade. In the face of this persistence of other important developmental skills we can expect to see persisting psychosocial difficulties. Stevenson (1996) proposed that these persisting language related problems, in particular reading problems, would result in greater and perhaps different behavior disorders in adolescence than were seen earlier.

The existing data that bear on this prediction are somewhat mixed. Early research performed with clinically ascertained samples has shown increased rates of behavioral and psychological problems in adolescents and adults (Baker & Cantwell, 1987; Rutter & Mawhood, 1991). Likewise, more recently, Durkin and Conti-Ramsden (2007) have reported poorer quality of friendships among adolescents with a history of SLI than typically developing children. These adolescents with histories of SLI were also found to be more at risk for anxiety and depression in adolescence. However, within the groups of adolescents with SLI and without, the individual differences in anxiety and depression were not associated with quantitative language status obtained in adolescence, nor were these associated with earlier language measures in childhood obtained for the children with SLI (Conti-Ramsden & Botting, 2008). These authors concluded that the relationship between language and emotional health was complex and weak. Beitchman and colleagues (Beitchman, Brownlie, Inglis, et al., 1996; Beitchman, Wilson, et al., 1996) found weak and generally non-significant relationships between speech and language impairment at 5 years of age, and psychiatric status at 12 years. Finally, Snowling and colleagues (Snowling, Bishop, Stothard, Chipchase, & Kaplan, 2006) also reported similar findings at age 16 for a group of children with language impairment in the preschool years; however, greater risk for problems of attention and social function was found among those children who had language problems that persisted into the school years.

Adolescent Psychosocial Outcomes in the Iowa Cohort

Recently, I examined the psychosocial outcomes of the youth in our longitudinal cohort (Tomblin, 2008). In this regard, we looked at both the extent to which the children with SLI and NLI (termed General Delay in Tomblin, 2008) showed positive resilient development as well as elevated problem behaviors. Thus we asked about social participation and friendships, conduct in the form of rule following and legal troubles, and well-being as reflected in self-concepts, satisfaction with life, and depression. The first question asked in this study was whether children who enter school with poor language differed from their TLD mates with respect to these domains of function. A second question concerned whether these adolescent outcomes differed between the

SLI or NLI groups. I will just summarize the findings of this study here and direct the reader to this paper for details.

With regard to the first question, our findings were generally consistent with the studies cited above. We used the Child Behavior Checklist 6/18 (CBCL) and the Youth Self-Report 6/18 (YSR) (Achenbach & Rescorla, 2001), and the Social Skills Rating Scale – Parent Report (SSRS; Gresham & Elliott, 1990) to obtain information on quantity of social participation. Across these measures we found that the two LI groups were less socially active than the TLD group and no differences were found between the SLI and NLI groups. We also asked about their sense of the adequacy of their social relationships using the UCLA Loneliness Scale (Russell, 1996). In this case, the children with SLI reported similar levels of satisfaction with their friendships as the TLD group; however, the NLI group reported significantly lower satisfaction than the TLD or the SLI group. Thus, somewhat lower social outcomes were found for the adolescents with histories of LI, and in particular, the adolescents with histories of NLI were less active and perceived themselves to be more lonely. The NLI group was more likely to have conduct problems than the SLI group; however, the differences were small. With regard to questions concerned with conduct contained in the TRF and CBCL, we found non-significant or marginally significant elevated rates between the LI and TLD controls. Likewise, the measures of well-being also showed that the language impaired adolescents had a lowered sense of mental competence and self-esteem compared with the TLD group, but again the effect sizes were small. Depression was measured via the YSR, and children with LI were more likely to have clinical levels of depression than the TLD group and this effect was concentrated in the children with NLI. Table 7.7 provides a summary of these results.

The Tomblin (2008) study did not focus on the problem behaviors other than depression contained within the Achenbach scales. Therefore we will compare the scores of these adolescents regarding Total Problems, Internalizing and Externalizing on the CBCL 6/18 and the TRF 6/18 so we can make a direct comparison with the scores these children obtained in fourth grade on these measures. Furthermore, in 10th grade, we also obtained measures of these behavioral domains via the YSR as noted earlier. These scores are summarized in Figure 7.10. Given that that Total Problems score combines Internalizing and Externalizing and there was no clear difference between these two subscores, we will focus on the summary Total Problems score. The Total Problems scores were significantly different across the three groups of children for both the TRF, $F(2, 298) = 15.86$, $\eta^2 = 0.09$, $p < 0.0001$, and

Table 7.7 Summary of the strength of relationships between outcomes in adolescence for children with specific language impairment (SLI) and children with nonspecific language impairment (NLI)

Outcome Domains		Strength of Relationship	
		SLI	NLI
Social	Social Participation	Moderate	Moderate
	Friendships	None	Small
Conduct	Rule Following	None	Small
	Legal Troubles	None	Small
Well Being	Mental Competence	Small	None
	Self Esteem	Small	Small
	Social Appearance	None	None
	Satisfaction with Life	None	None
	Depression	None	Small

CBCL, $F(2, 416) = 6.14$ $\eta^2 = 0.02$, $p = 0.002$; however, the adolescents themselves did not show an association between their reported problem behaviors on the YSR and their earlier language status, $F(2, 415) = 0.04$ $\eta^2 = 0.0$, $p = 0.96$. Also, follow-up post-hoc tests with regard to Total Problems showed that for both the TRF and the CBCL, the TLD group was significantly different from the SLI and NLI groups by having lower levels of problem behaviors, but the SLI and NLI groups were not different from each other ($p > 0.05$).

We can see that by comparing the data obtained in fourth grade shown in Figure 7.7 with the scores in Figure 7.10 for 10th grade, very similar levels of problem behaviors and patterns across groups can be seen. The same effect size ($\eta^2 = 0.09$) was found for the TRF in both 4th and 10th grades even though these are different teachers. A test for differences between the CBCL and TRF Total Problems scores showed that there were not significant differences in these scores between 4th and 10th grade across the full cohort (CBCL, $F(1,112) = 1.38$, $p = 0.24$; TRF, $F(1,1062) = 0.09$, $p = 0.76$). Furthermore, there was no support for an interaction between grade and language status (CBCL, $F(2,112) = 0.17$, $p = 0.84$; TRF, $F(2, 062) = 0.10$, $p = 0.90$). Thus, children with histories of language impairment (NLI or SLI) did not show a pattern of increased levels of problem behaviors.

This difference in results across the different informants is likely to be due to several factors. The teachers see these individuals in a different context than the parents. The school setting may be a place where the language skills of the youth are more often challenged and this could result in greater displays of problem behaviors as a function of language status than in the home. There is also the likelihood that the language skills of the youth could color the reports of behaviors provided by the teachers and to a lesser degree the parents and youth. Finally, informant differences could arise from differences in value systems of parents compared with teachers regarding the significance of problem behaviors.

Given the similarity in the effect sizes between kindergarten language and behavior problems at 4th and 10th grades, we find little support for the notion that behavior problems are the outgrowth of language problems that persist into adolescence. Rather, the current data suggest that, to the degree that there is a risk for behavior problems associated with language problems, it seems to be largely present by fourth grade. The evidence above consisted of a comparison of rates of behavior problems in 4th versus 10th grade, when language status was measured in kindergarten. We can test this further by asking whether there is any appreciable change in the strength of association between behavior problems in 10th grade and language status in kindergarten, versus language status in 10th grade. Table 7.8 summarizes the correlations between Total Problems on the CBCL, TRF, and the YSR and composite language scores at kindergarten and at 10th grade. The correlations of language measured at these two time points with the 10th grade Total Problems scores from the CBCL and the YSR are nearly identical, and the correlations with the TRF are also similar. Collectively, these results give further evidence that the risk of behavior problems in adolescence due to poor language is present fairly soon in development. The somewhat stronger association between 10th

Table 7.8 Correlations between Total Problems on the CBCL, TRF, and YSR with composite language scores obtained previously in kindergarten and later in 10th grade

Achenbach Scale	Kindergarten Language Composite	10th Grade Language Composite
CBCL Total Problems	−0.25	−0.24
	420	392
	$p < 0.0001$	$p < 0.0001$
TRF Total Problems	−0.34	−0.47
	302	275
	$p < 0.0001$	$p < 0.0001$
YSR Total Problems	−0.11	−0.10
	419	389
	$P = 0.02$	$p < 0.0001$

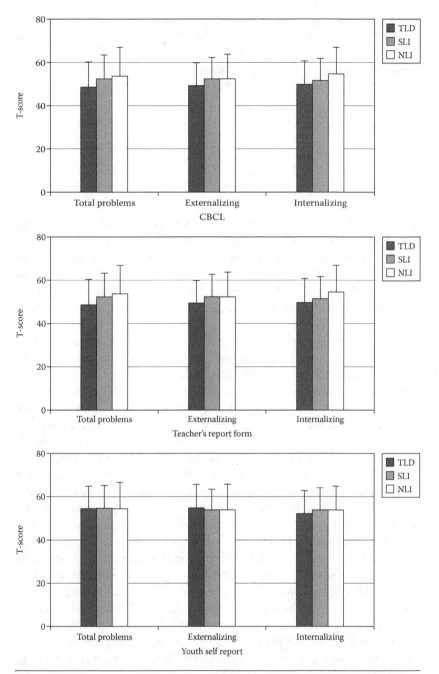

Figure 7.10 Mean T-scores for Total Problems, Internalizing behaviors, and Externalizing behaviors for children with typical language development (TLD) in kindergarten, specific language impairment (SLI), and nonspecific language impairment, using the CBCL, TRF, and YSR.

Table 7.9 Probabilities of clinically significant (T score > 65) Total Problems score on the Teacher's Report Form (TRF) or the Child Behavior Checklist (CBCL) obtained at 10th grade, associated with composite language scores in kindergarten

Composite Language Z-Score	Predicted Probability of Problems on TRF	Predicted Probability of Problems on CBCL
0	0.06	0.06
−1.0	0.12	0.12
−1.25	0.14	0.14
−1.50	0.16	0.15
−2.00	0.22	0.19
−2.50	0.29	0.25

grade TRF behavior problems and 10th grade language status compared with kindergarten language could be due to the teachers' reports of problem behaviors being influenced by the language skills of the adolescents or a local effect of the adolescents' language directly influencing problem behaviors. This effect, however, appears to be specific to the teacher reports and even here is not particularly large.

Because we can see that the risk for problem behaviors is well represented by the parent and teacher ratings in 10th grade, we can use these data to examine the level of risk for clinically significant problem behaviors for different levels of language ability as was done for academic problems. In this case we used guidelines from the Achenbach scales and therefore set a cut-off for clinically significant problems as scores greater than 65. Using this, we used a logistic model to compute the expected probability of having a total score greater than 65 on the TRF and the CBCL at 16 years of age, given a composite language score in kindergarten. Table 7.9 provides these values. You can see that the expected probabilities for the two scales are nearly the same, particularly with milder language deficits. When we compare these probabilities with those shown in Table 7.6 for poor reading, we can see the difference in the strength of association between later reading problems and later problem behaviors as language skills decline. Note that the base rates for children with average language ability in kindergarten for reading problems and behavior problems are quite similar (0.04 and 0.06 respectively). However, the growth in the risk for poor outcomes increases much more rapidly for poor reading than for problem behaviors as a function of language ability.

CONCLUSIONS

In this chapter we asked about how important outcomes in children's lives during the school years were related to their speaking and listening skills language status as they entered this phase of their lives. Earlier, in Chapter 4, we demonstrated that the relative language skills of these children remained quite stable across this time. Although it is very unlikely that all of the events during their school years had no effect on their language standing relative to their peers, we have a hard time showing this outcome. On the other hand, the data presented in this chapter show that individual differences in language at the beginning, as well as throughout the school years, clearly do have an impact on the lives of children. It is not surprising that the principal effect seems to be broadly in the area of academic and classroom performance, and, in particular, reading. Chapter 6 provided details of the association of language to reading, and because most measures of general academic achievement depend on tests that involve reading, it is difficult to know how much reading ability influences many of our measures of achievement, such as those based on the Iowa Tests of Basic Skills. We were able, within this study, to document that indicators that are not so directly coupled with reading, such as grade retention and teacher ratings, were also strongly associated with early language status and in particular poor language. Thus, the academic problems presented by these children are likely to be more than just poor reading.

Thus, the findings in this study underscore the very high importance of speaking and listening for long-term academic and classroom performance. Indeed, one could easily argue that a considerable fraction of the educational crisis that occupies political discourse is grounded in disparities of language skills by the students in classrooms. Unfortunately, a surrogate for these language skills has often been verbal IQ, which in turn is viewed naively as a largely innate trait that is not mutable. Indeed, it is not unreasonable to argue that language ability and the metacognitive system that it often serves make up most of what is considered to be verbal IQ; however, unlike verbal IQ, we have a considerably deeper understanding of how language is entailed in critical processes of message comprehension and production. In this sense, we can view language use as a mechanistic process that connects listeners and speakers, and, thus, students and teachers. In contrast, the construct of IQ, even the current theoretical forms, remains largely a mental trait with no power to explain how it serves learning (Gustafsson & Undlin, 1996). When viewed in this way, it becomes clear that we can begin to address the challenge of language barriers for some children in the classroom via careful research into the process of classroom language comprehension. However, this work needs to be extended into the processes of listening in the classroom as well. Our findings that language impairment and ADHD, particularly inattention, are comorbid with each other underscore this point. Many of the behaviors of inattention could be signs of comprehension failure. The fact that problems of inattention are often associated with academic problems (Lahey et al., 1994) supports the likelihood that language and inattention are on a common path that leads to poor academic performance.

Other than a substantial risk for ADHD, our data show reliable small to medium effects of early and persisting language problems on a wide array of problem behaviors, as well as behaviors that are reflective of positive well-being. These results are consistent with those of other studies cited earlier. Teachers consistently report a stronger association between language status and behavior problems, and it is very possible that this is a reflection of the fact that the classroom is a setting in which these children are being challenged, and no doubt experiencing a fair amount of failure. Despite this, we find that most of the data based on the adolescent's own report do not show much of an association between their language status and their behavior or sense of well-being. The measures we used to tap well-being were all self-report measures. These findings regarding well-being are consistent with results we obtained in an earlier study with young adults who had histories of language impairment (Records, Tomblin, & Freese, 1992), and can be useful in clinical settings as we counsel parents. It would appear that although these children face challenges during childhood and adolescence, they do not feel particularly bad about themselves, even when the parents and their teachers do have more of a negative perspective.

An over-arching issue in this study concerned the validity of diagnostic standards used for the diagnosis of language impairment. One issue that we examined concerned whether there was a justification for differentiating children with SLI from children with NLI. Recall that the children with NLI had slightly more severe language abilities and also poorer nonverbal IQs. Thus, we should expect that these children would have greater difficulties across the outcomes we examined. Where there were differences between the groups, we usually saw that the children with NLI fared less well. This was most noteworthy with respect to very poor reading comprehension by 10th grade. In only one case did we find a difference in the opposite direction. This was in the area of mental self-concept, which concerned the adolescents' view of themselves as learners. The children with SLI were somewhat more likely to view themselves negatively than the children with NLI. Since both groups were at similar risk for poor school performance, we might conclude that the children with SLI had more capability or experiences that lead them to view themselves as less capable in learning. Overall, however, the data showed that in most cases, the outcomes of these two groups with poor language were similar. Thus, once again, our data are not supportive of this distinction for clinical decision making.

Finally, we wanted to obtain data that would inform decision making regarding the region of severity that should be used to view these children as presenting language impairment. When we look at the nature of the relationship between quantitative measures of language skill and the various outcomes, as expected, we don't see a clear break point that allows us to separate the continuum of language into normal and impaired. Particularly in the area of academic performance, our cut-off for language impairment that fell at –1.14 is certainly in a region that is associated with uncomfortably high levels of poor outcome, and thus would seem to be a reasonable region of severity to justify clinical concern. The decision as to whether this is sufficient excessive risk requires a judgment based on how strongly one values outcomes such as academic achievement or psychosocial welfare. The data from this study can only provide the empirical evidence to be used in conjunction with these values.

REFERENCES

Achenbach, T. M. (1991a). *Manual for Child Behavior Checklist/4–18 and 1991 Profile*. Burlington, VT: University of Vermont, Dept. of Psychiatry.

Achenbach, T. M. (1991b). *Manual for the Teacher's Report Form and 1991 Profile*. Burlington, VT: University of Vermont, Dept. of Psychiatry.

Achenbach, T. M., & Rescorla, L. (2001). *Manual for the ASEBA School-Age Forms and Profiles*. Burlington, VT: Research Center for Children, Youth, & Families.

Aram, D. M., Ekelman, B. L., & Nation, J. E. (1984). Preschoolers with language disorders: Ten years later. *Journal of Speech and Hearing Research, 22,* 232.

Baker, L., & Cantwell, D. P. (1987). A prospective psychiatric follow-up of children with speech/language disorders. *Journal of the American Academy of Child & Adolescent Psychiatry, 26,* 546–553.

Beitchman, J. H., Brownlie, E. B., Inglis, J., Wild, J., Ferguson, B., & Schachter, D. (1996). Seven year follow-up of speech/language impaired and control children: Psychiatric outcome. *Journal of Child Psychology and Psychiatry, 37*, 961–970.

Beitchman, J. H., Brownlie, E. B., & Wilson, B. (1996). Linguistic impairment and psychiatric disorder: Pathways to outcome. In J. Beitchman, N. Cohen, M. Konstantareas, & R. Tannock (Eds.), *Language, learning, and behavior disorders*. New York: Cambridge University Press.

Beitchman, J. H., Hood, J., & Inglis, A. (1990). Psychiatric risk in children with speech and language disorders. *Journal of Abnormal Child Psychology, 18*, 283–296.

Beitchman, J. H., Hood, J., Rochon, J., & Peterson, M. (1989). Empirical classification of speech/language impairment in children: II. Behavioral characteristics. *Journal of the American Academy of Child & Adolescent Psychiatry, 28*, 118–123.

Beitchman, J. H., Nair, R., Clegg, M., Ferguson, B., & Patel, P. G. (1986). Prevalence of psychiatric disorders in children with speech and language disorders. *Journal of the American Academy of Child & Adolescent Psychiatry, 25*, 528–535.

Beitchman, J. H., Nair, R., Clegg, M., & Patel, P. G. (1986). Prevalence of speech and language disorders in 5-year-old kindergarten children in the Ottawa-Carleton region. *Journal of Speech and Hearing Disorders, 51*, 98–110.

Beitchman, J. H., Tuckett, M., & Batth, S. (1987). Language delay and hyperactivity in preschoolers: Evidence for a distinct subgroup of hyperactives. *Canadian Journal of Psychiatry, 32*, 683–687.

Beitchman, J. H., Wilson, B., Brownlie, E. B., Walters, H., Inglis, A., & Lancee, W. (1996). Long-term consistency in speech/language profiles: II. Behavioral, emotional, and social outcomes. *Journal of the American Academy of Child & Adolescent Psychiatry, 35*, 815–825.

Benasich, A. A., Curtiss, S., & Tallal, P. (1993). Language, learning, and behavioral disturbances in childhood: A longitudinal perspective. *Journal of the American Academy of Child & Adolescent Psychiatry, 32*, 585–594.

Bishop, D. V. M., & Adams, C. (1990). A prospective study of the relationship between specific language impairment, phonological disorders and reading retardation. *Journal of Child Psychology and Psychiatry and Allied Disciplines, 31*, 1027–1050.

Camarata, S. M., Hughes, C. A., & Ruhl, K. L. (1988). Mild/moderate behaviorally disordered students: A population at risk for language disorders. *Language, Speech, and Hearing Services in Schools, 19*, 191–200.

Cantwell, D., & Baker, L. (1987). *Developmental speech and language disorders*. New York: Guilford Press.

Catts, H. W. (1993). The relationship between speech-language impairments and reading disabilities. *Journal of Speech & Hearing Research, 36*, 948–958.

Center for Mental Health in Schools at UCLA. (2008 Update). Los Angeles, CA: Author.

Cohen, J. (1988). *Statistical power analysis for the behavioral sciences.* Hillsdale, NJ: Lawrence Erlbaum Associates.

Conti-Ramsden, G., & Botting, N. (2008). Emotional health in adolescents with and without a history of specific language impairment (SLI). *Journal of Child Psychology and Psychiatry, 49,* 516–525.

de Ajuriaguerra, J., Jeggi, A., Guignard, F., Kocher, F., Maquard, M., Roth, S., et al. (1976). The development and prognosis of dysphasia in children. In D. Morehead & A. Morehead (Eds.), *Normal and deficient child language* (pp. 345–410). Baltimore, MD: University Park Press.

Durkin, K., & Conti-Ramsden, G. (2007). Language, social behavior, and the quality of friendships in adolescents with and without a history of specific language impairment. *Child Development, 78,* 1441–1457.

Ehringhaus, C. C. (1990). Functional literacy assessment: Issues of interpretation. *Adult Education Quarterly, 40,* 187–196.

Feldt, L. S., Forsyth, R. A., Ansley, T. N., & Alnot, S. D. (1994). *Iowa Tests of Educational Development: Interpretive guide for teachers and counselors.* Chicago: Riverside.

Gresham, F., & Elliott, S. (1990). *Social Skills Rating System.* Circle Pines, MN: American Guidance Service.

Gustafsson, J., & Undlin, R. A. (1996). Individual differences in cognitive function. In D. Berliner & R. C. Calfee (Eds.), *Handbook of educational psychology* (pp. 186–242). London: Prentice Hall.

Hall, P. K., & Tomblin, J. B. (1978). A follow-up study of children with articulation and language disorders. *Journal of Speech and Hearing Disorders, 43,* 227–241.

Hoover, H. D., Dunbar, S. B., & Frisbie, D. A. (2001). *Iowa Tests of Basic Skills.* Rolling Meadows, IL: Riverside Press.

Jimerson, S. (2001) Meta-analysis of grade retention research: Implications for practice in the 21st century. *School Psychology Review, 30,* 420–437.

Johnson, D., & Myklebust, H. (1967). *Learning disabilities: Educational principles.* New York: Grune and Stratton.

Lahey, B. B., Applegate, B., McBurnett, K., Biederman, J., Greenhill, L., Hynd, G. W., et al. (1994). DSM-IV field trials for attention deficit and hyperactivity disorder in children and adolescents. *American Journal of Psychiatry, 151,* 1673–1685.

Masten, A. S., Hubbard, J. J., Gest, S. D., Tellegen, A., Garmezy, N., & Ramirez, M. (1999). Competence in the context of adversity: Pathways to resilience and maladaptation from childhood to late adolescence. *Development and Psychopathology, 11,* 143–169.

McGinnis, M. (1963). *Aphasic children.* Washington, DC: Alexander Graham Bell Association.

Mueller, K. L., & Tomblin, J. B. (2012). Examining the comorbidity of language disorders and ADHD. *Topics in Language Disorders, 32,* 228–246.

National Institute for Literacy. (1991). National Adult Literacy Act of 1991. 102nd Congr, 1st session.

Nelson, N. (1984). Beyond information processing: The language of teachers and textbooks. In G. Wallach & K. Butler (Eds.), *Language learning disabilities in school age children* (pp. 154–178). Baltimore, MD: Williams and Wilkins.

Peterson, J. J. (1983). *Iowa Testing Program: The first half-century.* Iowa City: University of Iowa.

Records, N., Tomblin, J. B., & Freese, P. R. (1992). The quality of life of young adults with histories of specific language impairment. *American Journal of Speech-Language Pathology, 1,* 44–54.

Redmond, S., & Rice, M. L. (1998). The socioemotional behaviors of children with SLI: Social adaptation or social deviance. *Journal of Speech, Language, and Hearing Research, 41,* 688–689.

Roisman, G. I., Masten, A. S., Coatsworth, J. D., & Tellegen, A. (2004). Salient and emerging developmental tasks in the transition to adulthood 1. *Child Development, 75,* 123–133.

Russell, D. (1996). The UCLA Loneliness Scale (Version 3): Reliability, validity, and factor structure. *Journal of Personality Assessment, 66,* 20–40.

Rutter, M., & Mawhood, L. (1991). The long-term psychosocial sequelae of specific developmental disorders of speech and language. In M. C. P. Rutter & P. Casaer (Eds.), *Biological risk factors for psychosocial disorders* (pp. 233–259). Cambridge: Cambridge University Press.

Silva, P., Justin, C., McGee, R., & Williams, S. (1984). Some developmental and behavioural characteristics of seven-year old children with delayed speech development. *British Journal of Disorders of Communication, 19,* 107–154.

Silva, P. A., Williams, S., & McGee, R. (1987). A longitudinal study of children with developmental language delay at age three: Later intelligence, reading and behaviour problems. *Developmental Medicine & Child Neurology, 29,* 630–640.

Snowling, M. J., Bishop, D. V. M., Stothard, S. E., Chipchase, B., & Kaplan, C. (2006). Psychosocial outcomes at 15 years of children with a preschool history of speech-language impairment. *Journal of Child Psychology and Psychiatry, 47,* 759–765.

Stark, R., Bernstein, L., Condino, R., Bender, M., Tallal, P., & Catts, H. (1984). Four-year follow-up study of language impaired children. *Annals of Dyslexia, 34,* 49–68.

Stark, R. E., & Tallal, P. (1988). *Language, speech, and reading disorders in children.* Boston: Little, Brown and Co.

Stevenson, J. (1996). Developmental changes in the mechanisms linking language disabilities and behavior disorders. In J. H. Beitchman, N. J.

Cohen, M. M. Konstantareas, & R. Tannock (Eds.), *Language, learning, and behavior disorders: Developmental, biological, and clinical perspectives* (pp. 78–99). New York: Cambridge University Press.

Stevenson, J., Richman, N., & Graham, P. (1985). Behaviour problems and language abilities at three years and behavioural deviance at eight years. *Journal of Child Psychology and Psychiatry and Allied Disciplines, 26,* 215–230.

Tallal, P., Dukette, D., & Curtiss, S. (1989). Behavioral/emotional profiles of preschool language-impaired children. *Development and Psychopathology, 1,* 51–67.

Tomblin, J. B. (2006). A normativist account of language-based learning disability. *Learning Disabilities: Research and Practice, 21,* 8–18.

Tomblin, J. B. (2008). Validating diagnostic standards for specific language impairment using adolescent outcomes. In C. F. Norbury, J. B. Tomblin, & D. V. M. Bishop (Eds.), *Understanding developmental language impairment* (pp. 93–116). New York: Psychology Press.

Tomblin, J. B., Zhang, X., & Buckwalter, P. (2000). The association of reading disability, behavioral disorders, and language impairment among second-grade children. *Journal of Child Psychology & Psychiatry & Allied Disciplines, 41,* 473–482.

Woodcock, R. (1998). *Woodcock Reading Mastery Tests-Revised/normative update.* Circle Pines, MN: American Guidance Service.

INDEX

Page numbers in *italics* denote tables, those in **bold** denote figures.

children 1–2, 6, 11–12, 15, 18–20, *23*, 24–5, **26**, 27–8, 31–2, 34, 37–8, 40–1, 48, 50–1, 54, 57, 59, 64, 70–1, 74, 79; background characteristics 72; communication 31, 59, *60*, 61, 95; developmental outcomes 7; kindergarten 13–14, **16**, 17, 148, 156; latent ability 63; lives 5, 197; language abilities 35; language delay 183; language disorder 4; language status 67–9, 73; monolingual 13, 25; pilot 29; poor language skills 21–2, 49, 69, 88–9, 167–8, 181, 189; poor readers 42; preschool 184; school-age 73, 80, 125–6; second grade 77, 83, **90**; social vulnerability 190; speech sound production 52; typically developing 80, 82, 84, 86, 120–2, 127–8, 132–3, 156, **171**, **186**, **188**, **190**, 191, **195**; urban 43

children with language impairment 23, 47, 80–3, **84–5**, *85*, 86–8, 117–19, 126, 144, 154, 155–6, *157*, **158–60**, 161, 168, 172, 184, 187, 191–2; nonspecific (NLI) 22, 89, **90**, 91–2, **93**, 94–5, 121–5, 154, 171, 173, 178, 182, 192, 198–9; specific (SLI) 8, 16, 35–6, 50, 89, **90**, 91–2, 94–5, 98, 119–26, 128–9, 133–8, 154, **155**, 156, 171, 173, 175, 177–8, 182–3, 185, 189, 191–2, 198–9

Children's Communication Checklist-2 (CCC-2) 31, 59, *60*, 61, 95

child's performance 54, 128, 130, 175

clausal density 54–5, *56*, *58*, 62, 101–2

Clinical Evaluation of Language Fundamentals (CELF-III) *33*, 34, *53*, *56*, 57, *58*, 59, *60*, *62*, *76*, 97

cognitive development 4, 89; nonverbal 98

Cognitive Hypothesis 89

Cohen, J. 171

Cole, K.N. 81, 89, 95, 123

comorbid 187, 198; comorbidity 137, 183

Competing Language Processing Task 37

complex syntax 96, 98–9, 104, 111

Conti-Ramsden, G. 81, 87, 96, 149, 191

conversational 99; aspect of language 54;

behaviors 55; discourse 36, 99; genre 111; initiation 189; language sample 18; tasks 101, **102**

conversations 31–2, 36, *55*, 59, 99; general 99; informal 19; initiate *54*

Cronbach, L.J. 4

C-Units 54, 100–1, *103*, *105*, *108*; grammatical 54–5, *56*, 57, *58*; with mazes 54, 56, *58*; Mean Length of C-Unit (MLCU) 101, **102**, **104**

depression 185, 191–2, *193*

diagnostic 17, 20, 22; Achievement Battery 145; assessment **16**, 17; battery 18, 52–4, 57, 66; categories 66, 83, 111, 124; core language measures 55, 57; cut-off 179; distinction 138; EpiSLI system 82; errors 84; framework 49–50, 87; groups 101–2, 119, 127, *174*; phase 21, 24, 67; protocol 53; schemes 86; stability 67, 80; standards 89, 187, 198; status 68, 173

dimensionality 48, 57, 64–5, 92; of individual differences 49, 63; of language 50, 52, 65; of language measures 62; of latent ability 63; second grade diagnostic protocol 53

disfluency 55

Dollaghan, C. 37, 125

Dual Processing Comprehension Task 37

Early Child Care Research Network (NICHD) 144

eighth grade *23*, 24, 34, 59, 61–3, 91, 94, 127; auditory tone processing 134–5; C-units 101, **102**, *103*; grade retention 169, 172, *173*, **175**; growth of vocabulary 74; language impaired **93**, 96; language samples 99; language testing protocol 58; nonverbal cognition 97–8; poor readers 151–3; reading achievement 147–9, 160; spoken language development 96

electrophysiological 137; measures 135, 138

Ellis Weismer, S. 73, 98, 118, 120, 125–9, 161n1

Vernacular Black English (VBE) 13, 19

Weber-Fox, C. 134–7
Wechsler, D. 20; Block Design and
    Picture Completion subtests 20, 35,
    97; Intelligence Scale for Children–III
    22, 97; Preschool and Primary Scale of
    Intelligence-Revised (WPPSI) 20
Woodcock, R. *39*; Reading Mastery
    Tests–Revised (WRMT-R) 20,
    144,178; subtests 145
working memory 8, 118, 127–8, 131–2,

135; abilities 125, 128; auditory task
128; capacity 125–6; limitations 119,
131; nonlinguistic task 126; nonverbal
128; performance 129; resources 37;
spatial 126, 128; tasks 126, 129; verbal
12630, 138

Youth Self-Report (YSR) 41, 185, 192–3,
    194, **195**

Zhang, X. 19, 21, 34, 53, 63, 82, 89, 92,
    123, 146, 148, 154, 161n1, 184